THE SKY DIARIES

THE SKY DIARIES

A True Story of Reincarnation

Andy Myers

gatekeeper press™

Columbus, Ohio

The Sky Diaries: A True Story of Reincarnation

Published by Gatekeeper Press
2167 Stringtown Rd, Suite 109
Columbus, OH 43123-2989
www.GatekeeperPress.com

The cover design, interior formatting, typesetting, and editorial work for this book are entirely the product of the author. Gatekeeper Press did not participate in and is not responsible for any aspect of these elements.

Library of Congress Control Number: 2021943393

ISBN (paperback): 9781662916878
eISBN: 9781662916885

For Toot Bug

Chapter 1

My grandma loved the sky. She was even known to chase the sunset. She often sat on her porch steps, chatting with her neighbor well into the evening. When Mother Nature was in the mood to show off, the western sky was ablaze with glorious shades of pink and gold. "Do you think we can catch it tonight?" her neighbor would ask.

With a hopeful twinkle in her eyes, Grandma answered, "Maybe if we drive far enough and fast enough, we can reach up and touch the sunset."

They were of retirement age, but scurried to the car with the enthusiasm of high school seniors on prom night. Westward bound with no particular destination in mind, they drove up and down the hilly side streets of Benson. Permanent smiles were etched on their faces as they rollercoastered up and down the neighborhood streets with their windows open. Each valley in the street made the sun appear to drop below the horizon. At the crest of each hill, the watercolor sunset appeared larger than life itself. The golden sky reflected in my grandma's soulful eyes. The breeze whipped through her wavy hair as the last of the sun's rays illuminated her face. Grandma was not a religious woman, but moments like that were her equivalent of church.

To her, the sun wasn't just a star. It wasn't merely a ball of hydrogen and helium 93 million miles from Earth. To her, the sun and the sky were tremendously more personal and meaningful. The sky represented wonder, possibility, and beauty. To Grandma, the sky was a creative masterpiece. Each sunset was a work of art that would never twice be duplicated. Each sunrise belonged in Mother Nature's art gallery.

Her fascination with the sky didn't stop after sunset. Grandma viewed meteor showers as the grand finale of nature's firework show. In my youth I vacationed with Grandma in rural Nebraska. We stayed in a cabin on a property called Flying Hawks Ranch. It wasn't a five-star resort by any stretch, but the place offered a night sky so dark it looked like God threw a handful of glitter across an infinite black canvas. With zero light pollution, we could see the spine of the Milky Way Galaxy. I felt like I was wearing a pair of 3-D glasses at the movie theater. The stars seemed so close I actually reached upward thinking I could touch them.

A meteor shower peaked while we were at Flying Hawks. Grandma allowed me to join her at 2:00 in the morning when the sky was darkest and viewing was at its best. I shuffled out into the warm summer night and collapsed on a blanket in the yard. For the short time I was able to stay awake, I don't remember seeing any shooting stars. I do remember how the crickets chirped and how the breeze wafted in the scent of the nearby lake. Grandma sat on the blanket next to me, cigarette in one hand, coffee in the other. The only time she looked away from the twinkling stars was to see the twinkle in my tired eyes. Grandma looked at me like she looked at the sky, and that was a real compliment.

She grew up in the picturesque town of Nebraska City, where creeks and tributaries of the Missouri River spider web out to shape the landscape. It's where my grandma and her younger sister Vilma got muddy, learned to fish, and captured bullfrogs. It was there at the birthplace of Arbor Day where they learned to climb crab apple, cottonwood, and hackberry trees. It's where my grandma and Vilma would play on the railcars along the train tracks. Grandma spoke of times she and Vilma swam in the river alongside water moccasins. Hearing her describe those snakes always made me squirm. "They're more afraid of *us* than we are of *them*," she assured me.

As the years went by, Grandma ended up in the Benson area of Omaha, Nebraska. It's an older, blue-collar district where the houses are made of brick and some folks still take the bus to work. As for Vilma, she settled in rural Missouri. They both retained their love of fishing and the two sisters remained close throughout the years. Vilma wrote letters telling of sixty-pound catfish they were catching down on the river in Missouri. My grandma phoned and told Vilma of all the road trips and adventures she was having with Boompa.

Boompa was my grandfather. His given name was Clarence, but everyone called him by his nickname. Boompa wore old fashioned newsboy hats, otherwise known as flat caps. Rather than wearing a belt, he preferred suspenders. Boompa liked betting on horse races and wasn't too shabby at ice skating for a man with short, bowed legs. Perhaps most of all, he enjoyed traveling.

Grandma and Boompa crisscrossed the country in their blue 1977 Pontiac station wagon. They made cars sturdier back then. The vehicle was essentially a steel tank with cup holders and an ashtray. In the back seat of the station wagon was a cooler full of ham sandwiches and ice-cold Pepsi. The only lifeline between them and civilization was the Rand McNally map Grandma clutched in her hands.

Boompa did the driving. Grandma did the navigating. They were weekend road warriors. During holiday breaks and three-day weekends, they'd travel to every corner of this big, beautiful country. More often than not, they'd end up lost or low on gas, driving on some godforsaken dirt road that wasn't listed on the map. There was no GPS. No itinerary. No plan in mind. Just a map, a carton of cigarettes, and a lot of empty highways to cover.

Her sense of adventure was second to none. My grandma was well traveled. She made it to all 48 of the continental United States – from the Badlands of South Dakota to the Grand Canyon, and from the Ozark forests to the Smoky mountains, she saw it all. As a child, I remember flipping through photo albums with Grandma, seeing pictures of these adventures she'd taken with Boompa. I couldn't help but wonder why she was wearing a red shirt in most of the photos.

She explained it was simply precautionary. She and Boompa would park the station wagon and then wander *really* far out into the empty prairie fields and deserts. By the time they were ready to leave, their station wagon was nothing more than a tiny speck off in the distance. Grandma said she'd often wear red in case they got lost or couldn't find their way back to the vehicle. She figured wearing a bright red shirt would make it easier for the search and rescue teams to find her, especially if they came by helicopter.

While traveling to all these locations, she collected interesting stories and new memories. And rocks. She collected *lots* of rocks – not just from gift shops and souvenir stores but from the prairie fields, beaches, and mountains they visited. She had big rocks, small rocks, geodes, and even a few meteorites. In addition, she found arrowheads, pottery shards, dinosaur bones, fossilized plants, and petrified wood.

She kept them all. Her basement was a treasure trove of history which reminded me of a museum. Rare artifacts were labeled and displayed on shelving units. Among these items were countless coin collections, all meticulously researched and impeccably catalogued. When the basement shelves were full, she'd squirrel her 'treasures' away in closets and kitchen drawers. Her treasures were plentiful, but perhaps the real treasure was Grandma herself. Because she was well-read and well-traveled, she was a geyser of information. To her friends she was known as Frances, but I viewed her as a female Indiana Jones, minus the fedora and whip.

On my tenth birthday, she gifted me a treasure chest full of goodies and artifacts. It was roughly the size of a shoebox and came complete with a little metal skull on the front. I wondered if real pirate treasure might be inside. Within the chest was a cornucopia of history. There were family heirlooms, including a wooden locket that belonged to my great-great-great-grandfather, Joseph Myers. He carved the little decoration by hand while sitting underneath a tree between battles in the Civil War. He served from 1862 to 1865 in the 89th Ohio Infantry. In hindsight, I'm honored that Grandma trusted me to care for such a priceless artifact, given that I was so young.

Grandma was always giving gifts and sharing her love of history, science, and the natural world. On another birthday, Grandma gave me a tackle box full of rocks and gemstones. Each was labeled and nestled in its own compartment. The collection contained, among other things, petrified wood, snowflake obsidian, fossilized sea shell, and my personal favorite, fool's gold, also known as pyrite. As a child, I held that chunk of fool's gold and pretended I was a dusty California prospector yelling, "There's gold in them thar hills!"

That's how it was to be around Grandma Myers. She somehow made the treasures come to life. With her impeccable memory, she told the story behind every rock, coin, and family heirloom. She made history itself leap off the pages of every book. She filled us with wonder, making us feel as though life was a treasure map and we were explorers.

We played Pick-Up-Sticks, Tiddlywinks, Dominoes, and Go Fish at her kitchen table. Next to her sat an ashtray full of Salem cigarette butts and a cup of lukewarm beige coffee. In hindsight, I think it was mostly creamer with a splash of coffee. A newspaper was always within arm's reach. A stick of butter rested at room temperature in a crystal butter dish on the counter. Buttered toast always tasted better at Grandma's house.

In the Benson home was a spare bedroom she referred to as the 'den.' It's where she read me countless books about dinosaurs, shipwrecks, black holes, mysterious animals, unexplored caves, and extraterrestrials. She read me books about African tribes, the Spanish Armada, the Revolutionary War, and Native Americans. She talked a *lot* about Native Americans. She told me how sixty million buffaloes once outnumbered humans on the midwestern plains. She spoke of Red Cloud, Sitting Bull, the Anasazi Indians of the Southwest, and the Trail of Tears. Grandma wondered how strange it must have been the first time Native Americans saw Europeans with white skin.

When she spoke of Native Americans, she did so with great reverence and respect. She had a way of captivating my imagination. I hung on her every word, becoming more and more fascinated with stories involving American Indians. Since Grandma knew so much about our family ancestry, I asked her if there was any chance that I, myself, was part Native American. I begged her to tell me that one of our ancestors had some Cherokee blood in them, or maybe some Sioux or Pawnee.

She relayed a story about one of my ancestors having very tan skin. Some family members speculated she was part Native American, perhaps having a different father than her siblings. Based on appearances, even a local group of Native Americans claimed she was one of their own. It was nothing conclusive, just speculation and hearsay. Yet, it was enough for my grandma to indulge my curiosity by saying I could be part Native American . . . even if it's just one percent.

Admittedly, I'm as pale as a cup of skim milk. I'm mostly a scoop of English and a scoop of Scottish with sprinkles of German and Irish heritage. During bath time in my childhood, my mom would wash my blond hair and freckled arms. I'd look up and ask, "When is my hair going to turn dark?" She laughed, assuming I wanted to be like my older brother, who has dark brown hair. She didn't realize I wanted dark hair because I wanted to look like a Native American . . . much like my past lifetime where I *was* one.

Grandma (left) and her sister, Vilma (right)

Boompa in unknown location

Grandma at Flying Hawks Ranch

Grandma gifting Andy a new 'treasure'

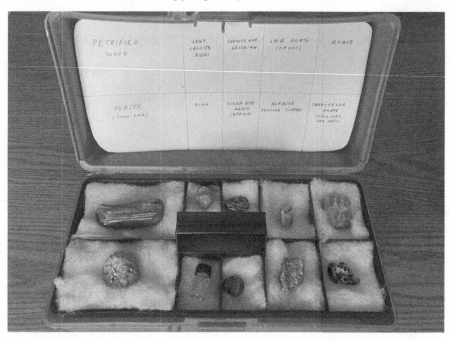

The tackle box of rocks given from Grandma

Treasure chest of family heirlooms given from Grandma

Chapter 2

"Sunkmanitu Tanka Owaci!" I screamed it at the top of my lungs as I hurled my tomahawk at the target. The herd of thundering bison kicked up dust that hung in the air like smoke over a battlefield. Having used my tomahawk, I resorted to my bow and arrows. A bead of sweat dripped from my forehead as I took aim. The half-ton buffalo charged me at thirty-five miles per hour, snorting and grunting. Its footsteps shook the ground like thunder. I exhaled as I released the arrow. I hoped it would hit its mark. A miss would cost me my life. Suddenly, I heard a guttural holler.

"Andyyyyyy . . . Daaaaavid . . . Come inside! Dinner's ready!"

It was my mom. I'd almost forgotten I was still in my backyard. My imagination flinched and the make-believe scene disappeared from all around me.

"Where did you get all those sticks, Andy?"

Half embarrassed and half annoyed, I responded, "Those are *arrows*, Mom!"

"And where did you get that plastic toy?" she interrogated as she opened a package of crackers. "Is that an *ax*?"

I sighed in frustration and rolled my eyes. "It's not an ax, Mom. It's a *tomahawk*. I found it at the park."

As the screen door shut, she hollered over her shoulder, "Well don't go hurting your brother with that thing. And please come inside. The chili is ready."

Although the toy *was* made of plastic, I made no promises. It was the spring of 1991. I had just turned ten years old. A few months prior, the movie *Dances with Wolves* was released in theaters. As Kevin Costner befriended members of the Sioux tribe, I could imagine myself in his moccasins. Hearing the Sioux speak their language in the movie also triggered something inside my soul. It was familiar and gave me a feeling of déjà vu. I remembered the foreign words and phrases from the movie long after the final credits scrolled up the screen. *Dances with Wolves* struck a chord with me in ways that were hard to express. I knew I had *literally* been there before, in a past lifetime as a Native American on the Midwestern plains.

Reincarnation wasn't a notion I was familiar with at a young age. My church didn't speak of past lives. From kindergarten through eighth grade at my Catholic school, they preached of Heaven and Hell. The good go to Heaven. The bad go to Hell. The inbetweeners like myself apparently hung out in a gray area called purgatory after death. They made it sound like the DMV waiting room of the afterlife.

I couldn't accept those ideas at face value. I was curious and had a lot of questions. *What parameters would a Higher Power use to determine if a person is good or bad? How does one judge such an intangible concept? Why would a Supreme Being judge anyone at all?* I couldn't get on board with a God who was angry and vengeful. After all, my own mom wasn't nearly that hard to please. If God was the most loving being in the Universe, I couldn't fathom why religion would make Him seem like such a temperamental guy.

As time went by, I slowly let go of the beliefs that were pushed upon me in my youth. I was on a new trajectory that was less religious and more spiritual. I suppose religion is akin to a journey where the path is clearly visible and marked with signs that show the rules. Spirituality is more like a hike through the forest where one can be a trailblazer without guidelines or restrictions. I've always been a sucker for adventure. I welcomed the twists and turns along my spiritual journey. I liked not knowing where it may someday lead me.

With time, the notion of reincarnation started to sound more plausible. I concluded that the concept of second chances made sense. If a higher power were to sentence us to an eternity of suffering for 'getting it wrong' on the first try, then this game of life must be horribly cruel. That would be like reprimanding a child for falling down on his very first attempt at walking. In order to master something, we humans need practice, repetition, and multiple chances. Mistakes are to be expected as they're part of the learning process.

Additionally, how can we possibly understand what it means to be human if we only live as one person, as one gender, in one culture, during one brief period of history? That would be like viewing the world through a keyhole rather than a picture window. They say variety is the spice of life. Reincarnation provides us with a buffet of options rather than one dish.

Furthermore, if we only get *one* lifetime here on Earth, our souls would hardly get a chance to participate in this game of life. It's proven that Homo sapiens have been around for approximately 200,000 years. So, if we only get one lifetime and we each live to be 100 years old, we would only participate in 0.0005% of human history. What would we do for the rest of eternity? Would we sit around feeling disappointed that we didn't have more time on Earth? Mathematically, that's the equivalent of an actress starring in one play and then being forced to sit in the audience as her fellow cast members performed in the next 1,999 shows. *How boring would that be?* As my mind wrestled with ideas like this, reincarnation seemed to make more sense.

I continued to ponder the mysteries of the afterlife, and still couldn't shake the feeling of déjà vu that *Dances with Wolves* had ignited within me. For a good six months after the film was released, I ran around shouting lines from the movie and chucking my plastic tomahawk at any object in my backyard that resembled a buffalo. I was Grandma's 'Honorary Chief', the one-percenter, the pale-skinned Indian warrior.

Like all ten-year-olds, I was prone to going through phases. I never outgrew my fascination of Native American culture or the Sioux tribe. Life just moved on and I got distracted with other things. Throughout my youth, playing soccer was a large piece of my social jigsaw puzzle. It kept me busy and out of trouble. At fifteen I began working at a local grocery store, carrying groceries to people's cars. I later got promoted to stocking the dairy cooler. Placing cottage cheese and milk on the shelves all evening gives a person plenty of time to think. It could be lonely work at times, but it gave me plenty of time to daydream about topics that were above my pay grade. *If God created us, who created God? Is there life on other planets? Why did my nightly dreams later come true in real life?*

I remained close with my grandma throughout high school and college. Together, we watched *Jeopardy* on TV. We ate Russell Stover chocolates and bet all of our make-believe money when a *Daily Double* came on the screen. Grandma was my sounding board when I wanted to discuss topics that had a little more substance to them. We talked about UFOs and time travel. We discussed ancient civilizations and the future of human technology. She cut out newspaper articles she thought I would find interesting, and we used them for topics of discussion. After we had our fill of deep conversations, she'd ask me about my work at the grocery store and how soccer was going.

When I was in high school, I finally shared with Grandma that I'd been having some precognitive dreams (nightly dreams that later came true in real life). She found it fascinating but a little scary at the same time. I asked if she'd ever experienced something similar. With hesitation, she recalled a time in her life when she frequently had odd premonitions and daydreams of future events that came to fruition.

When she was a young girl, Grandma and some of her cousins and friends were goofing around at a park. Some of them needed to relieve themselves, and without modern restrooms available, they decided to spread out into different areas of the woods for privacy. My grandma was the first to finish, so she walked to a clearing where everyone agreed to reconvene. From the corner of her eye, she saw someone up on the hillside about fifty yards away. It was her cousin Donald. He sat in a wheel chair, smiling at her. It was odd because Donald was perfectly able-bodied and had no wheelchair.

Grandma hollered up at him, "Hey Donald, what are you doing playing around on that wheelchair? Where did you find that thing?" She heard friends and cousins coming back out of the woods. To her surprise,

Donald was with all the others. Confused, my grandma glanced back toward the hillside. The image of Donald in the wheelchair had completely vanished. Perplexed, she asked the gang if anyone was messing around on the hill, or if anyone had found a wheelchair lying around. Everyone laughed and had no idea what she was talking about.

A few years later, an accident occurred that left her cousin Donald in a wheelchair for the rest of his life. Grandma said she always wondered if that vision was a premonition that had yet to transpire. The experience gave her the willies. This event, combined with a few other psychic moments left my grandma feeling unsettled. She decided it was a part of herself that she wasn't interested in further understanding. She had somehow turned it off. I never asked her to elaborate on how she managed to do that. I could only say that I completely believed her, because I had experienced similar events my whole life.

Chapter 3

Most humans have experienced an intuitive moment at one time or another. Whether one chalks it up to luck or probability, it's sometimes possible to sense an event is going to happen before it actually occurs. As a child, I experienced this so regularly I knew it couldn't be mere coincidence. I'd sense who was calling when the phone rang. On the way to school, I knew if a classmate would be absent due to illness. I was somehow able to foresee events before they took place. Admittedly, I wasn't sure how this was possible. I couldn't explain it, yet I couldn't deny it.

By high school, I was having precognitive dreams of sporting events. There were times I dreamt of an upcoming soccer match or football game. A day or two later, I'd watch it on TV and was shocked to see the final score was just as I dreamt it. Even specific plays and key moments of the game mirrored what I saw in my dreams. Eventually, I had precognitive dreams about events in my *own* life that would later transpire.

It was 1997. I was jolted awake by some commotion downstairs. As my heart pounded and my adrenaline surged, a bizarre and disturbing thought entered my mind. I pictured my dad lying dead on the floor. It was a silly notion, really, and I had no business jumping to such dramatic conclusions. My legs felt heavy running down the stairs, and as I entered the kitchen, the look on my mom's face confirmed my fears. There he lay, motionless on the kitchen floor. Heart attack. It's something you can't un-see no matter how much you wish you could go back in time and look the other way.

Just a few feet from my dad's body was my sixteenth birthday cake. It was wrapped in cellophane on the kitchen table, ready for my upcoming party. It was a home-made soccer ball cake with licorice hexagons and white frosting. I knew we wouldn't be celebrating anytime soon.

My dad was only forty-three years old. Sure, he hadn't been to the doctor since the Reagan administration and his diet consisted of anything battered and fried. Still, he had no known health conditions. Just days prior, I'd been playing basketball with him in the driveway and arm wrestling him at the kitchen table before dinner.

The days after his death were a bit of a blur. It felt like a bad dream. Upon waking up each morning, it would take a few moments to remember he was actually gone. The reality splashed me in the face like a bucket of ice water. When something exciting happened at school or during my soccer game, my initial thought was, "I'll have to tell Dad when I get home." Then, I remembered I couldn't. Like a rollercoaster at a carnival, life is a ride that eventually comes to a stop, no matter how much fun is being had. As time went on, the pain healed and turned into emotional scar tissue. We soothed our hearts by swapping funny stories of Dad to keep the memories alive.

Intuitively sensing my dad's death was the first and last time I've had a premonition involving tragedy. Through the grief, I was kept busy by my high school activities. It wasn't long before I was back at soccer practice, hanging out with friends, and going on dates. Ultimately, I knew Dad's absence meant he wouldn't be there for graduations, my wedding, or the birth of my first child. I realized it even back then, but didn't have time to dwell on it because life was simply too busy. In hindsight, maybe that was a blessing.

My mom, Sue, was an absolute rock during this time in our lives. She was the anchor that kept the family grounded, the glue that kept us together. Through her own grief and sleep deprivation, I'm not sure how she managed to be so strong. Admittedly, she kept my brother and me on a short leash for a while after Dad died. When we lose a family member, we tend to hold everyone else a bit tighter for a period of time. It's natural instinct. It's our heart's way of trying to prevent more pain, trying to keep more bad things from occurring. Unfortunately for my mom, this phase occurred when my brother and I were yearning for more independence and freedom. *Fortunately* for my mom, we were pretty good kids and didn't give her too many sleepless nights.

As time went by, I continued to have odd occurrences such as precognitive dreams and intuitive hunches. I began to wonder if I'd inherited that from Grandma Myers. *How was she able to "turn it off" at will?* During a time in my life when I was trying to make sense of it all, I had an experience that actually made me feel *grateful* for having these strange abilities.

It was an exceptionally vivid dream where everything seemed more colorful and life-like. My dad was in the dream, and I was aware that he'd passed. Yet, it was hard to keep that in perspective considering he looked so real, so vibrant and healthy. He was wearing his signature outfit of jeans and a flannel shirt with a blue checkered pattern on it. He didn't say anything. He merely smiled at me, and then walked up and gave me a tight hug. He felt strong and healthy. As we embraced, a small tear formed in the corner of my eye, and I felt the stubble from his five o'clock shadow brush against my cheek. I breathed in and smelled his Old Spice aftershave. It was a comforting and familiar scent.

As we released from the hug, I looked at him. He was still smiling, and there was a glimmer in his eyes that I had never seen before. It was a mischievous twinkle, like he had a secret but wasn't allowed to share it with me. He looked entirely peaceful and serene. The experience felt more real than reality itself. I opened my mouth, not quite sure what I was going to say. Before I could utter a word, the dream evaporated before my eyes and I woke up.

I sat up in bed and touched my cheek. I could still feel the sensation of rubbing against his chin stubble as we hugged. I had a tear in the corner of my eye, just like I had in the dream. Old Spice still lingered inside my nostrils. *Was it more than just a dream?* Part of me wondered if I'd just had a real encounter with my dad. *Was it a spiritual rendezvous that took place somewhere between Heaven and Earth?*

Andy with his dad, Steve

Steve fishing

Chapter 4

Time has a funny way of shuffling the card deck of our memories. I don't remember *everything* about my dad, Steve. I couldn't say what he aspired to be when he was a kid or why he decided to enlist in the Marines. I don't know what his greatest fear was, or what he considered to be his greatest accomplishment. I do remember the time he gave me a stick of gum before I took my date to the sophomore homecoming dance. He never had 'the talk' with me, but I think it was his way of telling me to make sure I had good breath if I planned on kissing a girl.

I remember his unique and endearing laugh. I remember how coordinated and competitive he was. Dad was skilled at anything requiring athleticism or hand-eye coordination. He was a natural when it came to golf, volleyball, basketball, shooting pool, foosball, darts, or tossing horseshoes. He was also a natural when it came to drinking beer. He was good at it. Maybe too good at times.

He taught me how to swing a baseball bat and shoot a three-pointer. During soccer games in my youth, Dad would pace the sidelines, smoking cigarettes and snacking on sunflower seeds. I'd give a little wave to him and he'd gesture for me to stay focused on the ball. I remember him raising his voice when he was mad and laughing when he was happy. I remember him watching black and white westerns on TV and how he liked John Wayne movies. His hair was always neatly combed, and he often sported a handlebar mustache. I don't ever remember seeing him cry. Not once. Not even when his dad, Boompa, died in 1990.

I remember the time my dad dressed up as a woman. It wasn't Halloween and it wasn't on a dare. It was just a Friday night at home. Perhaps he had one too many beers, or perhaps he was just in a good mood.

I couldn't tell and I never asked. But we were having a good time and one joke led to another, and before we knew it, Dad stuffed two balloons up the front of his shirt. They were half deflated but they filled out his chest enough that he strutted around the kitchen pushing up his 'cleavage' and making kissy faces at the rest of us. One of us found a blond wig in a toy box and tossed it in his direction. My dad gladly obliged, giving his best Marilyn Monroe impersonation.

I remember the music he listened to – those lazy summer days at the cabin where Dad and my uncles would sit around listening to Jackson Brown, Creedence Clearwater Revival, Led Zeppelin, AC/DC, and Norman Greenbaum. I remember the way Dad held a cigarette, tucking it discretely inside his palm so we could hardly see it. I imagined he smoked other things in that fashion once upon a time, maybe at a concert or in the back of a van. Again, I never asked. And he never told.

He worked night shifts at a printing press in downtown Omaha. When my brother, sister, and I were going to bed for the night, he was just waking up and getting ready for work. He'd come into my room and kiss me goodnight on my forehead before going downstairs and getting ready to leave. His breath always smelled like fresh toothpaste. His handlebar mustache always tickled my forehead. I pretended to be asleep, but I'm sure he knew I wasn't.

When he wasn't working, Dad had his line in the water along the banks of any lake within a twenty-mile radius. He loved to fish, whether they were biting or not. He had a bumper sticker on his '86 Oldsmobile that read, "My worst day of fishing is better than my best day at work."

I sometimes wonder what my dad thought about the afterlife, precognitive dreams, psychic phenomena, and similar subjects. I was so young when he passed that he was still ninety percent dad and ten percent friend. If he'd been around longer to become more of my friend and less of a rule-enforcer, I suppose we may have had those types of conversations. Aside from Christmas Eve mass, he never attended church with my mom and us kids. I envied him for that. Although I'm not sure where my dad stood spiritually, he did have a tattoo of a cross on his shoulder, accompanied with words that read, "In God I trust." I never asked him about the tattoo, but I asked my mom about it once. She rolled her eyes and shrugged her shoulders, saying he got it while in the Marines . . . probably on a bet . . . after having a few drinks.

Regardless of where he stood on religion, I'm pretty sure he believed in spirits. He once told me that when I get the chills, it's because a ghost or spirit is somewhere nearby. I was eight years old at the time, and Dad's little theory caused me a few sleepless nights that week. I believe he took a mild interest in occult topics. I once overheard my dad talking about a documentary he was excited to watch. It involved a prophet from France who predicted all sorts of important world events that later came true. My ears perked up and I asked if I could watch the show with him. My mom protested, suggesting that a show about Nostradamus was not exactly kid-friendly.

Although I wasn't permitted to watch the show in its entirety, I sneaked a few peeks as I passed through the living room. It was fascinating to think a person could intentionally see into the future. On a smaller scale, I'd been doing it for years, but my experiences were often mundane and accidental. I wondered if there were a way to harness the skill intentionally. *Could such a gift be used to help others?*

Chapter 5

My job at the grocery store was a good fit throughout high school and early into college because it provided me with a flexible schedule. In terms of my soccer games and social life, that was a plus. Ultimately, I knew that a career in retail wasn't for me. At work, I found myself getting into trouble for socializing too much in the back rooms and break rooms when I was supposed to be out on the floor working. My managers didn't realize I had become a makeshift counselor for many of my peers and fellow employees. I was a good listener. Sometimes I'd give them advice. Word got around that free counseling services were being offered in the back room, and before I knew it, I was an unofficial therapist for many of my fellow coworkers.

Unfortunately, this landed me in the 'friend zone' with a few girls I would have rather taken on dates. Ultimately though, it brought me to the realization that it felt good to troubleshoot problems with other people and offer them help. I was on the verge of needing to select a college major, so I decided on social work. Plus, I had once received some counseling services from a therapist who had a social work degree. She really helped me during a confusing time in my life, so I wanted to have a positive impact on others like she had on me.

Attending college full-time while holding down a job requires time management skills and the ability to operate on little sleep. I wish I could say that I felt my dad's presence with me and was inspired by the spiritual motivation he offered me along the way. Truth be told, I was so caught up with school, work, and my social life that I didn't often feel my dad looking over me in spirit. Sure, when I'd go fishing, I'd think of him. When I'd get a whiff of someone's Old Spice aftershave or would see someone wearing a flannel shirt, I'd nod to the heavens in his honor. Yet, I rarely felt his presence in any tangible way. I simply hoped he was proud of me and saw what I was doing.

I graduated with a Bachelor's Degree in Social Work from the University of Nebraska at Omaha. During college and a few years after, I worked at mental health facilities, after school programs, and youth centers. Social work provided me with a plethora of ways to be of service. I made wonderful memories with coworkers and clients alike.

Once college ended, I had more time to read and research subjects that were most interesting to me – namely, those involving metaphysics and the supernatural. All-night cram sessions and late-night research papers had made way for parties, road trips, and socializing with friends. I enjoyed my bachelorhood and my freedom. My life was a social bee hive of activity, and yet, I often felt very lonely. My friendships and social activities filled my time, but they didn't seem to fill my soul. I was searching for something to give my life more meaning. I didn't know it at the time, but as I was searching for my purpose, my purpose was also searching for me. On a crisp autumn night in 2006, an event happened that would forever change the direction of my life.

Chapter 6

I was twenty-five and living in an apartment. One night, I was awoken by a sensation I'd never felt before. It was a pleasant feeling that pulsed through my body, radiating through every cell of my being. I still don't have a reference point to compare it to any other sensation, but I imagine there's no drug on planet Earth that can make a person feel so wonderful, so euphoric. I was stone-cold sober, yet felt that every nerve ending in my body had been plugged into a universal consciousness that radiated pure, unconditional love.

The physical feeling was accompanied by a mental state of utter bliss. It was the absence of fear. Anxiety was nonexistent and time stood still. I was thinking nothing at all, yet my head was filled with infinite thoughts. I felt limitless. Endless. Like I was nowhere and everywhere all at once. For the first time in my conscious existence, I wasn't afraid of anything, not even death. Mentally and emotionally, I was intertwined with something far greater than myself.

Stranger still was what I *saw*. Above me on my bedroom ceiling was a breathtaking sight. It was the Universe itself – stars, planets, galaxies, and nebulas were all glowing in colors I never knew existed. It was as if someone had cut a six-foot hole in my ceiling and I was gazing straight into the cosmos through some all-powerful telescope.

In this moment of perfect clarity, a voice spoke to me. I didn't hear it with my ears, but rather felt it with my soul. The message was clear. It said that if I wanted to be reunited with my dad and see everyone who had crossed into the afterlife, I could float out of my body and into the galaxy above me. All I was seeking was waiting beyond the edge of my ceiling. It was unconditional love, acceptance, wisdom, answers, and unspeakable joy.

Without effort, I felt my spirit leave my body and begin to float upward toward my ceiling. The beautiful scene of stars and galaxies was drawing nearer. My capacity to feel joy had been multiplied by infinity. As I approached the threshold, I felt a homesickness for whatever it was beyond my bedroom ceiling.

Yet, a hesitation creeped in from somewhere down in the cellar of my soul. It was a feeling that I still belonged here on Earth. At the speed of thought, I expressed this to the consciousness I was speaking to. I felt my work here wasn't done, that I still had many people to help and important missions to accomplish.

The message was received. My request was granted. Suddenly, I felt my spirit drop down from the edge of my ceiling and slam back into my body. This jolted me enough to interrupt my hypnotic state. My muscles flexed and I inhaled deeply, like a swimmer breaching the surface after holding his breath underwater. The galaxies above my bed vanished, and I remained there on my back staring at the white textured ceiling. My heart raced and my extremities tingled.

I looked at the clock and it was the middle of the night. I sat upright in bed and glanced around the room, making sure I was actually awake and hadn't crossed into the afterlife. I never fell back to sleep that night. At the risk of upsetting my boss, I called in sick to work the next morning. The gravity of the experience left me reeling with questions. I needed more time to emotionally process the experience.

Had I nearly died in my sleep? I have, in fact, been diagnosed with sleep apnea. Perhaps I'd stopped breathing in the middle of the night. I've been told my apnea is not severe enough to warrant concern. Then again, conditions like that can fluctuate on a spectrum from one night to another.

The Sioux refer to our Milky Way galaxy as The Road of the Spirits. They believe the seven stars within the Big Dipper act as corridor through which souls transition from our world to the afterlife. The beauty of the cosmos had certainly called to me on that fateful night. Despite the option to depart this world, I was ultimately glad I decided to stay.

Yet, as glorious as it was, I felt myself slipping into a funk in the weeks and months that followed. It wasn't a depression per se, just a period of time where I felt a little *blah*. I began researching near-death experiences, wondering if that was, in fact, what happened to me. I learned that it's typical for a person to feel an emotional crash after the excitement of a near-death experience. It's the equivalent of a mental or spiritual hangover. I suppose once a person stands on the welcome mat of the afterlife, nothing here on Earth seems comparable. I could certainly relate. It felt like I'd seen color television for the first time and now I only had access to black and white TV. It was like a child visiting Disney World and then being sent back to live in the slums.

That being said, I had nothing to complain about. Nothing was outwardly wrong with my life. I had so much to feel grateful for. I just couldn't shake the feeling that I was missing something. *Why did it happen? What was I supposed to learn? What were the important missions I remained here to accomplish?* The experience seemed to release something inside of me. With more frequency than ever before, I began having psychic moments. I could feel the intuitive dial cranking up despite the funky mood I was trying to shake off. Meanwhile, my appetite for all things spiritual and metaphysical was insatiable. According to my research, this was all typical for people who'd survived a near-death experience.

This led me to wander into a book store one Friday night. I was looking for something, but wasn't quite sure what. I circled around the New Age section like a hungry man at a buffet. A purple book caught my eye and I picked it up off the shelf. It was titled *Conversations with the Other Side* by Sylvia Browne. Over the years, I'd seen her on *The Montel Williams Show*. She was a celebrity psychic. Sometimes I'd stop long enough to hear what she had to say. I held the book in my hand and curiosity got the better of me. I purchased it and read it that weekend.

One book led to two. Two books led to four. Soon, I was hooked. These books were my drug and I was a junkie who needed a fix. I craved more information. After work, I came home to a pile of books on my bed. I read until the wee hours of the morning, my eyes strained and bloodshot. I read about angels, astral travel, reincarnation, and the afterlife. I read about spiritualism, life charts, spirit guides, and déjà vu. I read books about psychic abilities and how they come in many forms. After reading most of Sylvia Browne's books, I began to binge on other authors as well.

These books were the story of my life. I finally felt understood. I learned definitions and terminology that made sense of things I'd experienced my whole life. I felt like an unidentified creature who'd just been assigned his order, genus, and species. These books made me feel sane, like I was not alone. I found solace and comfort within the pages of those books. I wished I was six inches tall so I could nestle into the pages and pull them over me like a comforter.

I was merely a caterpillar wanting to be a butterfly, and this spiritual metamorphosis was in full swing. I made conscious decisions to better my life, and some changes weren't easy. Over the years, I had surrounded myself with friends and acquaintances whose values and lifestyles greatly differed from mine. My naivety had allowed me to see only the good in people. Yet, after my near-death experience, it became increasingly difficult to hang around my old group of friends.

I started to distance myself from my friends, hoping nobody would notice. When that didn't work, I bluntly told them I would no longer be coming around. I felt horrible. The 'it's not you, it's me' line was too cheesy for me to say it, but it was the truth. *They* hadn't changed, but I certainly had. I didn't believe that I was better than them in any way. I just felt *different*. I needed to be around others who were in line with my values and the lifestyle I was trying to live. I wanted friends who allowed me to be a better person.

Rebuilding my social network was a lonely job. I rarely had plans on the weekends. Most days after work, my only company was a good book. I didn't feel sorry for myself. I accepted the need for a new life. I had dug myself into a social rut, and with time, I'd crawl out of it. With all this newfound free time, I had the opportunity to clear my head and contemplate my future.

During this time, I began to notice something peculiar. When coming in contact with strangers, I was somehow sensing personal details about their lives. I was at the gym and sensed that the lady next to me was going through a divorce and had two little girls at home. I looked over at the driver next to me in rush hour traffic and sensed that he was furious with his boss at work. I was at the grocery store and intuitively knew the lady in front of me had just bought her dream house. It was as though I was reading their thoughts or picking up on their energies.

A small part of me wondered if I was merely delusional. *Had I snapped? Was I nuttier than a squirrel at an acorn festival?* My education in social work and the mental health field allowed me to know exactly what types of diagnosis could apply to me. I wasn't experiencing other symptoms commonly associated with schizophrenia. Then again, most people lack the self-awareness to realize when they're in the throes of a mental breakdown.

I wasn't sure why or how I was suddenly sensing information about complete strangers. I didn't think I was making it up. At any rate, I didn't approach any of these strangers to verify my hunches one way or another. It was hard enough thinking I might be losing my mind. I certainly didn't want *others* to think so as well.

As all this happened, I couldn't help but wonder, "Okay . . . so now what?" I'd seen the Universe through my bedroom ceiling. I'd had a chat with some all-loving Higher Power and lived to tell about it. I'd spiritually centered myself, which had boosted my intuition. I had rid myself of people who may have been dragging me down. *Now what was supposed to happen?* It all felt a little anticlimactic.

I decided I wasn't going to find any answers sitting around my apartment reading books. I needed a road trip. The timing was perfect. I had just quit one job and had another one lined up. Between the two, I had one week off and intended to do some traveling. I was a modern-day Aboriginal and this was my 'walkabout.' I've always done my best thinking while driving, so figured I'd do some soul searching while cruising down the highway at sixty miles per hour.

I made a loop-de-loop around the Midwest of the United States, driving a big circle that stretched through the Dakotas, into Montana, down through Wyoming, and back across the midriff of Nebraska. Out on those highways and interstates, I thought of my grandma. I wondered if she and Boompa had driven those same roads in the past . . . back before every small town had a Pizza Hut . . . back when gas stations still had working pay phones.

Sadly, I knew my grandma's road trip days were nearly over. She was back in Omaha hooked up to an oxygen tank. She had recently quit smoking, but not before the cigarettes had strangled her lungs, causing emphysema and COPD. I wanted her to get better. It was a helpless feeling wondering how much time she had left. I kept driving westward, hoping I'd drive right into a gorgeous sunset. Perhaps Grandma would see the same sunset from her kitchen window back in Omaha.

I wasn't sure what I was looking for on my trip. I didn't know what I expected to find. Answers and enlightenment don't exactly smack you head on, like bugs on the windshield. I'd stop at motels when my eyes grew weary of staring at the road. I'd pull out some books I'd packed – books whose pages I had highlighted, dog-eared, and scribbled with notes.

I daydreamed about what the next chapter in my life would entail. *Marriage? Kids?* Perhaps. Some of my old friends had already started their families. I envisioned myself having a wife and a daughter and a two-story house someday. But I was still reveling in my independent lifestyle and couldn't foresee these things happening anytime soon. It's funny how our minds wander when the windows are rolled up and the radio is off.

On the last day of my road trip, I wondered if my journey had failed to produce any useful breakthroughs. I was to start my new job in a couple days, and I hadn't really accomplished anything on the trip other than blowing a bunch of money on gas, food, and motel rooms. On a social worker's salary, those expenses really add up. I wasn't any closer to having a sense of direction moving forward. *What was I supposed to do with this newfound intuition? Why was I sensing intimate details about the lives of total strangers?*

I was eastbound on Interstate 80, heading back to Omaha across the flat plains of western Nebraska. I would be home in a few hours and demanded some answers before I wrote the trip off as a total waste of time. I'd ask the heavens for answers but all I heard was tires on pavement. I gazed out the window and saw endless fields of sweet corn silently swaying in the warm August breeze – acre upon acre of green, glistening corn stalks. They looked like ocean waves rolling off into the distance.

The surreal beauty caused a blanket of calmness to fall over me. And right then, after I'd given up on obtaining any sort of messages from the spirit world, I heard a voice. It was the same voice that spoke to me on that crisp fall night only nine months prior when I saw the Universe through my bedroom ceiling. Rather than enter my ears like a sound wave, this voice originated from within. It was internal, yet came from somewhere else. "Take care of everyone else, and *you* will be taken care of."

I set the cruise control and took my foot off the gas. Suddenly, I didn't feel so alone in my car. I gave it a minute to sink in. Admittedly, the message itself wasn't anything overly profound. It sounded like a proverb one might find inside a fortune cookie. *Take care of everyone else, and I will be taken care of?* Yet, I couldn't dismiss the fact that it came from the same voice I'd heard before. Regardless of the words, I knew to take it to heart. Only time would tell if the message were true, and if so, to what extent. *Who were these people I was supposed to help?*

Regardless, come Monday morning, my new job beckoned. I pulled into my apartment complex and noticed I'd put nearly 3,000 miles on my vehicle since the trip started. Surely my new social work job would provide me with plenty of opportunities to take care of others. Still, the one person I most wanted to help was the one person I couldn't. Her health was quickly declining. Nobody wanted to admit it at the time, but Grandma was in the process of dying.

Chapter 7

Grandma's hands were soft and velvety like cocoa butter. Somehow, they always were. It was hard to believe, considering how many weeds she'd picked from her garden and how many dishes she'd washed by hand over the course of her life. Yet, her palm was so smooth it felt like I was touching baby powder. I gently squeezed her hand, careful to avoid the pulse oximeter that was attached to her index finger.

She looked up at me from her hospital bed and blinked her misty eyes. I asked how she was feeling and immediately regretted doing so. A sense of embarrassment overtook me as I realized she couldn't answer my question. Speaking wasn't easy for her. Grandma was hooked up to a breathing mask that was strapped tightly to her face. She looked so pale and vulnerable. It was hard to see her like this. I averted my eyes, not quite sure where to look.

Plastic tubes snaked from her oxygen mask to the breathing machine beside her bed. I could tell the mask was making Grandma feel claustrophobic. She uttered a word or two, but I couldn't make out what she was saying. It was like trying to hear someone speak under water. "You just save your strength, Grandma. I'll do all the talking, okay?"

I pulled up a chair bedside her and took a seat. "Alright, it's 'show and tell' day here at the hospital, so I brought something to share with you." I flashed her the book I was holding. It was titled *The Complete Guide to Mysterious Beings* by John A. Keel. She eyeballed it and nodded her head in silence. It was a book about mysterious happenings and unidentified creatures. I figured if she couldn't hold a conversation with me, I'd at least give her company by reading. She sat there in silence as I read to her, and Grandma never took her eyes off me.

In that moment, I realized everything had come full circle. I remembered the rainy afternoons from my childhood when Grandma read me books from the shelves in her den. I curled up next to the warm metal register vents on the floor and wrapped a blanket around me to trap in the heat. I looked up at Grandma as she read stories of myths, monsters, legends, and far-away lands. Here we were, twenty-some years later, still reading the same stories and still filled with wonder.

While reading to her, I occasionally looked up to make sure Grandma was still awake. She looked tired and weak. She'd been through a lot. It had been five months since I'd returned from my road trip. During that time, she bounced back and forth between the hospital and the nursing home, depending on the severity of her health issues. Every medication caused side effects which then required another medication. It was a vicious cycle.

I glanced at the clock on the wall and noticed it was getting late into the afternoon. As I finished reading one last short story to Grandma, I found myself fighting back tears and I had a lump in my throat. As I closed the book, I wondered if this was the last time I'd ever see my grandma. We sat there in silence for a moment. The hum and hiss of her oxygen machine was the only sound in the room. It had become the soundtrack of Grandma's life.

"Oh, hey . . . before I leave, I wanted to show you something." The sadness in my heart caused my voice to tremble a bit. I hoped she didn't notice. "You're gonna love this," I said, pulling my cell phone out of my coat pocket. I clicked on the photo album to display pictures I had saved. "Look at this little beauty. I took it last night while I was stopped at a red light." I held the image close to her face so she could see past the straps and plastic mask.

It was a picture I'd taken of a sunset – pinks, golds, and yellows, all mixed together from Mother Nature's paint palette. The clouds were nearly translucent from holding the light of the sun. They dotted the sky all the way to the horizon, like luminous stepping stones in a heavenly garden. Grandma wasn't the only one who loved sunsets. We shared a mutual admiration for them. When cell phones became equipped with cameras,

I'd take pictures of sunsets and show them to Grandma every chance I got. She was impressed with the new cell phone technology, but even more than that, she was impressed with the sunsets I showed her.

As she studied the one on my phone, she nodded. It was hard to make out her words, but I could tell she was *oooing* and *ahhhing* under her mask. Despite this short burst of enthusiasm, she was tired and needed to save her strength. I didn't want to overstay my welcome, so I slid my phone into my pocket and grabbed my book. "I'll check on you tomorrow, okay?"

Grandma reached out to grab my hand and she gave it a squeeze. I tried to sear that moment into my memory – the color of Grandma's eyes, the way she smelled, the softness of her hands. I didn't want my memory to rob me of these details in the years to come. I mustered up a half smile. She smiled back at me with her eyes. We were both pretending to be brave even though we were secretly scared. I told her I loved her and exited the room.

Walking through the hospital hallways, I felt helpless and worried, like my dog had just run away. Once I was back in the privacy of my car, I could no longer contain my emotions. Tears gushed out like there was a broken water pipe in my brain. I held my face and wept, hoping nobody in the parking lot was looking in my direction. Glancing in the rear-view mirror, I noticed how bloodshot my eyes had suddenly become. I needed to clear my head. So, I went for a drive.

The next day, I got the call from my mom. I'd been preparing for the call for nearly a year, but it didn't make it any easier.

"Sweetie, if you'd like to say goodbye to Grandma, you might want to head up to the hospital early this morning. They don't think she'll be around much longer."

I went up there immediately. My mom was already there. So was my aunt, Terry, who is Grandma's only daughter. They allowed me to go into Grandma's room by myself to say my goodbyes. Upon entering, it was clear she was heavily sedated. A ventilator was doing most of the breathing for her. She didn't look like herself. Much of the color was drained from her face. I gently held her hand and was pleasantly surprised to feel how warm it was. I touched her on the shoulder and bent down to speak softly in her ear.

"Hey Grandma, it's Andy. When you get to where you're going, can you please give us a sign that you made it there safely? We'll miss you, but we know you'll still be with us in spirit."

Her expression didn't change. Her eyes didn't open. While conscious the previous day, she'd been in so much distress that the nurses suggested it was best if she remain sedated. Still, I knew she was listening. She was still in there, spelunking somewhere deep down in the cavern of her subconscious. I told her one last time that I loved her, and I exited the room. Other family members stood in the hallway, misty-eyed and in a stupor.

One by one, close friends and family cycled in to have one last word with Grandma. After everyone had their chance to say goodbye, we gathered together and gave the hospital staff permission to unplug her from the breathing machine. It was surreal, like having an out of body experience. *These scenes only happen in movies, right?* The reality of it was hard to stomach. We stood arm in arm, watching helplessly as the hospital staff unhooked Grandma from the ventilator.

Unplugging her breathing machine wasn't followed by an immediate *beeeep*. She did not 'flatline' as they do in the movies. Real life is different. She didn't die right away. She held on. And on. And on. Without the breathing machine, her physical body reacted to the change in oxygen levels and she moved around ever-so-slightly in her bed without regaining consciousness.

As I stood at the foot of her bed, I began to hear a rapid grinding noise. It sounded like a plastic wind-up duck that waddles on its feet after the gears are turned. Nobody else seemed to hear it. I began looking around in confusion, trying to figure out where the sound was coming from. Suddenly, it dawned on me that it was the clock on the wall directly behind me. It wasn't a digital clock, but rather an analog one that was round and slightly larger than a dinner plate.

The clock had gone haywire! The second hand zipped around in circles so fast that it looked like a race car at the Daytona 500. This caused the minute hand to circle faster as well. Minutes whizzed by in just a few seconds. Hours were passing in mere minutes. I brought it to the attention of the others in the room. They took their focus off Grandma and looked at the clock. Everyone gasped. Some cried. Others laughed. A few of us scratched our heads. The hour, minute, and second hands continued to circle the clock at warp speed. We asked the nursing staff if any of the clocks in other patients' rooms were doing the same thing. Perhaps all the clocks were hardwired to the same power source and were all malfunctioning at once.

The nurses checked, but reported that ours was the only clock behaving in such a way. They didn't have an explanation. One of the nurses jotted notes on her clipboard in the doorway and said, "If you want to believe in miracles and signs from the afterlife, *be a nurse*! I've only been at this facility for a week and you wouldn't believe the things I've seen."

I told my family how I'd asked Grandma to give us a sign when she crossed into the afterlife. One of the more skeptical family members stated the obvious.

"She's not technically dead yet. If she's still alive, how could she be in Heaven giving us 'signs' already?"

It's commonly accepted that humans are comprised of a body, a mind, and a soul. The mind can be one place while the body is elsewhere. This makes it possible for a person to daydream about a beach in Mexico while shoveling snow in Minnesota.

Similarly, it's possible for the *body* to be in one place as the *soul* exists elsewhere. I experienced this previously when my soul floated toward my ceiling while by body was still in bed. Near-death experiences lend a lot of validity to the notion of the body, mind, and soul operating independently. Simply put, the soul can cross into the afterlife *before* the physical body actually expires. There's a delay between the body and the soul.

The concept is similar to unplugging an old TV set. If a person unplugged the cord from the outlet, the TV remained on for a second or two before the screen went dark. There was a slight delay. I knew that's what happened with Grandma. Her spirit had crossed into Heaven as soon as the nurse unhooked her from the ventilator. But her physical body still had enough *power* to hold on for a bit longer. On her way out of the hospital room, her spirit must have flown by and touched the clock with her silky-smooth hands, causing it to malfunction.

The clock on the wall fast-forwarded by exactly eleven hours and then suddenly began ticking at a normal speed again. Therefore, the clock displayed the wrong time for the rest of the day. For example, it was supposed to display 10:00 but it was showing 9:00. Although Grandma was still alive in the physical sense, I knew her soul had already transitioned.

It was a long day in her hospital room. The hours passed slowly. Grandma's body had yet to expire. Family members swapped stories of all the adventures Grandma had taken with Boompa. *How many times had they been lost and low on gas while driving around the country? How many Nebraska Cornhusker football games had they sat through in rain, wind, snow, and heat?* It was heartwarming to picture the two of them reunited in Heaven. We'd laugh until we remembered how much we'd miss Grandma, and then we'd cry again. Our emotions were on a string and this game of yo-yo went on all afternoon.

My mom and Aunt Terry suggested that my siblings and I take a mental break and go grab a late lunch. *Or was it an early dinner?* The stress of the day had thrown off our internal clocks.

"No need in everyone being up here since we have no idea how long her body is going to hold on," my mom said. She insisted we leave, and promised they'd keep us updated if anything happened. I glanced out the window and wasn't looking forward to going outside. It was a wet, sloppy, dreary January day. It was cold enough to chill a person to the bone marrow. Somehow, the rain hadn't yet frozen to the ground. We hadn't seen the sun all day.

After our meal, my siblings and I stopped back for a report at the hospital. Nothing had changed. Mom and Terry volunteered to stay there with Grandma and suggested we all head home. I glanced at the time on my cell phone. My screensaver picture was a sunset photo I had taken days earlier. It was the one I had shown Grandma. It saddened me that we'd no longer be able to admire sunsets together. Putting my phone back in my pocket, I looked at the clock on the wall. It still displayed the wrong time, remaining one hour behind. "Alright," I said to my mom and Terry. "Let us know if anything changes."

With that, I headed out of the room and down the hallway. Despite the emotional fatigue, I had a song stuck in my head. The playlist in my mind had been stuck on 'repeat' all day long. It was a song by Linkin Park called *Shadow of the Day*. The lyrics ran around in my head like a sprinter circling a track. I heard the lines over and over again.

"In cards and flowers on your window
Your friends all plead for you to stay
Sometimes beginnings aren't so simple
Sometimes goodbye's the only way
And the sun will set for you
The sun will set for you
And the shadow of the day
Will embrace the world in grey
And the sun will set for you."

The song and its lyrics reminded me of Grandma, my sunset buddy who I'd said goodbye to. Still humming this song inside my mind, I scurried to my car, stomping through the wet parking lot. I climbed inside and turned the key. The radio turned on, and the song that was playing was *Shadow of the Day*. In fact, it played the same exact line of the song I was simultaneously singing in my head. The timing was unreal. *What were the odds?* Surely this was beyond coincidence. I took it as assurance that Grandma was already enjoying sunsets in Heaven.

I put the car in gear and exited the parking lot. Turning onto the main street, I crested the top of a hill. The song was enveloping me. It soothed my soul and calmed me. I looked up through my windshield with misty eyes and a half smile on my face. I wondered if Grandma could see me in that moment. I wondered if she could hear the song.

The dark clouds in the western sky suddenly parted for the first time all day, and the sun was now visible just in time to set. Before I knew it, the sky was on fire! Colors pierced through the clouds like a train punching through a tunnel. Shades of dandelion yellow and burnt orange reflected on the sides of buildings. The light poured through my car windows and warmed my face. It was a symphony of emotions, and was almost too much to handle. A salty tear rolled downstream into the corner of my lip.

It was almost completely dark by the time I arrived home. The sun always seems to go down faster in January. I awaited a call from my mom about Grandma's status. It was late into the evening when the call came. My mom's tone was soft and sweet. "Hey sweetie, she finally went. She passed about an hour ago." I held the phone to my ear and nodded in silence. It was merely a formality. I had already grieved and made my peace with the situation. My mental gas tank was empty.

"Hey you know that clock on the wall in Grandma's room," my mom continued. "The one that was acting strange earlier in the day?"

"Yeah," I responded with an exhausted sigh. "Did they figure out what was wrong with it?"

"No, but you're not going to believe what happened after you all left. Terry and I were sitting there holding Grandma's hands, and a few minutes before she passed away, the clock sped itself up again."

Butterflies floated around in my stomach as I listened intently.

"But this time, the clock fast-forwarded exactly *one* hour and then promptly stopped and began ticking normally again."

"So that means . . . um . . ." My exhausted brain was trying to do basic math.

"So," my mom interrupted. "The first time the clock sped up eleven hours and this time it sped up one hour. So, the time on the clock was finally right again. And then moments later, Grandma officially passed away."

I was flabbergasted. The bizarre events of the day were faith-affirming to say the least.

"Sweetie, I've got to go. Terry and I need to make some phone calls. Grandma's sister Vilma in Missouri hasn't gotten an update, so we need to call her." I told my mom I loved her and reminded her to get some sleep.

Mom and Terry relayed Grandma's official time of death to Vilma. Upon hearing it, Vilma said, "Well, that's odd. That was the same exact time our ceiling fan turned on all by itself. The darn thing wouldn't turn off!" Apparently, Vilma and her husband, Jim, were stumped by the electrical anomaly and had never experienced anything like that before. Vilma eventually concluded that her sister may have paid her a visit.

The weeks that followed were a bit fuzzy. It's strange how the details of a funeral service fade away and we only recall the most obscure details. I don't remember what types of flowers were there or what I wore. I do remember writing a poem for Grandma's funeral service. It had to do with sunsets, of course. My uncle read the poem to those in attendance.

Grandma was cremated. Some of her ashes went to my siblings and me. Mom and Terry kept some as well. It took me a while to get used to speaking of her in the past tense. Grandma *loved* fishing, as opposed to Grandma *loves* fishing. I knew I had lost my grandma but it didn't occur to me until she was gone that I had also lost one of my very best friends. I wondered if she viewed me in the same light. My mom later told me that Grandma looked forward to my visits far more than I was aware of. She claims Grandma would practically clear her schedule when she knew I'd be stopping over. I hadn't realized this when Grandma was alive, but it was flattering to hear. It was heartwarming to know she enjoyed our quality time just as much as I did.

Grandma had been in the nursing home facility for almost exactly a year before she passed. After eight months, she accepted that she would never again be able to move back to her home in Benson. My mom and Aunt Terry hired a house flipper who was contracted to make some improvements before the house would be put up for sale. A lot was updated, including new kitchen counters, new cabinets, a completely renovated bathroom, and all new appliances. I had seen updates in previous months and it looked amazing.

However, it secretly pained me to think we'd never again have a family gathering at Grandma's house. We wouldn't have the chance to sit on her porch and watch a sunset. I knew I would miss the familiar smells of the house such as the scent of old books in the den or the aroma of tomatoes freshly picked from her garden. I'd miss the red brick exterior and the sound of the wood porch creaking beneath my feet. We'd no longer have access to the physical reminders of family memories and lore, like the laundry chute where Uncle Tim got lodged when he was a kid . . . or the bedroom that was rebuilt after the tornado of '75.

Grandma's house was ground zero for this Myers family folklore. Sure, those stories would survive and be passed down to younger generations even if Grandma's house was no longer in our family. Still, it was a hard pill to swallow. This was weighing heavily on my mind as I left Grandma's funeral service. Suddenly, I received an unexpected phone call.

"Meet me at Grandma's house this afternoon. I have some good news." It was my mom. She sounded surprisingly upbeat for a person who'd just lost her mother-in-law, especially considering how close the two of them were.

"I'll be there at 1:00," I said. As I hung up the phone, I couldn't help but wonder why her voice contained equal parts excitement and hope.

Andy's aunt, Terry Myers

Andy's family, left to right: David, Sue, Andy, Elizabeth

Chapter 8

We stood in the kitchen of Grandma's house. My mom wondered if I would be interested in buying the home. As the words left her mouth, my mom's eyes misted over with joy. I could tell she was trying to hold back a smile, but she's never had much of a poker face.

For a moment, I was speechless. The idea of buying Grandma's house had never occurred to me. At the time, I was eking by on a social worker's salary. I figured I might buy a house someday, but I figured that *someday* was still much further down the road. The idea of living there sounded appealing, but I wasn't sure I could afford the mortgage payments, even if they were rather low.

I shared these concerns with my mom, but she held up her pointer finger as if to politely interject. She informed me that with Grandma's passing and some additional assistance from Aunt Terry, my financial situation was about to change. I was in shock and nearly fainted. Purchasing my grandma's house was suddenly possible.

I interlaced my fingers as I clasped my hands together on top of my head. I needed a moment to take it all in. My eyes wandered from one part of the kitchen to another. I glanced at the empty floor below the windows where the kitchen table used to rest. It brought back memories of playing board games with Grandma. Inhaling a deep breath through my nose, I could still smell traces of my childhood.

My gaze fell upon the empty counter by the stove where the toaster used to be. I thought back to the time when Grandma overcooked some toast, and instead of throwing it away, she merely scraped off the black crumbs with a butter knife and claimed it was still edible. I couldn't fathom how a woman so frugal was able to leave a substantial inheritance to us all. This was a lady who would re-run the coffee maker in mid-afternoon using coffee grounds from breakfast. Wasteful she was not. I always assumed she lived that way because her budget required it. As it turned out, I was wrong. Apparently, she'd invested wisely a few decades prior, and living a modest lifestyle was simply her way of ensuring the rest of us would be okay once she departed this Earth.

I turned to my mom and said, "Do you think my foosball table will fit in the basement?"

She pulled me in for a bear hug. "You're going to love it here! And Grandma will be so happy to know you're enjoying the house. I'm sure she'll 'visit' you all the time! We better get ahold of the contractor soon though, because he was planning to list the house for sale on Monday."

I couldn't believe the timing of it all. If Grandma had died just a week later, the house would have been on the market and would have sold before I was financially able to make an offer. It was priced to sell. The timing of the situation made me wonder if some grand plan was in place. It felt as though the Universe was looking out for me. Perhaps Grandma herself was subconsciously part of this plan and chose to 'let go' when she did as a way of allowing this to happen.

It all happened so quickly it was a blur. The corner of Pinkney and 67th Avenue was my new residence. The month was nothing short of an emotional trampoline, providing enough lows and highs to make one's head spin. The sadness of losing her was mixed with the excitement of moving into her home.

Grandma's bedroom became *my* bedroom. I turned one of the spare bedrooms into a little art studio – a quiet place where I could draw and paint. I knew Grandma would approve since she always encouraged my artistic side. My mom and I mixed some of Grandma's ashes into the soil of the flower bed on the front side of the house, just below the day lilies. The rest of her ashes were sprinkled in Nebraska City where she grew up fishing and playing along the railcars with her sister, Vilma.

The Benson house felt like home immediately. Every nook, closet, and drawer brought back memories of the treasures once stored there. Cosmetically, the home was a bit different, but its personality remained intact. One aspect of the house that hadn't changed was the basement. In my youth, the basement (and the stairs leading down there) gave me the creeps. One might expect a person to outgrow such fears, but I still couldn't shake the feeling of being followed while walking up and down those basement stairs.

Perhaps basements belong in the same category as snakes and spiders, hardwired into our DNA as something that makes a person's skin crawl. Simply put, the basement of the Benson house felt haunted. As a child, Grandma or Boompa would sometimes ask my brother or I to grab something from the basement like a flashlight or a spare battery. We'd always look at each other wide-eyed in terror, as if they just asked us to handle a live scorpion. We'd often make up some excuse to use the buddy system.

Grandma would shrug her shoulders, wondering why it took two of us to accomplish a one-person job. We'd slowly shuffle down the stairs together, on edge and bumping into each other like the characters from a Scooby-Doo episode. We'd find the item we required and would bolt upstairs as quickly as possible, running like we had bumble bees down our undershorts. It always felt like some invisible presence was hot on our heels.

It wasn't long after moving in that I saved up enough money to have the basement finished. It's funny how adding some carpet and applying a fresh coat of paint can really change the energetic vibes of a place. It suddenly felt less ominous. Once I moved a TV down there, I was one pinball machine short of a rec room. It was a good space to unwind and relax . . . or so I thought.

Chapter 9

One afternoon, I fell asleep on the couch in the basement. I didn't mean to, but I was watching a documentary narrated by a British fellow. The hushed tones and cadence of his speech lulled me into a hypnotic stupor. Suddenly, I was awoken by an invisible presence shouting my name into my ear. *Andy!* I bolted upright like the house was on fire, and my heartbeat would have matched that of a hummingbird's. Goosebumps formed on my neck and forearms as my eyes darted back and forth around the empty room.

I wasn't dreaming when I heard the voice shout my name, so I didn't believe it was my imagination. The voice was audible and external rather than inside my own head. I looked at the TV, wondering if someone in the documentary might have loudly said my name. The British narrator was still speaking softly about the migration of humpback whales, so I ruled that out. I couldn't help but feel that I wasn't alone. I was being watched.

The presence felt mischievous but certainly not malicious. *Was I the butt of a paranormal joke? Had a ghost dared another ghost to wake me up by shouting my name?* I felt uneasy, like the space was not fully my own. It reminded me of the feeling I get when sitting in a chair that was recently occupied by someone else and I can still feel the person's body heat on my posterior. The fully-finished basement lured me into a false sense of security and caused me to let my intuitive guard down. If this was the consequence, I figured I could live with it. If my house was a deck of cards, the basement would have been the Joker. Thankfully, the rest of the home felt neutral in a paranormal sense.

The phenomena happened again just a few weeks later. While vacuuming the basement carpet, an urgent voice pierced my ears and my name was shouted. *Andy!* It was loud enough that I heard the voice over the deafening roar of the vacuum cleaner. It startled me so badly that I flinched and nearly stumbled into the wall.

In the years since this happened, I've discovered that this phenomenon is more common than one might think. People from all walks of life are prone to audibly hearing their name whispered or shouted when nobody else is around. *Who is the culprit?* In some cases it can be attributed to a ghost, which is an earthbound human who has died but hasn't yet crossed into the afterlife. Some ghosts attach themselves to a particular person for a period of time. Other ghosts are more interested in real estate and tend to hang around a physical location such as a house or building, regardless of the occupants.

In other instances, a guardian angel or a loved one in Heaven could audibly say a person's name as a form of, "Hello. I'm with you. I love you." Admittedly, the shock factor associated with this phenomenon is rather high. It tends to give a person heart flutters and goosebumps whether the voice is coming from a ghost or a loved one in Heaven. The fact remains that it's entirely possible for the deceased to communicate audibly with us. If they're trying to saying something, it's just a matter of time before we hear them. All it requires is for us to briefly be on their frequency.

At the Benson house, I had a CD player in the basement. It was a multi-disc changer that had about six discs in it. About once a month it would turn on in the middle of the night and begin blasting music from its speakers. It would startle me awake, and I'd hesitantly make my way down there to investigate.

It took some common-sense rationalizing to make sure there wasn't a logical explanation. I wondered if maybe it was on a timer and could turn itself on at a particular time. I quickly discovered that was not the case. Furthermore, it was not the type of CD player that would start playing music just by pushing the power button. You actually had to push the 'on' button followed by the 'play' button for a CD to begin. Therefore, the machine was clearly under intelligent control. It wasn't a mere glitch stemming from its power source.

I wondered who might be attempting to get my attention. Naturally, I thought of my grandma first. Then again, she was gentle and kind enough that she'd probably want me to sleep well and not be bothered in the middle of the night. I found it hard to believe she'd do something so inconvenient to get my attention at 2:00 in the morning. Next, I wondered if it could be my dad. This notion made more sense because he could be playful and a bit ornery at times. Plus, my dad was a real night owl due to working overnight shifts, so the middle of the night seemed like an appropriate time for him to be mischievous. The CD player antics were becoming a nuisance because they were causing me to lose sleep. I eventually said a prayer to my dad and grandma, asking them for a different type of sign. It didn't take long until my request was granted, but I never expected it to happen in such a bizarre manner.

Chapter 10

I was happy being a new home owner. It came with a sense of pride, a feeling of freedom. If I wanted to change the landscaping or repaint a room, I could. I decided to alter the color of the kitchen. It took me the better part of a Saturday, but I didn't mind. The rhythmic brushstrokes of painting tend to put my mind at ease and soothe my soul.

Once finished, I stood back to admire my handiwork. "Well, Grandma, how do you like the new paint color?" I'd gotten into the habit of talking to her out loud from time to time. On some level, I could sense her presence and knew she was never too far away.

Much like a chef loathes doing dishes after cooking, the cleanup process is never something a painter looks forward to. I had brushes, rags, tarps, and paint rollers to put away. I carried everything to the basement and put the supplies in the laundry room. It was an unfinished utility area with a concrete floor. There was a deep wash basin in the corner, and I began rinsing the paint off the metal paint rollers. As I was cleaning up, I kept thinking of my grandma and wondering what she thought of the changes I'd made to the house.

I set the paint roller inside the sink and turned around. I walked across the room to a cabinet and reached inside to get some clean rags for drying off the supplies. As I turned around to make my way back to the sink, I flinched as I saw an object in mid-air headed toward me. The metal paint roller was airborne, floating towards me like someone had tossed a Frisbee in my direction. Before my brain had time to process what I was seeing, the paint roller crashed to the floor and slid to a stop at my feet. I was standing approximately ten feet from the sink, so it was clear the paint roller hadn't simply *fallen* out of the sink. It had been *propelled* with a great deal of force.

I stood there motionless for what felt like an eternity as my body's fight or flight response teetered back and forth like a see-saw. I dared not move and instinctually held my breath. Either I had just witnessed an unexplained gravitational anomaly, or I was in the presence of an intelligent entity capable of moving inanimate objects. When one bears witness to an occurrence that defies the laws of physics, it makes one question everything. *What is real? What is not? What exists around us that cannot be seen?*

I scanned the room with my peripheral vision, my eyes darting back and forth like the ball in a ping-pong match. I bent down to pick up the paint roller, half expecting it to be a figment of my imagination. A psychotic break or a lapse in reality would have made more sense. Paint rollers cannot fly across the room on their own accord. When I touched it with my own hands, reality set in. I'd just witnessed something that science would classify as impossible.

In hindsight, I'm sure Grandma was standing somewhere nearby waiting for that lightbulb to turn on above my head. Tossing a paint roller across the room was merely her way of acknowledging my previous question when I asked if she liked the new paint color. *Did a flying paint roller indicate she liked the new kitchen color?* I guess the jury is still out on that one, but knowing how sweet and gentle Grandma was, she wouldn't have had strong opinions about the paint color either way. Nevertheless, if she were trying to get my attention, she had succeeded.

This instance alone was proof that it's possible to communicate with those in the afterlife. Little did I know at the time, the strange series of events had only just begun. The flying paint roller was the springboard that propelled me into the deep end of a paranormal swimming pool. In terms of my psychic senses, it was now time to sink or swim.

Chapter 11

I was driving home from a little getaway with a few friends. We were passing through Waterloo, Iowa, en route to Omaha. We were hungry and stopped at a restaurant. After we ate and paid our bill, I must have had a strange look on my face, because my friends asked me what was on my mind. "Nothing," I replied, as I grabbed the car keys and asked if everyone was ready to go. I was too timid to mention that I had sensed something about our waitress. The others in my party probed further until I admitted to having an intuitive hunch. They badgered me and insisted I go find the waitress. They wanted me to verify if my psychic hunch was correct.

"Oh, come on guys! She's busy waiting on other tables, and we need to make good time if we're going to get home before dark." Ignoring my protest, they playfully stole the car keys from my hands and refused to let us leave the restaurant until I marched over to the waitress and talked to her. Half annoyed and half terrified, I hesitantly agreed. If, after consulting with the waitress, I found my intuitive hunch to be incorrect, I would naturally conclude that all my recent intuitive thoughts about strangers were wrong. *Was it possible that my hunches were nothing more than my imagination playing tricks on me?*

"Excuse me," I said with a trembling voice. I was so embarrassed that my face must have been three shades of pink, like a Valentine's Day card.

"Can I help you? Was there a problem with your bill or something?"

"No," I replied, nervously scratching the back of my head. "I was just wondering . . . I had an intuition or something . . . and I was just curious to know if you take an interest in interior design. And also, my sixth sense led me to believe you have a three-year-old son."

I looked back at the entry way to see my friends smiling obnoxiously and giving me a cheesy thumbs up. I rolled my eyes in disgust and shooed them away with my hands as if to say, "Get lost." Turning my attention back to the waitress, I asked, "Does this make any sense? Sorry to bug you with these crazy questions."

She seemed a bit caught off guard, but clearly not annoyed. This was a relief to me. "Actually, it's funny you mention that. I actually just graduated with a degree in interior design. And, yeah, I have one child . . . a son. He just turned three last month. I can't believe how big he's getting."

I breathed such a big sigh of relief that it must have been audible to the cooks back in the kitchen.

"Are you a fortune teller or something?" she asked with a curious smile on her face.

"No," I replied. "Sometimes I just sense things about people."

After thanking the waitress for her time, I was gone in a flash. I darted off like a monkey who'd just stolen food from a tourist in India. I wanted to exit the restaurant as quickly as possible before people started to give me strange looks. The validation from the waitress made me feel sane, like there might be some substance to the hunches I'd been having.

Admittedly, I wasn't sure if there were any practical applications of sensing someone had an interior design degree and a toddler at home. I just figured that sensing those two things about the waitress defied statistical probability or chance. I wondered if I could harness my intuition to *really* help people. Perhaps I could give them detailed, practical insights that could benefit their lives. I suppose it was my inner social worker coming out.

After that experience at the restaurant, I was no longer a psychic virgin. Select family members slowly became more aware of my experiences, and thankfully they were tremendously supportive. Coming out of the psychic closet was a liberating experience. My mom and Aunt Terry not only accepted my intuitive side, they *encouraged* it. They reminded me that I come from psychic pedigree and that Grandma Myers had her own array of psychic occurrences throughout her life.

My sister caught wind of what was going on. She insisted I needed some psychic practice and volunteered her close friends to be used as guinea pigs. I was suddenly giving psychic readings for fun, as a way to practice. Only a few years prior, I could never have imagined I'd be doing such a thing. I laughed at the irony of a psychic who can't predict his own future.

I didn't have Tarot cards or a crystal ball. I wasn't performing behind a beaded curtain or wearing a turban. I guess some stereotypes are made to be broken. Initially, the psychic readings only lasted five minutes, maybe ten. I was a rookie who was learning his trade, trying my best to provide helpful insights for my newfound clients.

I found myself giving psychic sessions more and more frequently. At home, I turned one of the spare bedrooms into a cozy little office to meet with clients. It consisted of a bookshelf, a love seat, and a couple of chairs. It was the den – the spare bedroom where my grandma had read books to me in my youth which ignited my curiosity about life's mysteries. I thought it was very fitting to be using the room for my new endeavor. It felt like I had home field advantage. I couldn't think of a better place to conduct my appointments.

Meanwhile, I was invited to be a guest on Omaha's most popular radio station, Sweet 98. Pat and J.T. were the morning show disc jockeys and they had caught word of me through a mutual friend. To my surprise, they invited me on the show to talk about the paranormal. They thought it would make for an entertaining segment on their show. They wanted me to talk about psychic abilities and share a few ghost stories. After this, there was no going back. I'd publicly be known as a psychic. I agreed to come, having no idea how profoundly it would end up changing the rest of my life.

I was honored to have the opportunity, but on the inside I was secretly trembling like a freshman on the first day of high school. I was nervous and didn't want to make any blunders. Plus, I had to keep in mind that J.T. was the woman and Pat was the guy, not the other way around.

Compared to the pressure of being in the public spotlight, my social work job suddenly seemed very comfortable and safe.

With the microphone shoved into my lips and sweat forming underneath my headphones, the DJs ambushed me and took a call from a listener who wanted psychic information. Prior to the show, I was told I would *not* be giving psychic readings, but in the moment, there was nothing I could do but go along with it. In hindsight, I can't remember what the caller asked me. It all happened so quickly. I figured it must have gone well, because Pat and J.T. seemed very pleased. They invited me to come back again.

A few appearances turned into a regular gig, and before I knew it, I was appearing on their morning show every other Friday to chat about psychic abilities, ghost stories, dream interpretation, guardian angels, reincarnation, and a host of other topics. I took questions from callers and demonstrated how psychic abilities work. This gave me a platform to reach more people.

Word got around. Soon, the phones at the station were jammed with callers wanting me to demonstrate mediumship, which is the ability to communicate with deceased loved ones. I slowly improved my ability to relay messages from people in Heaven. My home office was then flooded with calls from people wanting private appointments. The psychic sessions began taking up all of my free time in the evenings after my social work job.

As all this was happening, I formed a discussion group called the Omaha Metaphysical Network. We shortened it to the OM Network, an appropriate name considering 'Om' is an ancient word for 'God' and our group was a spiritual gathering at its core. It was an open forum, a safe place for members of the general public to meet and discuss common interests. We talked about past lifetimes, near-death experiences, ghost stories, UFOs, inspiring books, meditation, and messages from loved ones in Heaven.

I facilitated the meetings and was surprised to see how well they were attended. At any given meeting, we'd welcome in twenty or thirty people. I was equally surprised to find that attendees were down to earth, everyday people. The discussions were attended by teachers, counselors, nurses, stay-at-home moms, construction workers, police officers, and other upstanding citizens. It broke the mold by proving normal, everyday people can express an interest in such topics. It was refreshing. Gone was the era of meeting in secret by candlelight to discuss these topics. We met at public library conference rooms. The meetings reminded us that a person's spiritual journey doesn't need to be a lonely one.

The meetings were refreshing, not just for others in attendance, but for myself as well. My spiritual journey had come a long way since seeing the Universe on my bedroom ceiling and spending countless hours reading all those books by myself. I suddenly had the best friends I could have ever hoped for. It was wonderful and I felt so blessed.

Back at my social work job, things were not so wonderful. I was employed at an alternative school, working with teens who had reputations for being violent. Some days, it was very rewarding work, and other days it was downright dangerous. Despite the fact that I have a gentle disposition and shy away from conflict, I had somehow managed to upset one of the teens. She had gang affiliations and had been in possession of a firearm in recent months. When she told me she was going to put a bullet in my head, I didn't brush it off as an empty threat. She and her fellow gang members had the means to actually do it.

I decided that I liked my head just how it was – free of holes. I did some soul searching one cold evening after work and concluded that the job wasn't worth risking my life. Over the years, my focus had shifted to more spiritual topics anyway, and I was beginning to wonder if it was my calling. I was busier than ever giving psychic readings from my home office and wondered if I could make a full-time job out of it.

I was now getting paid for delivering psychic readings, and although it wasn't much, I thought if I worked hard enough, I might be able to make ends meet. With a combination of fear and excitement, I put in my notice that I'd be leaving my social work job. On January 1, 2010, I became a full-time psychic medium and life coach. It seemed fitting to make a career change on the very first day of the decade. The timing seemed like an interesting synchronicity.

The decision was a risky one, but I wasn't making it alone. My grandma was behind me one hundred percent. I could feel her spiritual presence and support. My dad hadn't messed with the basement CD player in a few weeks, but I knew he was backing me as well.

It was around this time that I began to sense a regular presence around me. It was a spirit who called himself Henry, and he often seemed to be close by. I couldn't always see him, but I could sense his presence. I could even hear him, much like I could hear the words spoken by the deceased family members of my clients. Henry didn't burst into my life like a wrecking ball. He eased into the picture slowly, like a sloth moving down a tree. Perhaps he waded into my life so gradually as to not overwhelm me. I eventually concluded that Henry was one of my guardian angels.

Had he always been my guardian angel or was he a newly arrived member of my spiritual team? Perhaps my newfound intuition had finally allowed me to feel his presence even though he'd been with me my whole life. I wasn't entirely sure. One thing was for certain though. Henry was much more than an imaginary friend. He knew what he was talking about. He'd often speak to me through the psychic walkie talkie in my head during my psychic sessions. He'd help me with predictions and information that had a high degree of difficulty – the psychic equivalent of a triple Lutz in figure skating.

With Henry's help, I relayed information to my clients that was so specific, it had a low probability of actually being correct. For example, Henry once told me that my client Mary had a problem with her back, specifically in the T12/L1 area of her spinal column. Mary verified it as accurate, saying that just two weeks prior she'd gotten the same diagnosis from a spine surgeon.

In another session, Henry wanted me to mention that my client's husband had just bought a boat for their summer home in the Ozarks. . . and how Uncle Glen was flying in from Washington to join them on their boating trip. Again, the information was validated by my client. I was just as surprised as they were. Then again, spirits can be everywhere all at once, so with that kind of perspective, it's no wonder Henry was up to date on everyone's current events and whereabouts.

Messages and predictions like these became commonplace. Some days I felt like nothing more than a glorified delivery boy. I couldn't exactly take credit for the messages I was relaying. I was simply relying on what Henry was telling me and I was giving the information to my clients, like a parrot who mindlessly repeats what its owner says.

During this phase of my career, I felt like Henry was grooming me and helping me learn my trade. He was the master and I was the apprentice. As time went by, dozens of psychic readings turned into hundreds. Hundreds turned into thousands. I was still a regular guest on the radio, and was giving more private sessions than ever before. I found myself booked up months in advanced with people wanting private appointments. Meanwhile, the Omaha Metaphysical Network was still meeting each month. Life was good. I was happy beyond belief and truly grateful for all the blessings that had come my way.

Chapter 12

As I found my intuitive rhythm, I felt Henry begin to pull away a bit. He wasn't leaving. He was just giving me enough space to focus on my work without holding my hand the whole time. He insisted that I rely solely on other sources for intuitive information, such as the guardian angels and deceased relatives of my clients. Henry was done acting as the middle man. He encouraged me to spread my psychic wings and fly. At this point, my mediumship abilities began to fully bloom.

Henry was still active in my life. When I had a bad day or was in a pickle, I would consult with him for guidance. As my guardian angel, he never told me what to do with my life. Sometimes I wished he *would*, but he never did. My decisions were mine to make and he refused to interfere with my free will. Like a teacher coaching his student through a test, he didn't give me the answers. He merely gave me *hints* so I could make sound decisions on my own. As he continued to pull back, he was always accessible but shifted to an 'on-call' basis.

Ever since I first started sensing his presence, everything about him felt familiar – his energy, his demeanor, the way he talked. Even his appearance seemed familiar. It caused me to experience déjà vu, like I've known him before. Henry is Native American. His dark brown hair is pulled back into a pony tail and he has tan skin. He stands at an average height with fairly broad shoulders and a stocky build.

Seeing images of Henry in my mind's eye brought back the distinct feeling that I, myself, had been a Native American in a past lifetime. It brought me back to *Dances with Wolves* and what a profound impact that movie had on me. I remembered throwing plastic tomahawks and shouting lines from the movie in a language my soul still remembered.

Deep in my heart I knew that Henry was much more than just my guardian angel. He was my friend, my past life buddy who roamed the Midwestern plains with me in the 1800s, back when we were members of the Sioux tribe. I couldn't prove it, but I was certain of this truth. And I knew this was possible, because guardian angels do not have wings and halos. They're merely people who used to be alive. Often, they're individuals we've known in previous lifetimes.

It might seem strange, but it's absolutely true. It's possible to have a guardian angel who was a neighbor from a past life in London, a co-worker from a past life in Egypt, or a brother from a previous lifetime during the Industrial Revolution. The backstories of our guardian angels are as rich and intricate as the script of a Hollywood movie. In these previous lifetimes, we've grown to know and love our guardian angels. Our subconscious can't always recall these previous adventures. They tend to fade away like the misty details of a dream in the morning time. Yet, the *soul* never forgets. And when the intuitive winds are behind our sails, it's entirely possible to recall information about our guardian angels.

As I made the connection and realized Henry was my friend from the 1800s, the intuitive dam broke. Images and memories came pouring in from the past lifetime I'd shared with him. They fluttered around my head and consumed my thoughts. The images were crystal clear and I was mentally reliving the events that had transpired over a hundred years ago.

I saw myself inside a tent or teepee, daylight flickering through the flaps of the entry way. I was curled up in the fetal position, blood seeping from an open wound in my abdomen. I tried to block out the pain by thinking of something else, *anything* else. I focused on the noises outside. I heard children laughing off in the distance, dogs barking, the muffled and concerned voices of nearby tribe members, the sound of rustling leaves in the wind. I imagined my best friend Henry, nervously pacing outside my tent. He must have felt completely helpless.

I was dying. This much was clear. An arrow had pierced my stomach. The incident did not occur in battle. It was an accident, a matter of being in the wrong place at the wrong time as an inexperienced shooter was practicing with his bow and arrow. I was unlucky that it didn't kill me quickly. This was a slow death, and the pain was horrific. I had accepted my fate and intended to meet my maker with honor and dignity.

I chose to live out my remaining hours by myself in this tent. I didn't want my wife or children to see me in such agony. I was in pain but not scared. I was alone but not lonely. I felt connected to something greater than myself. Through the pain, I felt mental clarity and spiritual contentment. It was the end of that chapter, but not the end of my story. I knew that my soul was immortal, that I was an eternal being who would one day live again.

As the intensity of the pain increased, my breaths became shallow. Looking through the flap in my tent, the last thing I saw before everything went dark was the sunlight glistening off the quivering leaves in a nearby tree. I felt my body relax. Everything went dark, and my soul was free.

Chapter 13

These past life memories tumbled through my mind like socks in a dryer. Oddly enough, the memory of dying from the arrow in my stomach reminded me of something that happened in my youth. I was ten years old and was at a hockey game with my family. We had season tickets to watch the Omaha Lancers, and it became our tradition. Grandma always came with us and she'd sit next to me each game.

One particular night, we were enjoying the game when my stomach suddenly began to hurt. At first, it was just a moderate, dull pain, so I didn't think much of it. I figured that perhaps dinner wasn't agreeing with me. Minute by minute, the sensation grew more intense. Grandma brought it to the attention of my parents that I was nearly doubled over in pain. Clearly, something was very wrong. I'd never had stomach issues before, let alone pain so acute. It was something I'd never experienced before. It felt like I'd been shot or stabbed in the stomach.

With help from my mom, I got up, and she assisted me to the car. She drove me to the hospital faster than a NASCAR driver could have. I'm sure she feared the worst. *Was it a hernia? Appendicitis?* I had no clue and neither did my mom. She stared at me with a helpless look in her eyes as I writhed in agony. The only thing that made the pain more tolerable was balling myself up into the fetal position. Folded in half, I tried to focus on anything else but the pain. With my eyes closed and my jaw clenched, I gently rocked back and forth. The movement was soothing.

By the time I was seen by a doctor, the pain had started to decrease. They did some simple tests to rule out a few obvious conditions. And while the doctor was conversing with us, the pain had subsided to the point where it hardly bothered me anymore. As quickly and mysteriously as the condition had come on, it had simply gone away.

There was really nothing else to do. The doctor could only guess as to what may have caused the issue. He gave us permission to leave, but encouraged us to come back right away if the pain returned. The whole incident happened so quickly that my mom and I made it back to the hockey game in time for the start of the third period. Settling back into our seats, my grandma and the others asked how I was feeling. I said I felt perfect. Never better. I asked them to pass me the popcorn and I enjoyed the rest of my evening with no pain in my stomach whatsoever.

One must not get carried away in thinking that every incident has past life ties or paranormal implications. Most events have a down to earth explanation. However, it does make me wonder if that stomach pain was somehow left over from my Native American lifetime. Had the trauma crossed the divide between lifetimes? It's entirely possible for this to occur. What happened to me that night at the hockey game was rather tame compared to other past life case studies. There's some truly remarkable evidence when it comes to the concept of reincarnation and how past lives presently affect us.

Chapter 14

Even though we have a new body with each lifetime, it's possible for our souls to retain information from one life to the next. If the wires get crossed, so to speak, it's possible to be confused about which lifetime we're currently living, and therefore we could feel pain or have memories stemming from a past incarnation.

One subject that lends credibility to this idea is the phenomena of organ transplants. At one point in time, the *Science Channel* aired a show called *The Unexplained Files*. The show featured an interview with Dr. Gary Schwartz, a professor of neurology who is affiliated with the University of Arizona. He's the co-author of a research paper that discusses ten case studies in which organ recipients claimed to take on personality traits or memories of the donor.

One example was an incident involving an eight-year-old girl who received a new heart from a girl who was murdered. After receiving the new heart, the little girl started having frequent nightmares about her organ donor's murder. It felt like she was taking on the other girl's memories of the tragic incident. The dreams were so detailed that the information was passed on to police. Authorities used the new clues to positively identify the suspect, and ultimately it led to the murderer's conviction.

Dr. Schwartz believes there's enough evidence to suggest it's possible for personality traits, personal preferences, and even *memories* to be transferred from one person to another via organ transplants. How exactly this works is not yet understood. After all, hearts and kidneys and other organs are not known to possess consciousness. Unlike our brains, these organs are not known to have the capacity to store complex data such as memories. Yet, somehow, it seems that they do.

In terms of reincarnation, these implications are *huge*. If data, information, and memories can be stored in organs and passed from one body to another, then our soul/spirit would theoretically act in much the same way. This would make it possible for people to recall events they've experienced in previous lifetimes. We clearly get a new body with each new lifetime, but what if the data is still intact from previous versions of ourselves? What if the information is still there, tucked away in a file somewhere in our soul?

Computers offer a simple analogy of this notion. Accessing past life information (memories, pains, fears, or talents) is no different than taking a memory card out of one computer and plugging it into another computer. Think of our bodies as the hardware, the computer. Our souls are merely the software, the data, the information. Just like a portable memory card, the information can easily be transferred from one machine to another.

Unfortunately, this sometimes includes physical pains or emotional baggage in our current life that originates from a previous lifetime. The emotional baggage from past lifetimes can have a long-lasting effect on us, whereas physical issues, such as my stomach pain at the hockey game, are often short-lived. Thankfully, it's not always negative traits that are carried into our current life from previous incarnations. Talents, interests, and even a predisposition for speaking a particular language can also be carried over from previous versions of ourselves.

Take for example the 2016 case of a high school soccer player in Georgia named Reuben Nsemoh. Reuben was kicked in the head during a game and suffered a serious concussion. He was air-lifted to a hospital and remained in a coma for three days. Upon waking up from the coma, the first words out of his mouth were in Spanish. As Reuben became more alert, it was apparent to his friends and family that he was suddenly *fluent* in Spanish, despite only knowing a couple Spanish words before the head trauma. His ability to speak fluent Spanish faded with time, and slowly, his ability to speak English returned.

There's a medical term for this condition. Appropriately enough, it's referred to as Foreign Language Syndrome. It's related to a similar condition called Foreign Accent Syndrome. Doctors are still unable to explain how this occurs, but in my opinion, it's easy to connect the dots. Reuben spoke Spanish in one of his recent past lifetimes. Therefore, he's known Spanish all along. He just couldn't remember it until the head trauma made him confused as to which life he was actually living. The story made national news and was covered by a host of media outlets.

Although rare, cases like this *do* occur. Major news networks reported a case of a man named Michael Thomas Boatwright who was found unconscious inside a motel in Southern California. While medical staff was caring for him at Desert Regional Medical Center, authorities discovered he was a Navy veteran originally born in Florida. For unknown reasons, Michael could not remember anything about his own life. He didn't recall serving in the Navy and he didn't even recognize his own picture when authorities showed him his driver's license. He couldn't explain why there were tennis rackets in his bags, and he claimed that even his own name, Michael Thomas Boatwright, didn't ring a bell. He was adamant that his name was Johan Ek. As if that weren't bizarre enough, the 61-year-old man spoke fluent Swedish and didn't appear to know a word of English.

With time, his English slowly came back, and he attempted to accept his life as Michael, but only because doctors insisted it was the healthy thing to do. It doesn't take a rocket scientist to conclude that Michael had a recent past lifetime in Sweden, where his name was most likely Johan. It's the *only* explanation that makes any sense. After all, even if you dismiss this case by saying that Michael was merely having a mental breakdown, that still doesn't account for the fact that he inexplicably developed the ability to speak a new language overnight.

It's not just the ability to speak a foreign language that can seep through from one lifetime to the next. Head trauma can cause previously unknown *talents* to rise to the surface. This was the case for Derek Amato, who suffered a severe brain injury after diving into the shallow end of a pool. After he recovered, he somehow acquired the ability to play the piano at a skill level that would typically require a lifetime worth of training.

Before the head injury, Derek had received no classical piano training whatsoever.

To this day, he isn't able to read or write music. The notes just appear in his mind and he tickles the keys as if he's been doing it his entire life. Researchers were absolutely baffled and could come up with no logical explanation. Derek is one of a select few individuals worldwide to be diagnosed with Acquired Savant Syndrome – a condition where head trauma or bodily injury mysteriously unlocks a previously unknown talent within a person. Derek's story was covered by countless mainstream news stations.

Once again, it's not much of a stretch to assume Derek was a master pianist in a past lifetime. Like most of us, he simply came into this current lifetime with a blank slate, an amnesia that prevented him from remembering how to play the piano . . . that is, until the injury caused the long-lost talent to be unlocked.

Reincarnation provides us with a chance to come back for as many lifetimes as we wish. Life on Earth allows us to have experiences we cannot have in the afterlife. For example, one cannot play the role of firefighter in Heaven because Heaven is safe and there are no fires to put out. One cannot fulfill a life's passion as a therapist in the afterlife because there is no trauma, and therefore nobody who needs counseling.

We live lifetimes on Earth to try out a plethora of roles. In doing so, we acquire wisdom and experience. There are many roles to be tried, which is why we come back time and time again. We can experience life through the lens of teacher, student, doctor, patient, artist, advocate, forgiver, healer, adventurer, and even trouble maker. The list is endless. This makes the whole concept of reincarnation seem as though life itself is a community playhouse and we're merely actors who put on a new costume for each unique production.

As for my stomach pain at the hockey game, it was the one and only time I ever encountered that issue. I do believe it was an unfortunate side-effect of what happened in my past lifetime. The most interesting part of going to the emergency room was that it occurred right around my tenth birthday – just a couple of months after seeing *Dances with Wolves* at the movie theater. The film must have jarred something loose within my soul, and confused my body into reliving the last moments from my life in the Sioux tribe. Like most past life trauma, once it rose to the surface, it floated away and never affected me again.

The topic of past lives was quickly becoming my favorite paranormal niche. It was a subject that fascinated me more than anything else. I was hooked. Furthermore, I was shocked at how many of my clients were interested in discussing past lives. The vast majority of them believed in the subject . . . even those who were not raised to believe in such ideas.

Chapter 15

"I'd like to believe we can all live again, but why don't they mention reincarnation at church?" It was a lady who'd called into the radio station. I adjusted my headphones and turned up the volume to my microphone.

I covered the mic with my hand and whispered to Pat and J.T., asking permission to field the lady's question. After all, this was a top-40 station, not Christian radio. They each gave me a distracted thumbs up as they shuffled audio files on their computer screens.

I explained to the caller that reincarnation wasn't a New Age topic, but rather a very ancient concept. It's widely accepted in many parts of the world. Reincarnation is often scoffed at by Americans because the majority of Americans are Christian, and Christians do not believe in reincarnation.

"But they did a long time ago," I said to the caller.

The lady seemed interested, so I continued with a brief history lesson. I explained that in the fourth century A.D., the Roman Emperor Constantine got together with other religious and political big shots of that era to make some important decisions. This gathering was known as the Council of Nicaea, and the agenda for their meeting was to decide which books and scriptures would be included in the Bible and which ones would be left out. After all, Christianity was in its infancy. So, in an effort to have outsiders take their new religion seriously, they needed all their followers to be united under one belief system, reading and adhering only to the 'official' scriptures.

For controversial reasons, Emperor Constantine and his associates decided that all scriptures mentioning past lives and reincarnation would be excluded from the Bible. There were many scriptures suggestive of reincarnation. If they had decided to *include* those texts, modern Christians would have grown up believing in past lives. It's amazing how many of our modern beliefs are actually molded by the historical roll of the dice. One slight nudge in any direction can drastically change the societal norms of future generations.

Thanks to Roman Emperor Constantine, many people in the Western world now raise a skeptical eyebrow to the concept of reincarnation. It's not their fault though. People tend to believe what they were *taught* to believe, and have a habit of disregarding evidence that makes them question things outside their comfort zone. That being said, it's surprising that more Christians aren't open-minded to reincarnation. After all, it supports and substantiates the promise of life after death, which is a notion that's preached in churches every Sunday morning.

"Reincarnation just takes it a step further," I suggested to the lady on the phone. "It means that we not only survive death, but can come back to Earth as many times as we'd like."

"But if we come right back for another life," she asked, "how is it possible to be reunited with our loved ones in Heaven when we die? How can a medium like you communicate with people in the afterlife if they're already back on Earth again?"

J.T. looked up from her computer and leaned into her microphone. "Wow! That's a good point. I've never thought about it like that before." She glanced over at me and grimaced, hoping the question wouldn't leave me stumped or flustered.

"It's a great question," I assured the caller. "And it's actually one of the most common questions people ask me."

I explained that when we die, we don't immediately come back to Earth for another lifetime. We typically spend several decades in Heaven before incarnating again. Therefore, even if loved ones passed away twenty or thirty years prior, there's a very good chance we'll be reunited with them in the afterlife. There *have* been a few cases of a person coming back to Earth just five or ten years after their last lifetime, but that's extremely rare.

It's very likely we'll all be greeted by our departed loved ones when we eventually cross into Heaven. It will be a family reunion of epic proportions. And, since they're all hanging out in Heaven between lifetimes, that's what allows a psychic medium like me to communicate with them.

The caller continued by asking, "But what about animals? Can we come back to life as a pet?" she wanted to know.

Pat interjected, too excited to bite his tongue. "You mean like the Stephen King movie *Pet Cemetery*? That takes creepy to a whole other level . . . I mean, Fido dies and you bury him in a magical cemetery, and he comes back as a ghost-wolf. That's trippy stuff! What's your take on that, Andy?"

J.T. rolled her eyes and laughed as she smacked herself on the forehead with her palm. I laughed too, knowing that Pat wasn't entirely serious. Even the lady on the phone was chuckling. I could hear a small dog barking in the background, so I assumed the caller was an animal lover.

"I get asked that a lot," I assured her. "Everyone wants to know if we can reincarnate as animals."

I explained that I'm willing to believe anything is *possible*. However, over the years, I haven't seen conclusive evidence to suggest people can reincarnate as animals. "I'm willing to keep an open mind," I said, "but the jury is still out."

Pat was working on his third soda of the morning and had energy to spare. "I'd come back as some weird animal," he said. "Just to freak people out, you know . . . like one of those blue-butted monkeys or maybe a spider crab. Those things look totally alien."

J.T. laughed and began speaking about her own pets at home. She kindly thanked the lady for calling into the station and ended the call.

"So, assuming you don't reincarnate as a blue-butted monkey . . ." J.T. paused briefly to flash a condescending smile at Pat. "Do people generally remember their past lifetimes? I've heard that children are more prone to remembering those sorts of things because they're more psychic. Is that true?"

"Yeah, absolutely!" I affirmed.

"Do you have any examples that come to mind?" she asked.

"My Grandma Myers collected rocks when she was alive, but as for me, I collect *stories*. One in particular comes to mind. How much time do we have left?"

She looked to her computer screen. "'Bout ninety seconds. Go ahead."

I relayed a true story about a boy who was born in the Golan Heights region near the borders of Israel and Syria. From the time he could talk, he insisted that he was murdered in a past lifetime by an ax blow to the forehead. Interestingly enough, the boy was born with a noticeable birthmark on his forehead. I explained that birthmarks are believed to appear in places we've endured injury or trauma in past lifetimes. They can be an after effect of the previous lifetime, similar to a scar.

As time went on, the little boy claimed to remember the village he lived in during his previous life. It wasn't too far away, so his family took him there. Once inside the town, the boy remembered what his name was in the past life. What's more astonishing is that he also recalled the murderer's name. The boy insisted his family should confront the alleged killer. When they were finally able to track him down, the man looked astonished, as if he'd seen a ghost. He seemed nervous, but didn't admit to the crime.

The young boy insisted he remembered the exact site where the murder had taken place, so his family took him there. They grabbed some shovels and began digging. To their amazement, they not only found a body, they also found an ax buried nearby. Sure enough, the skull of the unidentified body showed a fracture in the forehead that perfectly matched up with the murder weapon. Family members slowly turned their gaze from the skull on the ground to the birthmark on the boy's forehead. It was in the same exact location. The family got authorities involved, and ultimately the man confessed to the crime. It had taken place approximately a decade earlier. This proved to be one of the rare cases of an individual coming back for another lifetime rather quickly.

Credibility is given to this story because the events were witnessed by Dr. Eli Lasch. He was involved with the story every step of the way and was present when the skeleton was dug up. Dr. Lasch worked in the 1960s as part of the Israeli government and helped develop medical systems near the Gaza region. Before Dr. Lasch died, he passed this story on to a German author and therapist named Trutz Hardo. The young boy's story appeared in Hardo's book titled *Children Who Have Lived Before: Reincarnation Today.*

Rubbing her forearms, J.T. looked to me and said, "Wow, I've got goose bumps!"

Pat took off his headphones and rubbed his clean-shaven head. "The dude came back for another lifetime and ratted out his own murderer? That's insane!"

J.T. interjected, "Moral of the story . . . if someone kills you, don't get mad, get *even*. Just come back to life and go to the authorities!"

Pat and J.T. wrapped up the segment by reminding listeners of my website and contact information. I thanked them for having me in, and took off my headphones. As I strolled out the studio doors, I hollered over my shoulder, "Later, Spider Crab!" Pat flashed me a peace sign and a friendly nod. I checked my social media accounts on my phone as I walked toward the parking lot. They were often buzzing with activity by the time I left the studio. I attempted to respond to as many comments as possible, and thanked people for listening to the live broadcast. The vast majority of questions and comments were supportive and positive. Occasionally, some were not.

I was in the public spotlight more with each passing month. In addition to the radio, I was giving lectures at various venues around the city. Business was going well and I felt blessed to have so many opportunities. Being in the public eye had some perks but it also painted a pretty big target on my back. Given that skeptics and religious extremists viewed my work as highly controversial, being on the radio attracted a few nay-sayers that I would rather have avoided.

Various people wrote on my Facebook page that I was a devil, that psychic abilities are evil, or that I was being possessed. These comments were usually accompanied by Bible quotes and suggestions that I needed Jesus in my life. It initially bothered me quite a bit. I'd respond to these strangers, explaining that intuition is rooted in love and can be used to help others. They'd write back with more Bible quotes and insults. On the other end of the spectrum were the skeptics and atheists who harassed me for discussing spiritual topics of *any* kind. I eventually grew thicker skin and decided it was a waste of time to try reasoning with people who were being *unreasonable*.

I've always figured that any spiritual path a person takes is a good path, as long as it gives the person a sense of peace and doesn't harm anyone else in the process. My naïve assumption was that other people abided by this *live and let live* mentality. Apparently, I was wrong.

I tried not to dwell on the negative comments because I didn't want to attract more negativity into my life. When we give attention to certain events, those events tend to find us more often. Emotionally, I made an effort to focus on the positive. I counted my blessings. I said prayers of gratitude. I welcomed the Universe to bring wonderful opportunities and good people into my life. As it turns out, the Universe was listening to my prayers and intentions and was on the verge of granting my request. I shouldn't have been surprised. The Universe is *always* listening.

Chapter 16

On Thursday, February 3, 2011, it was all of thirteen degrees outside. The wind chill factor made it feel even colder. I was waiting for my next appointment. She was scheduled for 11:00 and her name was Mackenzie. She had cancelled her psychic reading a few weeks prior due to a family emergency. Then, on our rescheduled appointment date, we mutually cancelled due to a blizzard and treacherous road conditions.

"Third time's a charm. Right, Zico?" He looked at me with a few curious blinks before gazing out the window at the tundra-like conditions. Zico (pronounced Zee-Ko) is my mixed-breed rescue dog. He was three years old at the time. His streamlined physique always leads people to wonder if there's some greyhound in his DNA. He has the sweet demeanor of a kindergarten teacher and the intelligence of a precocious toddler. Essentially, he's a therapy dog who never bothered getting certified.

A faint knock at the door prompted Zico to sit at full attention. "Okay, you know the routine, buddy. Wait right there." I held up my index finger and gave him a stern look. This was his cue to *sit* and *stay* until I gave him permission to approach our guest at the door. Despite his enthusiasm, he was eager to please and he remained sitting.

As I swung open the door, I immediately felt the cold wind scratching at my face. "Come on in. It's freezing outside!" I motioned for my client to come in. Zico couldn't help himself. He trotted up to the stranger, his tail flipping back and forth like windshield wipers set to full speed. She bent down to pet Zico and he welcomed the affection.

"I *love* dogs," she said in a friendly and high-pitched tone. Zico was soaking up the attention. "You're a good boy, aren't you? *Aren't* you?" She practically kissed Zico on the nose as she scratched behind both his ears at the same time.

"I'm Andy, by the way," I said with a smile on my face.

As she stood to officially introduce herself, I noticed she was truly beautiful. "I'm Kenzie," she said as she squeezed my hand. I was surprised by the grip and strength of her handshake. Her enthusiasm matched Zico's, and her personality warmed the chilly entryway. "I like your hat. What are those called?"

"I think it's called a flat cap or a newsboy hat. My grandpa used to wear these kinds too."

She unzipped her coat and began taking her shoes off in the entryway. "Yeah, you don't see that style of hat very often."

"Nobody recognizes me without it," I chuckled.

After meeting our quota for small talk, she followed me to the home office. She perused the small collection of Sylvia Browne books displayed on the shelf, and mentioned how she'd read a few of them. Upon taking her seat, it was clear Kenzie was very excited to get started.

She was kind and bubbly with a gentle disposition. She had a familiar quality I couldn't quite place. It felt like she was an old friend as opposed to someone I'd just met. In chatting with her, I discovered Kenzie is part Native American. "I'm about one-fourth Sioux," she explained. "It's from my dad's side of the family."

Looking more closely at her high cheek bones, tan skin, and dark hair, I couldn't believe I hadn't noticed earlier. Her Native American features were obvious. They reminded me of a time and place I had never quite forgotten. I wanted to divulge how fascinated I was with Native American culture. However, I refrained from doing so. During psychic sessions, I like to keep the focus on my client rather than myself.

She was holding a little green journal in her hands and kept looking at it throughout our session. She had written down her questions so she wouldn't forget what she wanted to ask. She held the little journal close to her chest, glancing down at it like a poker player eyeing her cards. "Do

I have any guardian angels or spirit guides around me?" she asked in a hopeful tone.

Adjusting the invisible, psychic satellite dish above my head, I concentrated for a second or two. I sensed the presence of a spirit directly behind Kenzie and I intuitively knew the spirit's name. "Sarah is one of your guardian angels. She's right behind you. You actually have five guardian angels altogether, but Sarah is your primary one."

Kenzie's eyes grew wide and a smirk formed on her face.

"What's so funny?" I wondered.

"I already knew that."

"You already knew *what*?"

She set her green journal on her lap and sat up straight in her chair. "Sarah. I've always had a feeling that one of my guardian angels was named Sarah. This might sound crazy, but I've always had little intuitions about certain things. Anyway, I'm glad you can sense her behind me, too." It was a validating moment for us both.

We dove into all the usual topics I discuss with my clients. We talked about finances, career, love life, health, and various purposes that Kenzie's soul came here to experience. Eventually, she asked, "What about kids in the future? I don't have any now, but someday I hope to."

Like a catcher gloving a 95 mile per hour fast ball, it hit me quickly. "One girl," I replied without hesitation. I was certain of it. I said there would be something special about this girl. She'd be different than other kids. I envisioned her being highly intuitive, very creative, and would possess a tremendous amount of empathy. I predicted that Kenzie's daughter would reach developmental milestones earlier than expected. She'd be very intelligent, wise beyond her years, and would be passionate about animals.

I found myself trailing off, almost in a daydream state of mind. Suddenly, I was staring at the floor. A sense of déjà vu washed over me. It was like I'd just remembered something but wasn't quite sure what it was. I shifted my gaze back to Kenzie only to discover she was misty eyed. This description of her future daughter had struck a chord with Kenzie. She informed me that she, too, had always pictured having the little girl I'd just described.

I connected more with Sarah and the other guardian angels. They were giving me insight about Kenzie's future daughter. Just then, the two of us heard a loud *POP*. The noise jolted us upright in our seats. It sounded like someone had just cracked a whip next to our ears. Zico nervously stood to his feet and the hair on his back stood straight up.

Tiny shards of broken glass rained down on the floor like ice pellets during a sleet storm. I hurried to the wall and blew out a candle that rested on a decorative shelf. The glass candle holder had shattered, or rather, *exploded*. Candle wax dripped onto the carpet. "Oh great," I sighed in frustration. "I've only lived in Grandma's house for a few years and here I go nearly setting it on fire."

As I cleaned up the mess and tried to keep Zico away from the slivers of glass, Kenzie asked, "What do you think caused that? Was the candle flame just too hot for the glass?"

I threw my hands up and shook my head. "I guess so. I'm not really sure. I've been lighting candles every day for years and this has never happened."

I returned to my chair and sat down as I gave Zico a gentle pat to calm his nerves. He gave me the cold shoulder and walked back over to have a seat near Kenzie's feet.

"Wow, sorry about that. What were we talking about?"

"My daughter, and how amazing she'll be." Kenzie's smile was infectious.

We had so much fun conversing that we eventually went a few minutes past our allotted time. Almost as if Zico knew we were done, he stood up to escort Kenzie out of the room. I joked that he was a traitor because he seemed to like Kenzie better than me. The two of us made more small talk on our way to the door. She asked about the house and wondered if it had recently been renovated. I informed her that many updates were made just before I'd purchased the home. "*It even comes equipped with flying paint rollers in the basement,*" I thought to myself.

"Hey, you should come to my monthly discussion group," I told her. "It's called the Omaha Metaphysical Network. It's a great way to make new friends who are also interested in past lives and guardian angels and all that good stuff." She seemed excited.

"Everyone is very welcoming so I promise you won't feel like an outsider."

As Kenzie zipped her coat, she promised she would be present at the next meeting. She bent down to pet Zico one last time. It seemed like she was stalling. I wondered if she was dreading going back into the cold. "Do you think it was my guardian angel Sarah who caused that glass candle holder to explode?"

I inhaled deeply as I looked to the ceiling and pondered her question. "Yeah, anything is possible," I said. "The thing you have to remember is that guardian angels are masters of *timing*. When the votive shattered, we were talking about your future daughter. I wonder if it was Sarah's way of saying, 'pay attention to the significance of this conversation!'"

"Maybe it means my daughter will be a little firecracker."

I couldn't help but laugh. "In today's world, I'd rather a girl have too much feistiness than not enough. In terms of a fighting spirit, you can always dial it down a notch, but you can't inject more fire into her than she's born with."

I typically offer a hug to my clients before they leave my office. That being said, many of them are old enough to be my grandparent. Considering Kenzie was a young attractive female, I thought a handshake might be more appropriate. Once again, she practically crushed my hand with her grip. "Stay warm out there," I said as I opened the door for her.

"I'll try, but I don't think that's possible," she said over her shoulder as she walked away.

Closing the door behind me, I turned to Zico. "Well buddy, do you think we should grab some lunch before our next appointment?" He inquisitively cocked his head and looked at me with a twinge of sadness in his eyes. "Hey, I'm sorry pal. I know you really liked her, but you can't go home with her."

I walked back to the room and began cleaning up the shards of broken glass. Through the loud hum of the Shop-Vac, my mind was unusually calm and clear. For some reason, I was in a fantastic mood. I wondered if I'd ever cross paths with Kenzie again. *Would she really come to the OM Network meetings?*

I stared at the dried candle wax on the carpet, and pondered the implications of the candle holder exploding. *Was it merely a coincidence . . . perhaps just a combination of pressure change, temperature, and cheaply made glass? Or, was it something else?* One thing was for sure. If someone from the spirit world was trying to get our attention, it worked.

Chapter 17

"*What the Bleep Do We Know?*"

"That's really the name of it?" I asked with confusion.

"Yeah, but it's a documentary, not a movie."

My friend Craig looked as animated as a Disney cartoon character. He just couldn't contain himself, and he wanted the meeting to get underway.

"It's kind of about spiritual topics, but from a quantum level. Have you ever heard of something called the God particle? It's a . . ."

"Hey, you made it!" I shouted across the room. Kenzie had kept her promise and had just arrived at the meeting. I stepped away from Craig to greet Kenzie. He kept talking, assuming others were listening and not even noticing that I'd walked off.

I asked Kenzie how she was doing. We chatted casually, and she informed me she had gotten a little lost trying to find the meeting location. Soon, we all took our seats and the meeting officially began. We hopped from one topic to the next. As the facilitator, I tried to ensure everyone got a chance to talk. After the meeting concluded, some of the group members suggested we continue our discussions over dinner at a nearby restaurant.

Everyone was invited, but only a dozen of our group members were able to come. After a short game of musical chairs, Kenzie and I happened to be seated next to each other. She ordered a veggie omelet with no mushrooms, and I ordered a southwestern skillet. We shared a pot of coffee.

We joined in other conversations at the table, and it was a free-flowing jumble of stories and laughter. I thought to myself, this must be what it's like to have dinner with a big, Italian family . . . just with a few more ghost stories and a little less pasta. We all left the restaurant and stepped out into the cold air. Craig reminded me to watch that documentary, and I assured him I would.

Our group continued to meet once a month. It was refreshing to be around positive and open-minded individuals. Members of the group became my friends. It was nice to have such a support system, especially since I was going through a divorce at the time. The whole process was emotionally draining, but I was relieved to finally be out of an unhealthy marriage. Members of the Omaha Metaphysical Network were there for me and made it easy to keep my spirits high.

After a fun night out with the gang, I'd come home to my newly decorated house. Since I was single once again and no longer felt I was walking on egg shells, I granted myself permission to purchase some new home décor items. One such purchase was admittedly a bit tacky. It was a model of the Milky Way galaxy that was rather large. It was the diameter of a kiddie pool and dangled from my bedroom ceiling. 3-D planets were attached to metal rods and spun in circles around the sun. Jupiter was the size of a soccer ball. Earth was comparable to a grapefruit. The size of the planets wasn't to scale, but they made me happy and kept me entertained.

Gazing at the planets reminded me of that autumn night back in 2006 when I spoke to a Higher Power and saw stars and planets through my bedroom ceiling. Now, I had planets of a different kind above me. A slight breeze from the register vent sent planet Earth on a circular journey around my bedroom. Inch by inch, it glided a full rotation around the sun – a complete 'year' in the cosmos of my bedroom. Looking at Earth made me feel like I was a small part of something much larger than myself. Surely, astronauts feel this way when looking at our beautiful blue and green marble from space.

It's amazing how our solar system is arranged in such a perfect manner. There is balance and order. Our planet has come to find its unique orbit around the sun. Likewise, our moon is held in place by Earth's gravity. The Earth and moon's rotations are tidally locked with each other, meaning we always see the same side of the moon. It's nothing short of miraculous how two celestial bodies can dance in circles together for billions of years, always maintaining eye contact. I wondered if we humans are much the same. *Is it possible for one person to fall into another's orbit? Could one soul be tidally locked with another, held together by the gravity of fate and destiny?*

Chapter 18

I stayed in touch with Kenzie and continued to see her at the Omaha Metaphysical Network meetings. She happened to be wrapping up a divorce of her own, and was renting an apartment that she hardly had enough belongings to furnish. Kenzie didn't have children either, so her divorce process was rather uncomplicated, much like my own. As time went by, I began sending text messages back and forth with Kenzie just as I did with many of my other friends from the Omaha Metaphysical Network. Legal matters with the divorces were heading down the home stretch, and when the timing was finally right, we began spending time together outside of the OM Network meetings.

We had coffee together and took our dogs for walks at the park. We swapped stories of all the bizarre experiences we'd encountered through the years. I told her about the day Grandma died, and all the small miracles we witnessed during her passing. Kenzie told me about the first time she ever saw a ghost. It happened in her Aunt Kim's back yard in Albion, Nebraska.

Spending time with Kenzie filled my soul with something I didn't even know I was missing. Our core values and beliefs synched up like the gears in a Swiss watch. I could relate to her easy-going nature and free-spirited tendencies. Spending time with her was easy. It was natural. We could both truly be ourselves. To vibrate at the same frequency as another person is very rare. Neither of us had ever experienced it before. We began falling for each other, and as the days passed, our energies became more and more intertwined. Some days, I felt as though we shared the same brain or could read each other's thoughts on some level.

One morning, Kenzie described to me a dream she had the previous night. In the dream, she was walking on the ocean floor and was able to breath under water without the use of an oxygen tank. Crystal clear water enveloped her. Sparks of light glistened from the sun rays above. With outstretched arms, she felt the ocean current slipping through her fingertips. It felt smooth and silky, like sticking a hand out the window and feeling the air while driving on the highway. The buoyancy of the salty water caused her hair to float upward, like an astronaut in zero gravity space. Fish of every size and shape circled around her in a kaleidoscope of brilliant colors. Along the ocean floor she continued to walk, but she dared not blink. She couldn't bear to miss one second of this otherworldly beauty.

I was left speechless when Kenzie shared this dream with me, because it perfectly described *my* dream from the previous night as well – down to every last detail. *Had our souls taken a trip together in dreamworld? Is that even possible?* The odds of such a bizarre coincidence were so beyond staggering they bordered on impossible. Yet somehow, in the vastness of the dreamworld, our souls had traversed the same location on the same night – an underwater haven of unparalleled serenity.

It seemed like our weeks were a blur of making love, laughing, going on dates, and talking late into the night. She'd often get off work from her nursing job around 11:00 at night and would come straight to my house. We ate leftover pizza and sprawled out on the basement floor watching *Twister, Jurassic Park,* or other movies from the 90s we'd seen a hundred times.

We'd cuddle inside a cocoon of twisted blankets, staying up so late that Zico could no longer keep his eyes open. His legs twitched and he huffed and puffed in his sleep, dreaming the dreams of a happy dog. I took the scenic route through the terrain of Kenzie's life, asking her questions about her family and her childhood.

I found it heartwarming how she agreed to go to her sophomore homecoming dance with a special needs student, despite being asked by several other boys. I fell in love with her depth of character, how she'd been pretty enough to do some modeling in high school, but quickly dropped it because she was more interested in extracurricular activities such as science club, math club, and the Health Occupations Students of America.

She shared with me that she endured some bullying in high school. The very thought of it gave me pause. *How? Why?* She was witty, fun, approachable, and beautiful inside and out. Some of her female classmates must have felt threatened by Kenzie. They made up some unflattering rumors that were untrue and horribly cruel. It wasn't an easy four years. Thankfully, she graduated a semester early while carrying a 4.0 grade point average, and she never looked back.

I enjoyed learning more about her. *What were her future plans? What was her childhood like?* She told me of the time her mom made her attend a confirmation class at a Lutheran church. Kenzie was curious about reincarnation, so she raised her hand to ask their opinion on it. They scoffed at her, saying the church doesn't subscribe to those ideas. She felt singled out, but it only further ignited her curiosity in such topics. She snuck into her mom's bedroom and borrowed some Sylvia Browne books that discussed past lifetimes.

Her mom is a devout Christian but a closet believer in reincarnation, so the two of them often gifted each other Sylvia Browne books at Christmas time. Kenzie would rush home from school on weekday afternoons before golf practice to see Sylvia Browne talk about spirituality and paranormal topics on the *Montel Williams Show.*

I fell in love with the way Kenzie sometimes snorts when she laughs. I discovered she doesn't like ice cubes in her water but she does like orange wedges in her beer. I learned she wanted to be a marine biologist when she was young and was obsessed with animals from an early age. On rainy days, her mom would take her to the pet store to get a new critter. Over the years, she became the proud owner of a menagerie of animals. There was her guinea pig named Sparky, a bunny named Patches Rainbow, and a Dalmatian named Maggie.

Her Aunt Rhonda taught her how to groom show dogs in her youth. Her Grandpa Hartford taught her how to work with goats. At the Weeping Water County Fair, an ornery Toggenburg goat broke free from its leash and trampled over Kenzie. She got away with little more than a bruise and a funny story to tell.

I loved Kenzie's sense of adventure, her appreciation for history, science, and the natural world. She grew up living by the river in Plattsmouth, Nebraska. It was the prime location for finding rocks, fossils, shells, and gold pyrite along the river banks. She'd then convince her younger brother they were worth hundreds of dollars. He'd do Kenzie's chores for her and would earn the priceless artifacts she'd found along the river. I laughed, knowing my brother had taken advantage of me in similar ways in our youth. I suppose that's the God-given right of the oldest sibling.

Kenzie asked more questions about Grandma Myers and the items she'd collected. I'd point over to the corner of the basement and explain that's where she used to keep the storage shelves of dinosaur bones, petrified wood, and fossilized remains. I wished Kenzie had met Grandma before she passed away. The two of them would have gotten along so well. They had a lot in common.

These endless conversations and late nights always ended the same. Kenzie would fall asleep in my arms well before the movie credits rolled up the TV screen. Thankfully, we were able to sleep in most mornings. Her nursing shifts didn't start until afternoon, and my psychic readings didn't generally begin until ten or eleven o'clock. Once awake in the morning, we liked to discuss our dreams and interpret their meanings.

One particular morning, Kenzie rolled over and woke me by planting a kiss right on my lips. As always, I asked how it was possible that she look so stunning first thing in the morning without a trace of makeup on. She humbly thanked me and then insisted I get my eyes checked.

"On second thought, you kind of look like a rooster with that awesome hairdo," I joked. She touched the top of her head and laughed.

I asked if she remembered her dreams. She said she did, and insisted she had dreamt about my dad. "That's odd," I said. "How do you know it was him? You've never even seen a picture of him before."

"He just seemed familiar and I intuitively felt connected to him in some way."

"Um. Okay." As it left my lips, I felt guilty for the skeptical tone in my voice.

"I swear it was him. I'm not making this up."

"So what was the dream about?" I asked. "What did he look like?"

She squinted her eyes, as though she was trying to remember the dream. "When he was alive, did he ever wear a blue flannel shirt?"

She had my attention.

"Did he have a mustache?"

"Yeah, actually he did." I was flabbergasted. A hurricane of déjà vu circled counterclockwise inside my head. "His mustache would tickle my forehead when he'd kiss me goodnight."

"And in my dream, he smelled like Old Spice cologne or Old Spice aftershave. Is that a scent you remember him wearing?"

I hopped out of bed and opened my closet door. "I've never told you *any* of this about my dad." I rummaged through a bin that was buried behind clothes in my closet. I found an old photo of my dad wearing his blue flannel shirt and sporting a handlebar mustache. I held it up for Kenzie to see.

"I can't see that far away without my contacts."

Like a detective interrogating a suspect, I shoved the photo close to Kenzie's face and asked, "Does this guy look familiar?" Her smile said it all. "And he was wearing Old Spice aftershave, you said?"

She nodded as her eyes glistened with a misty mix of emotions.

"To this day, I can't smell Old Spice without thinking of him."

"Do you think he would have liked me?" she asked in a hopeful tone. "I mean, if he were still alive, do you think he would approve of you and me dating?"

I sat back on the bed next to Kenzie and gently held her cheek in my hand. "He would *love* you. Are you kidding me? Hell, the three of us would probably be out fishing right now if he were still alive."

She smiled, hoping I was right.

"My grandma would have loved you too. I was always her little Chief, since I'm one percent Native American and what not. Grandma would think it was so cool that I was dating a *real* Native American."

Kenzie looked at me with a pitiful expression. "Babe, you're about as Native American as Zico is."

"Hey now, I could be one percent. You never know."

She grabbed me by both cheeks and playfully said, "Come here, white boy. Give me a kiss." With that, she pulled me in and planted one on my lips.

I stood up and gently propped my dad's picture on the dresser. I rummaged through my drawers for clean clothes. "Ever since we started dating, I can't seem to stay caught up on laundry."

She looked up at me and winked. "That's because you've been a little preoccupied lately."

"Are you almost packed? Our flight leaves really early tomorrow."

"Yeah, I need to stop back at my apartment later today," Kenzie mumbled through a yawn. She extended her arms over her head and stretched out her 5'2" frame. "I'm caught up on laundry but I need to find my swimsuit. Hey, do you think we can go fishing in the ocean while we're in the Outer Banks?"

I balanced on one foot as I put on a sock. "Heck yeah! I plan on reeling in a marlin."

"Oh really?" She asked in a challenging tone. "And what happens when you get pulled overboard and get eaten by Jaws?"

Putting my hand on top of my head like a shark fin, I gently jumped on top of Kenzie. I snorted into the side of her neck, hoping it would tickle. She squealed and laughed as she threw the covers over her head. Her voice was muffled through the comforter as she shouted, "Sharks don't snort. You're thinking of pigs, you dork!"

Kenzie, 2011

Chapter 19

Kenzie was set to accompany my family on a vacation to the Outer Banks in North Carolina. I figured it was a great way for my family to get to know her. Aunt Terry made all the preparations. She booked a multi-level beach house where everyone could stay. My mom came, as did Terry's husband, Al. My two siblings joined us as well, along with their significant others. We were instructed to come and go as we pleased but to be present for dinner each night so we could all spend some quality time together.

Kenzie and I rented some fishing equipment from a local fishing shack. The guy who ran the place looked like he belonged in a Jimmy Buffett song. I asked him which equipment would be best to help me reel in a trophy fish. As a tourist, he saw me coming from a mile away. He suggested I upgrade to the deluxe equipment package. I eagerly agreed, figuring it was okay to splurge just a bit while on vacation.

We only had the fishing equipment for a day or two when I managed to sink a fishing hook so deep into my finger that I required a tetanus shot from a nearby medical clinic. With nine good fingers still intact, we continued getting up before sunrise to fish in the ocean. We launched our lines out into the water and waited patiently in our beach chairs.

One morning we saw a thunderstorm forming way off in the distance over the ocean. Clouds grew and stacked upon each other like bubbles foaming out of a bathtub. Out of cumulonimbus clouds, lightning kissed the orange sky like a snake's tongue tasting the air. I wondered how far away the thunderstorm was. It was difficult to gauge since the ocean stretched all the way to the horizon.

Seeing lightning off in the distance reminded me of my grandma. When I was young, she told me of a time she and Boompa were enjoying the afternoon together at a lake. Boompa was out in the tall grass, wandering around and looking for rocks. Grandma was fishing. As she held her pole, she felt a static charge envelop her entire body. All the hairs on her arms and neck stood on end, and she swore she could taste electricity in the air. She felt like she was being charged up to receive a lightning strike.

Overhead she could see nothing but clear blue skies. Yet, darker clouds were rolling in from the west. Her instincts kicked in and she threw down her fishing pole. She ran to the car, jumped in, and slammed the door shut. Boompa jokingly gave her a hard time about it, claiming she'd overreacted. That is, until they drove home and saw cloud-to-ground lightning strikes all around them.

As I recalled that story, I suggested to Kenzie that we pack up our gear and head inside before the lightning got any closer. Since both of us are typically night owls, waking up before the sun left us feeling a bit fatigued. On a daily basis, we'd retreat to our bedroom and take a nap together. Relaxing in bed together one afternoon, we continued a conversation that began several months prior. We talked about Kenzie's future daughter I had predicted during the psychic reading.

During that appointment, I had no idea Kenzie and I would end up together. The irony of being psychic is that it's easier to see a stranger's future than my own. When I spoke of the very special daughter Kenzie was destined to have, neither of us had any clue we were meant to have the baby *together*. I'm sure Kenzie's guardian angel, Sarah, found this hilarious during the psychic reading.

We were snuggled up in a tangle of body parts that resembled a fisherman's knot. With fingers interlaced, we began to discuss our future together. We daydreamed about the baby girl. We knew we were getting way ahead of ourselves by even discussing such things. After all, we had no plans to get married anytime soon, let alone have children. We were merely letting our minds wander. I suppose we were so comfortable with one another that Kenzie and I could speak openly about such things without hesitation.

"If she's going to be as amazing and unique as you predicted, she'll need an original name."

"Yeah," I replied, "Her name has to be strong yet gentle. Classy but easy going."

"And nothing *too* weird," Kenzie said with a scrunched nose. "It can be whimsical, just as long as it's *normal* enough for others to take her seriously."

"We could name her Raindrop Moonbeam Twinkle Star," I said sarcastically.

Kenzie rolled her eyes and laughed. "Poor kid. She'd have to live at a hippie commune."

We assumed my premonition was correct in that we'd have a girl, so we never seriously considered boy names. We tossed around several ideas for girl names and Kenzie half-seriously suggested "Lennon" as an option. She's always been a big Beatles fan. We decided that it was good, but not quite fitting enough.

Staring at the textured ceiling reminded me of when my spiritual journey first started – when I saw the Universe through my bedroom ceiling. I remembered the colors that glowed and the stars that sparkled inside of vast, swirling galaxies. I thought back to my grandma and watching meteor showers with her on clear summer nights. I recalled our mutual admiration for sunsets and how I showed her those pictures on my phone. I remember being a child and how the sky made me feel so small, so curious, so special.

"How about Sky?" I asked, as I turned to Kenzie and looked in her eyes.

"Sky . . . as in S-K-Y-E?" Kenzie inquired. "I like it."

"No," I said, shaking my head and pointing upwards toward the ceiling. "Sky . . . like S-K-Y . . . as in the stars and the moon and sunsets."

She cocked her head and looked to the ceiling as if she were trying to see what I was seeing. Kenzie's gaze fell back to me, and she could tell by the look on my face that I was already in love with the name. As she ran her fingers through my saltwater-ridden hair, she agreed it sounded like the perfect name. *Sky Myers.* It was settled.

We were two love birds taking a flight through uncharted airspace. We were naïve. And fearless. And hopelessly in love. We had no idea where life would take us, but we were ready for the journey. Much like Grandma and Boompa's road trips, we knew there would be unexpected twists and turns on our adventure. We might get turned around from time to time, but we figured everything would turn out okay as long as we had each other.

In that moment, our guardian angels Henry and Sarah must have been grinning, for they knew something we didn't. Unbeknownst to Kenzie and me at the time, Sky wasn't a new name at all, but a very old one indeed. The name had a deeper meaning. It originated from a time and place where our souls had once crossed paths . . . a place where teepees dotted the landscape and buffaloes roamed the Midwestern plains by the millions.

Chapter 20

I was scheduled to give some lectures at a paranormal convention. It was a fundraiser for the Nebraska Boston Terrier Rescue organization. Combining psychic phenomena with animal charities might sound like a weird mixture, but it actually makes a lot of sense. People who are spiritually open-minded and into the holistic arts tend to be kind-hearted individuals. Naturally, many of them are animal lovers. The proceeds from the event would help save countless dogs, so when I was asked to participate as the main speaker, I was delighted. It was a real honor.

The event took place at the Joslyn Castle, a historical location in Omaha. The castle is stunningly gorgeous, but is reported to be haunted. It was the perfect venue for a paranormal convention. Kenzie tagged along with me to the event. I was on the fourth floor giving lectures all day on the subjects of past lives and guardian angels. Having heard all my lectures before, Kenzie wandered around the castle, perusing the hallways and bumping into mutual friends from the spiritual community. There were numerous vendors there, such as pet psychics, energy healers, Tarot card readers, and ghost hunting teams.

Kenzie stumbled upon a room where a local hypnotherapist was conducting past life regressions. She was professionally certified to practice hypnosis and had a good reputation throughout the community. The castle was buzzing with chatter, but thankfully the hypnotherapist had a quiet room to conduct her sessions.

Between my talks, I was busy socializing with audience members and answering questions. I lost track of time, and suddenly I saw Kenzie walking up the stairs towards me. She'd finished her past life regression with the hypnotherapist. I was eager to hear about her experience.

"Hey babe," she said enthusiastically.

I envied her energy levels as I was feeling a bit exhausted from talking all day. With a raspy voice, I asked, "How did your hypnosis session go?"

"Great! You won't believe what happened."

Distracted by all the noise and commotion around us, I motioned for Kenzie to follow me. We walked a few steps and stood in the corner of the room where it was a tad quieter. She told me about her experience. The hypnotherapist had guided her through the process of accessing her past lifetimes. She helped Kenzie to feel relaxed. Although she was conscious and still awake, Kenzie was in a meditative state. She was then able to dive deep into her subconscious. Under the right conditions, this can allow a person to see information related to previous lifetimes.

As Kenzie slipped into a past lifetime, she saw things from a first-person perspective, as though she were reliving the events. She looked down and saw her bare feet. She held her hands up to her face and noticed her hands were dark brown. Based on her surroundings and the clothes she wore, Kenzie felt she was a full-blooded member of the Sioux tribe. As for the time period, she deduced it was in the 1800s.

With a lump in my throat and goose bumps forming on my arms, I asked, "What else did you see?"

"This was the cool part," Kenzie continued. "The hypnotherapist asked who was present with me, and I said my husband was there. She asked who my husband was, and I replied, 'Andy is my husband.'"

My ears perked up. "Oh my God. Are you for real?"

"Your name probably wasn't *Andy* back in that lifetime, obviously."

"Obviously," I said, while fidgeting with the pen in my hand. "Then what? Did you discover anything else?"

"Yeah," she replied, as her voice suddenly sounded more serious. "In my mind, I saw images of something kind of freaky." She paused, as if she was hesitant to tell me.

"What? What is it?"

"The hypnotherapist asked me what else I could sense regarding my husband. I said he eventually died from getting hit in the stomach by an arrow. He died alone in a tent or something because nobody was able to help him. Isn't that weird?"

I felt like my heart had just fallen into my stomach. Suddenly, I was lightheaded and felt like I was drowning in a storm surge of déjà vu. I shook my head as if to dust off some mental cobwebs. A thought occurred to me which left me utterly perplexed.

"How did you know that?" I asked.

Kenzie was startled by my serious tone. She suddenly seemed more concerned as she replied, "How did I know *what*?"

"How did you know that I died from an arrow in my stomach when I was a Native American? I've always known it to be true, but I've never, *ever* told you that."

She took half a step backwards and was silent for a second. It seemed like she wasn't sure what to say.

I stood there trying to process everything. I rubbed my stomach, half expecting to feel an arrow still embedded in my abdomen.

Kenzie tried to lighten the mood by playfully saying, "Well, thank goodness we get a new body with each lifetime. You weren't born with a birthmark on your belly or anything, so I guess you're all healed."

She leaned in for a kiss but I was so dazed that I hardly kissed her back. I exhaled deeply, as though I was attempting to blow away the painful memories. "What else did you discover? Is that all?"

"There's actually a lot more," she continued. "So, when the hypnotherapist asked who else was with me, I replied 'Henry and Sarah Cloud.' It was strange. I said it without even thinking, like my lips knew the answer even though my brain was half asleep."

I opened my mouth to ask a question, but nothing came out. The pen fell from my hand and hit the floor. *What? How? When?* I was dumbfounded.

"Yeah, the hypnotherapist wrote it all down and took notes on what I said."

"Henry? As in my *guardian angel* Henry? And Sarah? Like . . ."

Kenzie grew impatient as I tried to connect the dots. "Yes, Henry and Sarah . . . our guardian angels! In the regression I identified them as our best friends. The four of us were always together."

"What's with the name *Cloud*? Was it their last name? Were they married or something?"

Kenzie threw her hands up in confusion and replied, "I don't know. I mean . . . I guess so. That's what I would assume."

I scratched the stubble on my cheek and stared at the floor.

"The weird thing is," Kenzie continued. "The last name Cloud sounds so familiar and I'm not sure why."

"Wasn't there a famous chief named Red Cloud or something? Could that be it?"

She shook her head as she looked up at the ceiling, deep in thought. "Yeah, I've heard of Red Cloud, but that's not what I'm thinking of. I'll have to do some research. I know it rings a bell for some reason."

We stood in silence for a moment letting it all sink in. I already knew Henry was my past life buddy, but it blew my mind that Kenzie unknowingly validated details of my death through her regression. Furthermore, it had never even crossed my mind that Kenzie was present in that past lifetime as well, not to mention her guardian angel Sarah. It was almost too much to comprehend. I imagined the four of us going on double dates in the 1800s. Henry and Sarah, Kenzie and I – just the four of us going for a joy ride on a Friday night by horseback. "*Nobody is going to believe this,*" I thought to myself.

A nearby stranger overheard our conversation and leaned in. "This was a past life regression, you say? Where do I go for that? I gotta get me one of those." Without breaking eye contact with me, Kenzie pointed in the general direction of the past life regression room.

"You okay? You still look a little shaken up."

I wasn't sure what to say, so I cracked a joke. "You're such a stalker. You didn't get enough of me back then, so you followed me into *this* lifetime?"

"Yeah, well, I figured you'd get into trouble without my help, so count yourself lucky," she replied.

I gathered my belongings and we made our way down the staircases from the fourth floor of Joslyn Castle. My lectures were over and it was time to leave.

"Seriously though, was there anything else you learned from the regression?"

"Actually, yeah," Kenzie said with an excited look on her face. "When the hypnotherapist asked what *my* name was back in that lifetime, I responded with a word that I couldn't quite pronounce. It almost sounded Lakota or Dakota."

I nodded. "Those are languages spoken by the Sioux, right?"

"Yep," Kenzie assured me. "But since I've never had much contact with my dad's side of the family, I don't speak a single word of it."

"You could do an internet search for the name and maybe find a translation that way," I said. We exited the facility and made our way down the outside staircase. "It would be so cool to find out what your name was in that lifetime we shared together."

"Yeah, the lady wrote down the word but wasn't really sure how to spell it." Kenzie shrugged. "Anyways, I've been meaning to get in touch with my dad's family for a while now, so this will give me an excuse. Maybe I have some aunts or uncles or grandparents who could translate the word . . . if there's even a translation."

We walked towards our car near 39th and Davenport Street. Kenzie got into the passenger seat while I placed my belongings in the back of the vehicle. I closed the trunk and sighed. I knew there was more to the past life story. I just didn't know what it was. We were hot on the heels of our guardian angels, and I knew they were leaving a trail of breadcrumbs for us to follow.

Chapter 21

I don't pretend to be an extrovert. Despite my public speaking and radio appearances, I still enjoy quiet time to myself after a busy day of socializing. Kenzie was now spending the night at my house a couple nights per week, but after the charity event at the Joslyn Castle, she let me have a night to myself. We mutually agreed it was healthy to spend some time apart so as to not smother each other.

That evening, I watched a documentary about Bigfoot and sent her a text that read, "I wonder if Bigfoot is simply *too* good at hide and seek. Maybe that's why nobody can find him?" I tried my hardest not to text her, but I just couldn't help myself.

She responded with, "Nah, he's probably just hanging out with the Loch Ness Monster." Via text, she informed me she was rummaging through her bedroom closet, organizing belongings, and unpacking items from when she first moved in. An hour or so went by and I hadn't received another text from her. I figured she had fallen asleep. Meanwhile, at her apartment, she'd found a tattered shoebox at the bottom of a storage bin. She'd forgotten all about it and couldn't remember what it was. Upon opening the lid, she found old receipts and random paperwork that needed shredding.

At the bottom of the box was a document that looked vaguely familiar. She saw dates and names printed in shaky handwriting. It was a family tree. Her biological father had given it to her several years prior, back when she still kept tabs on his whereabouts. Her dad is one-half Yankton Sioux, and the family tree mapped Kenzie's Native American ancestry back to the early 1800s.

Earlier in the day, the past life regression had sparked Kenzie's curiosity of her own heritage. Coming across this document on the very same day was interesting timing. She'd always been proud of her Native lineage, but felt a little guilty that she didn't know much about that side of the family. In her defense, her biological father was never consistently in her life. She only knew a little about his past. She said he'd been a track star in high school, and she remembered that he gave her a pair of dreamcatcher earrings and a bundle of sage grass on her nineteenth birthday.

She traced her finger from left to right across the page, looking closely at each name and date. Suddenly, she noticed two familiar names. "*Holy shit,*" she whispered under her breath. The entire family tree began with Henry and Sarah Cloud.

She batted her eyelashes, trying to keep a tear from falling onto the paper in her hands. All the pieces were fitting together now. It was surreal. She was looking at tangible evidence that our guardian angels were real people. Back in the 1800s, Kenzie and I were best friends with her great, great, great grandparents, Henry and Sarah Cloud.

Kenzie thought back to the part of the regression where the hypnotherapist asked what *her* name was in the 1800s. Kenzie recalled her response, and used her cell phone to look online for Sioux words that were similar. The Sioux language is a complicated Rubik's Cube of dialects and variations. Her ancestors were Yankton Sioux and had migrated from Canada once upon a time. They primarily spoke Dakota, and that was at least a starting point for her internet search.

She scrolled through one list after another, looking for a Dakota word or name that was similar to what she mumbled during her past life regression. When she finally saw it, she gasped and nearly dropped her phone. What really floored Kenzie was the English translation. It was a word of great importance to us both. With hands trembling, she steadied her fingers and immediately began texting me. "Oh my God." she whispered to herself. "*Oh my God . . .*"

Kenzie's family tree

Chapter 22

Still watching my Bigfoot documentaries at home, I was on the verge of falling asleep. It was late when I received the text message. It simply read, "My name was Sky."

I turned off the television and rubbed my heavy eyes. I held my phone closer to my face in order to make sure I had read the words correctly. "*My name was Sky?*" I whispered to myself. "What the heck does that mean?" I walked upstairs from the basement and called for Zico to follow me. He trotted right behind me as I made my way up to the main floor. This made me walk a bit faster, and reminded me of the times in my youth I had sprinted up those stairs while feeling a ghost was hot on my heels. I let Zico out to go potty in the yard, and while he did his business, I sent a text back to Kenzie.

"Your name was Sky? You must be delirious. Haha. What are you talking about?"

The reply came so fast I wondered how her thumbs were moving that quickly. "In our past lifetime . . . my name was Sky!!!! The Dakota word for Sky is Mahpiya. It's the word I said when the hypnotist asked what my name was :) How insane is this??!!"

Reading the words on my phone was like having an out of body experience. I had unknowingly selected a name for our future daughter that was actually *Kenzie's* name when she was my wife in our past lifetime. I wanted to write something back to Kenzie but couldn't gather my thoughts. Zico was beginning to growl at a stray cat who was mocking him from outside the chain link fence. I snapped my fingers and called for him to come.

We went back inside and I took a seat at the kitchen table. Still staring at the text message on my phone, I leaned against the table. It was in the same corner of the kitchen where Grandma used to sit. I thought back to how she would stay up late into the night listening to the *Coast to Coast* radio show, hearing stories of world mysteries and bizarre happenings. As I gave Zico a scratch behind the ears, I wondered what Grandma would think about the discoveries Kenzie and I were making.

I grabbed my phone from the kitchen table and decided I better not leave Kenzie hanging for too long. "What about Henry and Sarah, our BFFs from that lifetime . . . were you able to make sense of that last name *Cloud*?"

"Yup!"

"Do tell!" I wrote back immediately.

"I could tell you, but I'd rather *show* you," she replied.

"You're coming over right now? It's after midnight!"

"Your intuition must be broken, my dear :) No, I'm not coming over right now. I'm exhausted. Wanna have coffee in the morning though and I can show you what I'm talking about?"

"Roger that," I replied.

"I love you."

"I love you more." As I hit the send button, I shut off my phone and headed for bed. I wondered what she had up her sleeve. A new development in the case? I felt like we were past life archaeologists digging for clues and piecing together evidence. I wasn't sure exactly what we would find, but it was shaping up to be a memorable weekend.

I collapsed onto my bed. Zico hopped up beside me and nestled into my ribs. I watched the planets on my ceiling dangle on their metal rods and slowly move around my bedroom, propelled by the air from the register vents. And as my eyes grew heavy and my thoughts slowed down, I gazed upon planet Earth. Through the nothingness, I dreamed of buffaloes, arrows, and the sound of Native American drums. The night was still, and dawn would bring the promise of new clues.

Chapter 23

I woke up the next morning and made a pot of coffee that was bolder than a Spanish conquistador. It was so strong it practically walked out of the pot and into my cup. I was still recovering from being around so much energy at the Joslyn Castle the day before. I was groggy and looking forward to a lazy day of doing nothing.

Kenzie eventually showed up. I opened the door and said, "Hello, Sky." I just couldn't help myself. We shared the same sense of humor, and giving each other a hard time was the equivalent of saying *I love you.*

"Hey babe," she chimed back with a smile. Kenzie made her way to the coffee pot and joked that she wanted to insert an I.V. of coffee into her arm. "Man, I'm so tired today."

"Maybe the past life regression took a lot out of you. Tell me again, what's the Sioux word for Sky? Is it *Miah*? *Myapa*? How do you say it?"

"Mahpiya. But it's pronounced like *Mog-pee-uh.* I think the Dakota language is kind of tricky."

"I bet a lot of people would totally butcher that pronunciation." I held my cup to hers and proposed a toast. She clinked her coffee cup into mine and asked, "Cheers for what?"

"To us and our recent discoveries. I can't believe Sky was *your* name in our past lifetime."

She smiled at me. I studied her high cheekbones, her full red lips, her perfect complexion, and her almond shaped eyes. I wondered if she looked similar in the past life we shared together. With my free hand, I guided a strand of Kenzie's straight, black hair behind her ear and leaned in for a kiss. Her hair smelled like pomegranate shampoo, and the scent filled my nostrils.

"So, you have something to show me?" I asked her.

"Yeah, you're not going to believe this . . ."

Kenzie pulled a sheet of paper from her purse and set it on the kitchen counter. Together, we leaned over it, shoulder to shoulder, like two pirates studying a treasure map. "What is it?" I whispered.

"It's a family tree of the Native American side of my family."

I instinctively grabbed our cups of coffee and carefully moved them to the opposite end of the counter. I didn't want to take any chances. Kenzie may have the gentle touch of a pediatric nurse, but she has the self-awareness of a rhinoceros. She'll admit to being clumsy. Her knack for spilling drinks is as predictable as the moon phases.

"I found it in a shoebox last night when I was organizing my closet," Kenzie said. "I forgot I even had it. My dad gave it to me years ago."

We studied the paper together. Kenzie didn't point it out to me. Like a teacher coaching a student through his test, she wanted me to figure it out myself. I traced my finger up and down the sheet, studying the names. *Herr. Drapeau. Zephier. Cloud.*

"Cloud!" I shouted. My voice was so loud it startled Zico. I covered my mouth with my hand, shocked that my voice had gotten so shrill amidst my excitement. I looked at Kenzie. She just smiled back with a mischievous grin on her face. "You're related to Henry and Sarah?" I asked. "Our guardian angels are *relatives* of yours?" I was surprised by how high pitched and squeaky my voice had suddenly become.

"Crazy, isn't it?"

"Did you have any . . ."

"No," she interrupted. "I had no idea. I haven't seen this thing in years. My dad gave it to me a long time ago, and even then, I don't think I even looked at it closely. I think I was so annoyed with him that I just tucked it away somewhere."

I marveled at the family tree and couldn't stop looking at it. *Should we have it laminated? Should we get it framed?* I wanted to protect it, as though it was the Declaration of Independence. The inner-detective residing in us both wanted more answers. In the weeks that followed, we signed up for an account on an ancestry website. After some searching, we found further evidence of Henry and Sarah's existence. It was a Native American census from the mid-1800s which showed Henry Cloud was age 62 at the time, and his wife, Sarah, was 58.

We were certain Kenzie's name was Mahpiya (Sky) back then, but we soon learned it's actually a fairly common name in the Sioux culture. It's the Native American equivalent of an Ashley or Jennifer in modern-day America. We came across many Mahpiyas on the ancestry websites, but without a last name or further information, we were unable to find Kenzie. As for me, we had no clue what my name was in the 1800s so we didn't even know where to start. Obviously, the ancestry websites didn't mention who Henry and Sarah's best friends were, so our search was at a standstill. Nevertheless, it was amazing to have documented evidence of our guardian angels from multiple sources.

Many of Kenzie's ancestors were fur trappers who came down from Canada, making their way across Minnesota and into the Dakotas. Due to our recent discovery, Kenzie and I knew we were a part of that chapter in history. For me, it made perfect sense because it explained why I've always felt a sense of déjà vu while driving though the rolling plains of Minnesota. The same can be said for the Badlands and Black Hills of South Dakota. I've always felt drawn to those areas. They resonate with my soul in ways that are hard to explain That's often the case when we find ourselves passing through a location we lived in a past lifetime. It beckons to us and makes us feel like we've come home.

Census showing Henry and Sarah Cloud

Chapter 24

I was on my hands and knees, applying a fresh coat of paint to the wood floor of the porch. My home in Benson would soon be on the market, and some cosmetic updates were needed. Selling the home came with mixed emotions. *What would Grandma think? Would Aunt Terry be disappointed?* Regardless, we needed to start planning for the future. Kenzie and I wanted to eventually start a family. Crime rates in the area were steadily increasing, and we wanted to live in a quieter neighborhood, ideally one with younger families and plenty of kids for our future child to play with.

I glided the paint roller back and forth along the porch, touching up the very spot where Grandma's rocking chair once rested. *How many sunsets had she watched from there?* Often times when I'd drive over to visit, she'd be sitting right there on the porch, reading the newspaper and sipping coffee. She'd take off her reading glasses and give a little wave as I pulled up.

My knees and shoulders needed a rest, so I stopped painting and sat there on the porch for a while. My mind began to wander. I looked down at the garden below the porch. The hostas were getting big. Grandma had planted them years earlier. I wondered if the new owners would care for them. I wondered if they'd appreciate the house as much as I did. I gazed over at the front porch staircase where my siblings and I would pose for pictures on Christmas and Easter. The staircase suddenly seemed smaller than it did back then.

Some of Grandma's favorite rocks were displayed on the steps. Others rested below in the garden. They had been there as long as I could remember. I suppose they'd always been Grandma's equivalent of a garden gnome or pink flamingos – a conversation starter to liven up the entryway.

One was roughly the circumference of a cantaloupe. I believe it's called a stromatolite, but by appearance, one might think it was a fossilized bird nest. Another rock was adorned with marks that looked like fossilized sea shells. I could only speculate as to its origin or how it was formed. It was certainly eye-catching.

Additionally, there were two hunks of petrified wood. One was roughly the size of a phone book and another which was more elongated like a football. They consisted of various swirls of brown, black, and umber. I wondered where they came from. Perhaps Grandma found them in a forest in Washington. Maybe Boompa bought them from a collector in Oregon. I wished they were still around to tell me.

Part of me wished we could physically pick up and move the Benson house to a different neighborhood. While a feat like that was technically possible, I knew it was more practical to buy a new house. Grandma's rocks and fossils were coming with me. I'd place them on the front steps and garden of the new place as an homage to our humble beginnings, a tribute to Grandma and the house in Benson.

Grandma's rocks and fossils

Chapter 25

It was the equivalent of taking the fuzzy dice from the old car and hanging them from the rear-view mirror of the new one. Grandma's rocks looked nice on the steps and in the garden of the new house. The new house felt like home immediately, and I was certain we'd make memories there to last a lifetime. Our back yard sloped down to a walking trail that hugged the edge of a nature preserve. Our back deck was elevated, allowing us to overlook the nature preserve in all its glory. Our view made it hard to believe we were still inside city limits.

We spent the week unpacking boxes and hanging décor around the house. One day, while walking into the front living room, I was stopped in my tracks by a peculiar sight. The window cornice had been mysteriously moved. It was a large, decorative pad roughly the size of a pool table. It had been hanging above the large, picture window. Yet, I found it propped upright behind a lamp several feet away. Had it simply *fallen*, we would have found it lying on the floor directly beneath the window, not standing up vertically in a different part of the room. Clearly, the object had been deliberately moved. *But, by whom?*

Naturally, I tried to rule out logical explanations. I asked Kenzie about it, and she was as dumbfounded as I was. I called my mom and sister. They were the only other people who had keys to our new house. They swore adamantly they hadn't touched the decoration, and claimed the last time they were in the house, the cornice was hanging in its place above the picture window.

We eventually concluded that it was a sign from Grandma. It was her way of assuring us she wasn't upset about the Benson house being sold. It eased some feelings of guilt I'd been having. As for the feat itself, it was quite remarkable. She had graduated from levitating paint rollers to moving large home décor items. Clearly, she had followed us to the new house. The inconvenience of rehanging the cornice was nothing compared to the comfort we felt in knowing Grandma was still around us in spirit.

So much was changing in our lives, it was hard to keep up. New love. New home. There were even new professional opportunities. In the midst of moving, I'd been invited onto Kansas City's most popular radio station. I gave psychic readings live on the air during the station's morning show. This turned into a regular gig. The publicity from the radio station allowed me to reach a whole new population in Missouri and Kansas.

I soon began conducting psychic events in Kansas City every other month, and I was entirely grateful for the opportunity. With all the frequent trips to Kansas City for my work, it was the last place Kenzie expected me to take her on vacation. Still, I had an idea, and the planetarium in Kansas City was an integral part of my plan.

Chapter 26

Kenzie nodded along to the music as it poured through the speakers of my Toyota Camry. She sang along and occasionally mumbled the wrong lyrics. I found it endearing, and it was one of her quirks I'd grown to love. We were cruising along I-29 South, bound for Kansas City at seventy miles per hour.

"I bet this was the kind of song your dad loved when he was alive," Kenzie pondered as she cracked open a shell and popped a sunflower seed in her mouth.

"Goin' up to the spirit in the sky
That's where I'm gonna go when I die
When I die and they lay me to rest
Gonna go to the place that's the best."

"Is this Credence Clearwater Revival?" I asked.

She tossed me a look of pity. "No way. Come on man . . . It's *Spirit in the Sky* by Norman Greenbaum."

"Kind of reminds me of lazy summer days out at the cabin. Dad and my uncles would have a stereo playing classic rock songs as they tossed horseshoes and drank beer."

Kenzie smiled. She liked knowing she had my dad's taste in music. Kenzie has always been young at heart, but the old soul in her gravitates towards music and interests from generations past. She's always claimed she 'misses' the 1960s and 1970s even though she was born in 1987.

The drive to Kansas City was a pretty one. Looking out our windows, we could see it was finally springtime. Everything was green again. The previous winter had been unseasonably warm, so now everything was blooming a few weeks earlier than usual.

Kenzie reclined her seat as she quietly sang along with the lyrics. *"Oh set me up with the spirit in the sky. That's where I'm gonna go when I die. When I die and they lay me to rest, I'm gonna go to the place that's the best. Go to the place that's the best."*

Suddenly, I had an idea. "From now on, let's designate this song as a sign from my dad. When it happens to come on, we'll take it to mean he's dropping by to visit us."

She loved the idea. It was refreshing to be in the company of someone so easy going and optimistic. She cracked open another sunflower seed and popped it in her mouth. Her legs were outstretched. Her bare, size seven feet were propped up on the dashboard, and her toenails were painted turquoise. I steered with my left hand and placed my right hand on Kenzie's knee. "Careful now," she said with humor in her voice. "I haven't shaved in a couple days. I feel like Bigfoot's long-lost cousin." Her smile was so warm that I considered turning on the air conditioner.

I playfully patted her on the leg, taking my eyes off the road just long enough to notice the faint, white scar on her knee. She acquired it as a child when she cut her leg going down the turtle-shaped water slide at an amusement park. Scars are a quality I admire in a person. People with a lot of scars have the best stories to tell. They're people who have lived life, gotten dirty, had adventures, and made memories.

"Hearing *Spirit in the Sky* has got me craving some more good jams," Kenzie said, as she flipped the car's music setting from radio to CD mode. It was a six-disc changer, but there was no way to tell which CDs were in there already. Most of the CDs were a random assortment of songs I'd mixed together and burned onto discs from my computer.

Kenzie hit the play button as she said, "Let's see what's on this one." The first track of the mix began playing.

When I die and they lay me to rest
Gonna go to the place that's the best.

When I lay me down to die
Going up to the spirit in the sky.

With jaws hanging open in disbelief, we looked at each other and laughed. My dad must have been listening to our conversation moments earlier and was willing to play along. He knew the song was on one of my CDs and nudged Kenzie to play that very disc. At my lectures, I'm always telling people that loved ones in Heaven are clever and resourceful. They're able to use whatever is available in our surroundings to deliver a sign we'll find validating. They're masters of timing, often grabbing our attention when we're thinking of them or missing them dearly. I had to applaud my dad for his creativity and sense of humor.

We passed by Percival, Hamburg, Craig, and St. Joseph en route to Kansas City. It was a very familiar drive. We could have navigated there with our eyes closed. The vibe was different this time though. I wasn't scheduled to give psychic readings. I didn't have to be intuitively focused. We were there for pleasure.

We rolled into the parking lot of Union Station and were blown away by its grandeur and size. It's quite an imposing piece of architecture. Built in 1914 and originally used as a train station, it consists of over 900 rooms and nearly a million square feet. The ceilings are high enough for Paul Bunyan to walk through without hunching over.

We made our way to the wing of the building where the planetarium was located. The whole time, I'd been carrying a mystery package with me. Kenzie begged to know what it was, but I refused to tell her until later in the day. It was a rectangular cardboard box, roughly the dimensions of a briefcase. The package was covered in wrapping paper.

We looked at the list of show times and were intrigued by a presentation on black holes. Both of us have been fascinated by outer space for as long as we can remember. As we entered the planetarium and took our seats, it was apparent that we practically had the place to ourselves. It was a weekday afternoon, and there were only five or six others in the theater. We sunk down into our chairs and angled our heads upwards to see the show. The room went dark, and as the show began, I took Kenzie's hand in mine. We felt like astronauts aboard a space shuttle, embarking on an epic journey into the cosmos.

As the show concluded, people began to shuffle out of the small auditorium. Kenzie stood and asked if I was ready to go. I gently took her by the hand and asked her to take a seat. I handed her the wrapped package and said she could now open it. Like a kid on Christmas morning, she held it and looked at it for a moment. "Is it a puppy?" she joked. I nervously chuckled and cracked my knuckles in anticipation.

She opened the package slowly and gently. She squinted, attempting to make sense of the gift she was holding. It was a cream-colored sheet of paper that was thick like heavy card stock. It was decorated with stars and colorful swirling nebulas. It displayed the coordinates of a star. Constellation: Sagittarius. RA 18h 32m 23s D-15° 57'. The main focal point of the document was a name printed in large letters. It read *Kenzie Renae Myers*.

She studied the paper with a confused expression. With a trembling hand, I pointed to the star coordinates and explained I had named a star after her. As her eyes darted from the paper to me, tears welled up. "Yeah, it's through an organization called the International Star Registry," I said. "Somewhere up in the cosmos, there's a beautiful, glowing star with your name on it."

She exhaled as she slouched down into her seat. Holding her hand to her chest, she searched for words. "Babe, I can't believe you did this." Her smile was radiant. Looking more closely at the document, she cocked her head. "But it says Kenzie Renae *Myers*. Did they make a mistake or something?" As she turned to look at me, she noticed I was holding something in my hand. It was a blue sapphire ring.

With a shaky voice, I muttered, "Well, I was hoping you would do me the honor of taking my last name." She held her face between her shaky hands. She was speechless, but I took her smile as a good sign.

"Kenzie, will you marry me?"

She nodded emphatically. Two tears rolled down her beautiful, high cheeks bones. A second or two later, she responded, "Yes! Absolutely!"

We hugged tightly. The planetarium was now empty, but somewhere nearby I could feel a spiritual crowd beginning to form. Henry and Sarah were standing arm in arm, squealing with excitement. I pictured my dad in his flannel shirt, pumping his fist in the air. I imagined Grandma, Boompa, and Uncle Tim smiling down on us from Heaven while giving us a thumbs up.

She stopped hugging me and asked, "Hey, is that why you proposed to me in a planetarium? Because it fit in with your star-themed proposal?"

"Maybe," I replied with a mischievous wink.

A faint voice from the edge of the auditorium disrupted our private moment. "Is everything okay?" It was a teenage boy who was an employee of the planetarium. He approached us, but quickly stopped in his tracks once he saw the look on our faces. He must have known we were in the middle of something important.

"Everything's okay," I assured him. "We just got engaged! Would you mind taking our picture?" He obliged. I handed him my digital camera, hoping it would produce a clearer photo than the camera on my cell phone. As he snapped a few pictures, Kenzie held up her hand to show the sparkly blue gem on her ring finger. Its color was deep blue like the ocean, and it was enclosed by two half circles of small diamonds. It reminded me of a yin-yang symbol.

I began to tell Kenzie more about the star I'd named after her. "It's in the constellation Sagittarius because that's your astrological sign." Kenzie nodded, studying the beautiful designs on the document and tracing her finger over the letters. "Apparently, the best view of your star is in the southern sky, but I'm not sure if it's actually visible with the naked eye here in the U.S." She found it very interesting and wanted to do more research on its location.

We exited the planetarium, intending to explore other areas of the facility. Had we been cartoons, our feet would have floated above the floor as we meandered around Union Station. Being drunk on love tends to have that effect on newly engaged couples. We visited the gift shop outside a little area called Science City, and we purchased some t-shirts as souvenirs. Mine displayed a floating planet with a caption that read, "Rest in Peace, Pluto." Kenzie bought a shirt that displayed colorful images of super-enlarged germs and bacteria. I lovingly teased her for being a biology nerd. She jabbed back, calling me an astronomy geek.

Two days later, we left Kansas City. As we merged onto the interstate, Kenzie asked me what kinds of radio stations we could pick up in the area. I was only familiar with the one I'd been making guest appearances on, so I wasn't really sure what other stations existed. Hopeful to scan through the stations and find some good tunes, she flipped on the radio. It must have already been set to an oldies station, because the song that came blaring through the car speakers was a familiar one.

"Goin' up to the spirit in the sky
That's where I'm gonna go when I die
When I die and they lay me to rest
Gonna go to the place that's the best."

We didn't say a word. We didn't need to. We just smiled at each other and sang along with the song lyrics, confidently knowing my dad was somewhere in the car with us. I peered out my window and looked to the southern sky. Somewhere just above the cloud cover and beyond the stratosphere was a star named after my fiancé. Although I couldn't see it with my eyes, I made a silent wish on that star. I wished that our marriage would be filled with love, laughter, and plenty of adventures. I looked back at Kenzie. The twinkle in her eyes assured me the wish would come true.

Chapter 27

"So, your guardian angel and Kenzie's guardian angel were married in a past lifetime?"

"Yeah, but it took us a while to figure it out. We . . ."

"Now, Andy," J.T. interjected. "You always tell us that our guardian angels never get frustrated with us, but I'm sure that Henry must have been smacking himself on the forehead while you two were trying to piece it all together." J.T. chuckled a raspy laugh. "And the four of you were best friends back when you were Native Americans in the 1800s?"

"Yeah, it's quite a story. There's a synchronicity involving Kenzie's name in that past life. But it would take a long time to explain it all."

"Well in that case, let's get right to the phone lines," Pat interrupted as he hit some buttons on a switchboard. The buttons were glowing, and it reminded me of a Lite Brite toy from my childhood.

"Dana is on the line," Pat said with enthusiasm. He was two Red Bulls into a four pack and it was only 9:00 in the morning. "Dana, you're live on the air. What's your question for Andy?"

"Hi Andy," she said as her voice trembled. "I'm a little nervous because I've always thought about calling, but I always chicken out."

I attempted to ease her nerves by telling her to imagine Pat in his underwear. "Isn't that what they say to do when you're nervous? Just picture people in their underwear and you'll loosen up?"

"Trust me dude, nobody wants to see that," said Pat. He was loving the attention and jumped into the joke like it was a game of hop-scotch. "It's laundry day at my house and I've resorted to wearing my old undies that I've had since O.J. was on trial."

"Oh dear God," J.T. interjected as she rolled her eyes and shook her head. "Pat, I'm going to call your wife and tell her to take you shopping. Dana, please go ahead with your question for Andy."

It took Dana a moment to compose herself through the laughter. She finally worded her question, and she essentially wanted to know how she could better communicate with her guardian angels. She said she often *thinks* she feels their presence, but then she second guesses herself and wonders if it's just her imagination.

"Great question, Dana," Pat assured her. "Can you answer that one, Andy? How does a person like Dana speak with her guardian angels like you do with Henry? And, most importantly, do our guardian angels see us when we're wearing nothing but our undies?"

"Thankfully for *you*, Pat, our guardian angels are very good at respecting our boundaries, so they often disappear when we're doing something that requires privacy." I explained there are a number of ways a person can establish communication with his or her guardian angels.

"They use any means possible to get our attention," I said. "Maybe your dearly departed grandpa Ned subconsciously causes you switch lanes while driving. You then find yourself at a red light behind a car with the license plate NED 721. In that moment, you realize today is the anniversary of his death, and his birthday was July twenty-first."

J.T. interjected, "So it's like they gently guide us into situations where we'll see something meaningful?"

"Yes, exactly," I said. "They're aware of our surroundings and know which license plates, billboards, bumper stickers, and other visual cues will have significant meaning for us."

Pat weighed in. "Can they use animals to deliver a message? Because a few weeks ago, I was thinking about my deceased aunt and suddenly a cardinal landed on my deck. She loved cardinals, so I thought it might be more than a coincidence."

"Or numbers," J.T. said. "It seems like every time I look at the clock, it's 11:11 or 4:44. Surely, that has to be a wink from our guardian angels, right?"

"Yep, often times that's the case," I assured her. "Keep in mind, guardian angels and loved ones in Heaven don't control the time. I mean, it's gonna be 11:11 whether we look at the clock or not. But they subconsciously cause us to notice the clock when it's that time because they know it puts a smile on our face."

Continuing with the theme of the conversation, I wanted to explain how the spirit world can even use music and song to deliver a message. "Recently, we were driving to Kansas City, and *Spirit in the Sky* came on . . ." My words came to a halt as I winced in pain. The simple act of bending to adjust the headphone volume had tweaked a nerve in my back.

Pat looked up from his computer screen. "Hey buddy, do you need a minute? You okay over there?"

I gritted my teeth while placing my hand on my lower back. I arched the other way, hoping to stretch out the muscles. "Yeah, I'm alright," I said as I let out a nervous giggle. We were still live on the air.

J.T. butted in with a joke. "Should we cut to commercial break so you can head over to human resources and demand some workman's comp?"

"I'll live," I assured her. "It's the family legacy . . . heightened intuition and bad backs."

Pat nudged the conversation back on track by saying, "Well, if guardian angels can speak to us through music, can I blame them when I get *The Village People* song *YMCA* stuck in my head?"

I laughed, but it only seemed to aggravate my back more. I'd become accustomed to back pain, but this felt entirely different. It was a sharper pain, like a hunting knife was lodged in my spine. I knew our segment was nearly over, and I was secretly counting down the seconds. By this time, I was leaning into the studio desk and holding myself up by my elbows for support.

Pat decided to wrap things up. "You take care of that back, buddy. Everyone tuning in can find more information on Andy's website. Thanks for stopping in, Andy."

"Thanks for having me, guys."

With that, they cut to a commercial, and I nearly collapsed to the floor. With help, I gingerly made my way to my car in the parking lot. I had a few appointments scheduled for later that afternoon, but I knew I was in no shape to be giving readings. I had no choice but to cancel them and schedule a trip to the doctor's office. Given my lifelong struggle with back pain, my doctor suggested a surgery might be in my future. However, he wanted to wait a while to see how this flare-up calmed down.

A few days later, I was still recovering. Kenzie left for work early in the morning and I was home alone. When I finally got out of bed for the morning, I carefully walked into the hallway and started making my way down the staircase. I walked gingerly, like I was barefoot on a floor full of Legos. Every muscle in my back was tense and flexed. I felt like a Victorian era woman who was wearing a corset that strangled my torso.

With each passing step, my hope diminished that I could actually make it down the stairs to retrieve my prescribed muscle relaxers. I could no longer walk, and resorted to crawling on my hands and knees. Inch by painful inch, I scooted backwards down the stairs like a toddler who was just learning to walk.

I reached a point where I could no longer move. The pain was unbearable. Stranded on the stairs on my hands and knees, I wondered if Henry was somewhere nearby. Perhaps my dad and grandma were nearby as well. I was in too much pain to sense anything intuitively. Even if they were around, I knew there was nothing they could physically do to help me. There's a limit to what spirits can assist with. I feared this situation was beyond their control. Thankfully, I had tucked my phone in my pants pocket. I was too embarrassed to call 911, and I couldn't call Kenzie because she wasn't allowed to check her phone at work.

I called my mom and she quickly arrived, but there wasn't much she could do to help me, so she called an ambulance. It was the most painful physical experience of my life. A large medical bill was my party favor after visiting the emergency room that afternoon. After consulting with doctors, my surgery was scheduled. I was to have a fusion in the lower section of my spine. My mom calmed my nerves by telling me it was pretty routine procedure as far as back surgeries go. I trusted her, given that she'd worked as an x-ray technician for many years with some of the best back surgeons in the country.

However, my anxiety shot up like a bottle rocket when I learned more details about the surgery. The doc explained that they'd actually cut me open just below my belly button. Then they'd stick a device through my innards all the way to my spine and do the fusion that way. Hearing these descriptions left me feeling woozy. I asked him to spare me the details. It was easier to imagine they'd fix my back with magic and good intentions. I felt like the little guy on the children's board game *Operation*. I wondered if I would jitter and vibrate if the surgeon made a mistake with his instruments.

After hearing more, I learned there was a risk of doing the surgery this way. If they accidentally damaged some crucial 'wires' in there, it could render me sterile for the rest of my life. I couldn't believe it. It was in the small print of the brochures and everything. Since I wanted a little Sky someday soon, I took the precautions that were suggested. I went to a sperm bank and made a deposit. It was a way to preserve some of my swimmers. This way, I could still make a baby even if the surgeon didn't have a steady hand on the day of my surgery.

The experience at the sperm clinic was awkward. I tried to lighten the mood by cracking a sperm joke to the nurse. She looked at me like I was a complete idiot. "Here's your cup. Place it on the counter when you're finished," she said with a monotone voice.

A few days later, I received an unexpected call from the reproductive center. They said they had done the standard tests to analyze my specimen, and wanted to inform me that my sperm count was low. On the plus side, my sperm's mobility was pretty good. In other words, I didn't have many swimmers in the pool, but at least the ones available had a good work ethic.

I asked how this issue might affect our ability to conceive a child down the road when we were married. She wouldn't initially give me a straight answer, but assured me there's always a chance. "I've seen couples with worse odds still conceive a baby." I knew she was trying to be helpful, but still, it wasn't exactly reassuring. I asked her to give me some solid numbers. "Four percent," she said in a matter-of-fact tone. "Assuming Kenzie doesn't have any reproductive issues herself, you two have a four percent chance of getting pregnant."

Four percent? *Was she kidding?* Not five or ten percent, but *four*. I told Kenzie about the situation. As always, she was optimistic. Her words were positive, but she couldn't hide the glimmer of worry in her beautiful eyes. My sperm was suddenly the elephant in the room. It was ironic how the smallest cell in the human body was causing us the biggest worry. Having a child was far from impossible, but the odds were certainly not in our favor.

Chapter 28

"Oh my God, this is so painful!" I cried out. "I can't take this anymore!" I threw my arms up in disgust as I looked away from the TV. "This is painful to watch," I hollered at Kenzie. "The defense looks like they're on vacation. Of course Portugal is going to score if you give them that much space! Did you see that, honey?"

"Calm down," Kenzie said. "Quit shouting at the TV. It tightens up your back muscles." She handed me my 2:00 meds along with a glass of water. I used my crutches to elevate myself off the couch enough to take a sip of water. I tossed back my meds and swallowed them like a crocodile eating a fish. The surgery went well and I was home recovering for a few weeks. My recovery coincided with the European soccer championship. Multiple games from the tournament were on TV each day, and I watched them all. British accents from the commentators became the soundtrack of the summer. Kenzie was kind enough to tolerate my soccer addiction while simultaneously playing nurse for me.

It was the summer of 2012, and it was the hottest summer I can remember. With all the time off from work, I decided to finally work on writing my first book. It had been a lifelong dream of mine. I'd been keeping journals since I was seven years old and writing had always been a passion of mine. I supposed I inherited the habit from Grandma Myers. Throughout her life, she also kept several journals of her travel adventures.

Had it not been for the back surgery and the ensuing recovery, I'm not sure I would have found time to write my first book. I'd been giving so many psychic readings that by the time I got home from work each day, I was too mentally fatigued to write. Sometimes, the Universe puts our life into slow motion for a period of time. This allows us to rest, reflect, or attend to projects we've been putting off.

Between soccer games, my only company was a warm cup of coffee and my keyboard. Kenzie was at work most days, so the house was still and quiet. With my back brace strapped on tightly, I sat at the kitchen table for a good portion of every day, clicking away at my computer.

Included in my book were all the odd occurrences and spiritual synchronicities Kenzie and I had witnessed. I even mentioned the time Grandma tossed a paint roller across the room to get my attention. Appropriately enough, I titled the book *Flying Paint Rollers from Heaven*.

Although I had written most of the book during the month I was recovering, it would remain a work in progress for more than a year. I eventually reached a point where wedding plans took precedence over writing. Putting my manuscript to the side nearly gave me withdrawals as writing had become an obsession. That being said, there was plenty to be excited about. I was on the verge of marrying the love of all my lifetimes.

Chapter 29

It was a simple yet beautiful back yard wedding at Aunt Terry's house. My sister officiated. No groomsmen. No bridesmaids. Just an intimate gathering of friends and family in Terry's garden. As Kenzie walked down the patio and joined me near the butterfly bushes, I knew I should have been nervous, but for some reason, I wasn't.

It was warm, and there wasn't a cloud in sight. Cicadas hummed in the distant trees. Bees buzzed around the nearby flowers. A gentle breeze filled our noses with the scent of summer. I tightened the flat cap on my head and prepared to marry Kenzie. Again. A lot had changed since our past life together, but in another sense, nothing had changed at all. Our souls still recognized each other. My soul was drawn to Kenzie's soul like the magnets I used to play with at Grandma's kitchen table.

We exchanged the vows we had written, and somehow managed to get through it without crying. Henry and Sarah must have been smiling and shaking their heads. They'd surely played the equivalent of best man and maid of honor for us a very long time ago. Sometimes, history really *does* repeat itself.

As the ceremony concluded, guests met us at a local pizza place for the reception. We had the place all to ourselves. People drank beer and mimosas. The reception was perfect in its simplicity. The focus was merely on the best things in life – fantastic friends, endless laughter, true love, and good food.

We had our first dance in the corner by the game room as our wedding song played through the speakers of our portable sound system. Some people noticed we were dancing. Others didn't. We had no interest in being the center of attention. Kenzie and I were lost in our own little world.

It felt like we were slow dancing alone in our kitchen, which was something we often did on Saturday mornings while waiting for the coffee to brew.

Our wedding song was *Hoppípolla*. It played during our ceremony, and it's by an Icelandic band called *Sigur Rós*. Nobody at our reception had ever heard of them before. It's such a beautiful song, I imagine it's played through the loudspeakers in Heaven. I embraced my bride as we swayed back and forth to the ethereal melody. The song overtook us and we closed our eyes as we held each other tighter.

The day of the wedding went by so quickly it was hardly fair. *Had I thanked Aunt Jean and Uncle Jim for coming? Was my cousin McKenna there? Did I say hi to my brother-in-law?* It was all a blur. That's what happens when you're in the eye of the wedding hurricane and so much commotion is going on. The details slip away and all you're left with is a bunch of pictures and leftover wedding cake.

A week later, we were on a plane headed to the Pacific Northwest on our honeymoon. The timing of the trip was difficult in a way. My sister and I were in the process of opening a brand new office space. During the honeymoon, I had no choice but to field a few time-sensitive phone calls regarding the office and its build-out. Thankfully, Kenzie was understanding.

The new facility would provide Elizabeth with an office to conduct her intuitive healing sessions, and I'd have my own room for my psychic readings. Additionally, there was a large conference room which could accommodate up to 100 people. It would work well for my lectures and for the Omaha Metaphysical Network meetings. It was just what we needed.

As for the honeymoon, it was a weeklong excursion through Portland, Seattle, and a sleepy town called Forks, Washington. The two of us were giddy and uninhibited. Like carefree teenagers, we threw rocks from the top of the bridge at Multnomah Falls near the Colombia River Gorge. We giggled as we watched them splash down to the water below. We stopped for handpicked blueberries on our way to Cannon Beach. In Forks, Washington, we pulled onto an empty logging road and relieved ourselves inside a forest so quiet a mouse's heartbeat would have been audible. We

kept nervously looking over our shoulders, thinking we'd see a bear or wolf
. . . or maybe Bigfoot himself.

In Seattle we signed up for an underground tour that winds through
the dusty, dark underbelly of the city. Afterward, I pulled the tour guide
aside, asking if people report seeing ghosts down there. She looked from
side to side, as if she weren't supposed to share this with paying customers.
"All the time!" she emphatically whispered to me.

Inside the Seattle Space Needle, we purchased a onesie for our future
daughter. It displayed the logo of the Seattle Sounders, the city's professional
soccer team. We hoped buying children's clothes wouldn't jinx our chances
of getting pregnant. As Kenzie held up the outfit, she sighed at how little
and cute it was. She was ready to be a mom, and I knew we'd be trying to
have a baby soon enough.

Kenzie and I strolled through Pike Place market in Seattle. A
fisherman tossed a freshly caught fish across the room like an NFL
quarterback throwing a football. It was caught by the butcher as the crowd
cheered. While still in the coffee capital of America, we booked a motel
room and later discovered it was in a seedy part of town – ironically situated
between an adult video store and a bar called Woody's.

In the city of roses, we attended a Portland Timbers soccer match.
The game was a sellout, and as 22,000 people looked to the jumbo TV
screen, Kenzie and I kissed each other on camera. It was a blistering hot
day, especially by Portland's standards. Our newly purchased soccer jerseys
clung to our sticky skin as we rooted for our favorite team.

We later attended an outdoor concert featuring our favorite band,
Sigur Rós. The venue smelled like marijuana as dreadlocked fans sprawled
out on blankets and meditated to the New Age music. As the band played
our wedding song, Kenzie and I wrapped our arms around each other and
slow danced. With eyes closed, we didn't care if anyone was watching. It's
a memory that will stay with us for the rest of our lives. Just two weeks
earlier, we'd danced to the very same song at our wedding reception.

We didn't want the fun to end. We weren't ready to return to the
real world. As our plane touched down in Omaha, I wished we had a

vacation to recover from the vacation itself. It's strange how having such a great time can be so exhausting. I eyeballed my work schedule. Dozens of appointments were sprinkled on my calendar for the upcoming week. It was time to adjust my psychic satellite dish and get back to work.

I looked out the window as the airplane slowly rolled towards the jetway. Kenzie hadn't noticed that we'd landed. She was sound asleep. I studied her facial features. She looked so peaceful, so beautiful. My gaze fell from her eyes down to her flat stomach. I wondered if there would ever be a soccer ball sized bump at her midsection.

I looked at my wedding ring and traced my finger over its smooth surface. I was happy being Kenzie's husband. Still, I wanted something more. I wanted to be a dad. I thought back to my nearly-finished book. It included details of our journey and mentioned a daughter we were destined to have together. *Were there missing pieces of the story? Would we ever meet our precious Sky?* I was starting to wonder if it was possible to miss someone I'd never even met.

Wedding ceremony

Chapter 30

Life has a way of picking us up in its current and taking us along for a ride. I was busier than ever with psychic sessions, radio appearances, and giving lectures in multiple cities throughout the Midwest. It was nothing short of a dream come true. At the time, it was also a great deal of pressure. People were waiting up to ten months for a private session with me. When expectations are that high, there's no room for mistakes. Every single day, I was expected to be at my intuitive best. Energetically, it was hard to keep up at times, and ultimately it was a crash course in time management. I was fortunate enough to have help when it came to bookkeeping, answering phones, and scheduling appointments. This allowed me to focus more on my appointments.

Yet, my intuition would not allow me to predict when Kenzie would become pregnant. I was too close to the situation, and therefore my psychic senses were clouded on the matter. A few months had passed since our honeymoon and we were actively trying to conceive a child. In some ways, making a baby is a rather fun process. At the same time, it can be emotionally draining. I suppose it's the anticipation, the not knowing, the waiting, the hoping. Several months went by and Kenzie still wasn't pregnant.

I found it ironic that trying to conceive a child can take much of the romance out of love making. The process was suddenly about the end result more than the act itself. If Kenzie was ovulating, she expected me to be readily available to perform my husbandly duty. Like anything in life, it was all a matter of timing, and we were shooting for that window when she was most fertile. Time and time again, we were unsuccessful.

Life is weird like that sometimes. I'd heard of couples who did little more than wink at each other and then discovered they were pregnant. Meanwhile, other couples may try for years to have a child but to no avail. It was easy to be frustrated at the old clichés. *God's time is different than our time. Everything happens for a reason. Just stop trying so hard and it will finally happen.* We'd heard it all before. And, while these sayings might be completely true, it's the last thing a couple wants to hear when they're so desperately wanting a child.

One fall evening, I was in a contemplative mood and was sitting on my back deck. My eyes gravitated towards the line of trees that served as the perimeter of the nature preserve behind my house. The leaves were ablaze in yellows and oranges, made even more luminous from the setting sun on the western horizon. Autumn in Nebraska is a beautiful sight. A caravan of yellow leaves corkscrewed downward like the attached cars of a rollercoaster. Falling equally fast was my confidence that Kenzie and I would conceive a child without the help of a fertility specialist.

As always, I looked to the sky for answers. The sky serves as the symbolic middle ground between Heaven and Earth. I hoped some insight would tumble out of the heavens and fall within reaching distance. I looked westward towards the setting sun and pondered what the future held. The sky made me think of the daughter we didn't yet have. It made me think of the name Mahpiya and the past life Kenzie and I shared together.

The sunset also made me think of Grandma. I remembered her telling me stories of how Lewis and Clark traveled westward in search of adventure, new lands, and hopes of discoveries. I was on a journey of a different kind, but I wondered what awaited us just over the horizon on our life's voyage.

Deep in thought, I was interrupted by a gentle tapping at the sliding glass door. Kenzie slid it open and poked out her head to ask, "Hey babe, you coming inside before it gets dark? Let's pick out a movie." It sounded like a great idea and a welcome distraction from my worries.

We dimmed the lights and nestled into the couch. Zico wedged himself between us as Kenzie covered him with a blanket. After plenty of searching on our streaming movie service, we agreed on a movie we'd never heard of. We hit the play button, knowing we could pick a different movie if it turned out to be a dud. As the opening scene unfolded, we quickly realized the main character was a female named Sky. We didn't say anything, but Kenzie looked at me with a shocked expression on her face.

We had been seeing signs related to Sky for several months. The previous week, we saw the word "sky" carved into a picnic table we were sitting at. A few days later we saw the word etched into a tree at a theme park. We even saw "sky" written in sand at a beach while on a recent trip. We couldn't escape the name. It was everywhere. While it's possible we were hypersensitive to seeing the word, it sure felt like the Universe was plopping it down in our path repeatedly for a reason. It left us feeling even more impatient.

The movie wasn't keeping our attention, so I exited out and searched for another one. I turned to Kenzie and asked, "So, have you given any more thought to a middle name?" Her jaw was clenched and her posture was tense. I wondered if she was feeling deflated. "I don't want to talk about it," she replied in a stoic tone. We'd previously entertained the idea of naming her Sky Azura, which was the equivalent of Sky Blue.

Tossing a kernel of popcorn into my mouth, I said, "Ooooo, this one looks good. Whatcha think?" She avoided eye contact with me and ignored the question as she scratched Zico behind the ear. I clicked on the highlighted science fiction movie and hit the play button. I hoped it would be more exciting than the previous movie. The opening credits flashed on the screen and displayed the name *Azura Skye*, apparently one of the main actresses in the film.

Kenzie sighed audibly and rolled her eyes. Zico sprang from the couch and looked at us with a concerned expression on his face. He sensed the change in energy and wondered what was going on. I could only grit my teeth and shake my head in silence. I didn't know what to say. *Out of all the movies, why did I have to choose that one?* All these signs involving the name Sky made it feel like the Universe was mocking us rather than reassuring us. Deep down, I knew that wasn't the case. Sometimes, perspective is skewed when one is feeling frustrated.

We continued watching, determined to finish at least one movie that evening. The plot involved a post-apocalyptic Earth where a woman named Sarah treks across a barren landscape in search of help. She is pregnant and is set to deliver the first baby born on Earth in fifteen years. After a while, we decided we weren't in the mood for something so serious, and we began watching old reruns of *Friends*.

It wasn't long before Kenzie fell asleep in my arms. I gently kissed her forehead. Her eyes darted back and forth beneath her eyelids. I wondered what she was dreaming. Little did I know, she was dreaming of future events that would come to fruition . . . a prophetic glimpse into a reality we weren't yet living.

Chapter 31

"Something blue on two twenty-two." It was the next morning, and we were relaxing in bed together. As I rubbed the sleep from my eyes, Kenzie repeated her strange words. "Something blue on two twenty-two."

"What in the world are you talking about? It's too early for riddles."

"I'm not sure what it means, but I heard those words over and over again in my dream right before I woke up."

Propping myself up with my elbow and still squinting one eye shut from the morning light, I asked, "What do you think it means?"

"I have no idea," she responded in a curious tone. "But we better write it down in case it's a premonition or actually means something."

"Okay, I'll add it to my journal," I said. She knew which journal I was referring to. Back when my spiritual journey began, I started a log of all of my interesting occurrences involving psychic phenomena. It had grown to be over fifty pages long.

"Something blue on two twenty-two?" I whispered the words to myself, attempting to decipher what it could mean. "You don't think it means we'll have a baby boy on February 22nd, do you?"

Kenzie looked aimlessly at the corner of the room, lost in thought. "Ummmm . . . I don't *think* so." Her inflection indicated it was more of a question than a statement. "But if so, the baby wouldn't be born this coming February. I mean, it's already November. It would have to be February 22nd of *next* year . . . if that's what the dream even means."

"I guess we'll see," I said through a yawn.

Soon, the leaves on the trees behind my house were gone. Nature's cruelest trick is windy days in late October and early November when it strips the colorful foliage from the trees. Eventually, the gratitude of Thanksgiving collided with the consumerism of Black Friday shopping deals. November quickly turned into December. Kenzie and I are spiritual people but we don't claim to be religious. That being said, we still celebrate the Christmas holiday and relish in the joy it brings everyone.

We bought each other a few holiday gifts. On Christmas morning, I tore into one of my presents. As I slid off the wrapping paper, I felt perplexed. I wondered if I had accidentally unwrapped one of the presents I'd bought for Kenzie. It was a blue t-shirt displaying a picture of a caffeine molecule on the front. Scratching my head, I couldn't help but chuckle.

"I hope you like it. What's so funny?" she asked me.

"You'll see," I replied, handing her a package to open. I tried to hide the smug grin on my face. She erupted with laugher when she saw it.

"Oh my God, it's the *same thing!*"

"Pretty close. Your shirt is a lighter shade of blue, but the molecule is the same," I agreed.

"What are the odds?" Kenzie giggled as she checked the tag for the shirt size.

"I figured it was appropriate given how much coffee we've been drinking."

"I think we share the same brain sometimes," she said.

"Are we going to be one of those couples who wears matching outfits in public?" I groaned in a loving tone. "God help us."

Christmas passed. A week later the ball dropped in Times Square, ushering in 2013. The previous two years had been a whirlwind of change. Reflecting back, I couldn't believe how entirely different our lives looked in such a short amount of time. Yet, one thing remained the same. Kenzie still wasn't pregnant.

As the laughter and cheer of the holiday season subsided, there were fewer distractions. Unfortunately, this allowed us to dwell on our situation even more. We tossed around the idea of consulting with a fertility specialist. We weren't ready to schedule any appointments just yet, but did some research on fertility doctors in our area.

All the while, life moved forward. I continued to make progress on my book, and had gotten in touch with a publishing agency who seemed interested in working with me. Business was going well and I was staying busy at work. Life was great, but it was becoming a juggling act trying to balance my work life and my personal life. It was hard not to bring my work home with me, at least in a mental aspect.

Most of my private appointments consisted of communicating with the deceased. Relaying messages from the dead brings a lot of closure and validating to the living. For a person to *know* their loved ones are still alive Heaven is very faith-affirming and healing. Yet, in talking with my clients, they'd often share the details of their loved ones' deaths, which included tearful descriptions of suicides, murders, battles with cancer, car accidents, and heart attacks . . . complete with details of who found the body and how the family was ripped apart by grief.

I suppose my clients used the medium sessions as an alternate form of grief counseling. They always felt better afterwards. From my perspective, the work was fulfilling, but I felt like I had absorbed much of their sadness. I often felt emotionally devastated after a day's work, like I had attended half a dozen funerals in one day.

After thousands upon thousands of these sessions, it began taking a toll on me. I learned it's possible for counselors to develop second-hand post traumatic stress disorder (PTSD) from guiding their clients through traumatic events. Helping my clients cope with death was causing me to think of my own mortality a great deal. I thought of my dad who passed at age forty-three, and dreaded the thought of having a similar fate. Some work days were more lighthearted, but others really wore me down. There were countless times I came home from my office in tears. Kenzie would ask what's wrong and what types of things I'd heard in my sessions. My response was always the same. "You don't want to know."

Over the years, I've found that one of the best ways to shake off work stress is to surround myself with good company. And, thanks to the Omaha Metaphysical Network, I had the best friends a guy could ask for. One particular evening after I'd had an emotional day at work, Kenzie and

I went over to our friend Craig's house for dinner. We needed some laughs and lighthearted discussion.

Craig has a son named Patrick who was almost four years old at the time. Craig and I mutually agreed Patrick was an old soul. It's a term describing a child who is wise beyond his years, highly intuitive, creative, empathetic, and intelligent. He was going through a 'Santa phase' at the time, and Craig's house was practically an art gallery of Patrick's drawings of the jolly fellow. After having some dinner and good conversation, Kenzie and I were getting ready to head out for the night. We were in the hallway putting on our coats and shoes while admiring some of Patrick's drawings. Suddenly, Patrick turned to me and said, "You need to take really good care of Kenzie."

I was caught off guard and didn't really know how to respond. After a few seconds, I asked, "Oh, okay. Why is that, little buddy?"

While fidgeting with his Batman pajamas, he casually replied, "Because you two need to take care of Sky together."

I looked at Kenzie and she stared blankly back at me with raised eyebrows. Placing my hands on my hips, I asked, "What do you mean? How do you . . . how do you know about Sky?"

Patrick ignored my question and pranced down the stairs into the living room. Within seconds, he was sitting cross-legged on the floor, engrossed in a cartoon on TV. He'd clearly lost interest in our conversation and left us without any clarification.

Craig returned from grabbing a book from the bedroom. "Here it is, man. This is the book I was telling you . . ." He stopped speaking mid-sentence and looked at Kenzie and I with concern. "What's up with you two? You look like you just saw a ghost."

I pointed to Patrick, who was quietly watching his show, and I told Craig what he'd just said. The three of us mutually agreed we hadn't talked about Sky or even mentioned her name that evening, so there's no way Patrick could have eavesdropped on an earlier conversation. *Had he intuitively sensed something about our future? A psychic premonition about our daughter?* "Hey little man, why did you say that to Kenzie and Andy? And where did you hear the name Sky from?"

Without looking away from his cartoons, Patrick mumbled, "I don't know." Craig held up his hands in frustration and asked Patrick again, but he was too focused on his cartoon to respond.

I shrugged and patted Craig on the back. I reminded him it's important not to pry *too* much when questioning kids for answers in matters like this. I'd heard hundreds of cases like this. A child says something odd that may have psychic implications, and when the parent probes for more information, the child loses interest and skips away without a care in the world.

It seems that for a brief second, the child has access to information beyond his or her scope of understanding, like a glimpse into the future or a memory from a past lifetime. Yet, the moment is fleeting, and doesn't hold the child's attention. These incidents happen most frequently when a child is between the ages of three and four, just like Patrick was at the time.

I asked Craig to keep us posted if Patrick said anything else peculiar. He promised he would, and with that, Kenzie and I walked to our car and waved goodbye. On the way home, we further discussed Patrick's comment. We figured it was an isolated incident. Little did we know that others were beginning to have premonitions about Sky as well.

Chapter 32

It was February 16, 2013. My 32nd birthday was the very next day, so I celebrated with those attending the Omaha Metaphysical Network. A lady in the corner sheepishly raised her hand like she wanted to say something. It was Monica. She was a regular of the group and usually wasn't timid about sharing her thoughts. I wondered why she was suddenly acting so hesitantly. "Well, I know you might think this is weird or whatever, but I had the strangest dream last night involving Sky." I sat upright in my chair as I anxiously fidgeted with the cap on my water bottle.

Monica continued, "She was a newborn baby and I was holding her. I could see her eyes so clearly, and they were mesmerizing . . . almost piercing in a way. She just seemed so peaceful and serene. I *knew* it was Sky. I just *knew* it. And the dream was so vivid, I thought maybe it was a glimpse into the future or something."

Glancing around the room, I noticed some of the 'regulars' were nodding and whispering among themselves. We were a close group of friends. Many group members already knew Kenzie and I were trying for a child. Suddenly, another person in the room raised her hand, indicating she had something to share.

"Just last week, I also dreamt of Sky."

Hushed whispers filled the room as participants awaited further explanation. I prompted the lady to continue.

"Yeah, it was crystal clear. I saw a little girl who was . . . I don't know, maybe two or three years old. You were on one side holding her hand. I knew it was you because of your hat. And, Kenzie was on the other side, and you were both holding her hand like you were about to swing her up into the air."

Inhaling a deep breath, I took my hat off and ran my fingers through my hair.

"Of course, I couldn't see your faces because you had your backs to me. But I know it was you and Kenzie. And I'm sure it was Sky because the child wore pink leggings and had long hair."

"Is Mercury in retrograde or has there been a full moon recently?" I smiled and took a sip of water. I thanked Monica and the other lady for sharing their dreams. It was certainly interesting. *What were the odds of two individuals having a dream about a child who was not yet born?* Secretly, I hoped their dreams were a glimpse into the future. I would have welcomed Monica to hold Sky and look into her beautiful eyes. I wanted nothing more than to hold my daughter's hand and swing her into the air.

Not wanting to hog the spotlight, I suggested we change the topic. A gentleman named Fred took this as his chance to share some thoughts about UFOs and extraterrestrials. I hardly heard a word he was saying because I found myself thinking about Sky and the dreams we'd just discussed.

At our group meetings, we often talked about the law of attraction, a concept also known as manifestation. It's a belief that our thoughts and intentions quite literally create our own futures. The Universe is always paying attention and is willing to grant our wishes, for better or worse, based on what we focus our energies toward. Positive thoughts attract positive things. A negative mindset draws more misfortune. Fixating on a particular desire is like throwing a lasso around the event and pulling it into our reality. In its simplest form, all manifestation requires is faith mixed with effort. Thoughts become things, because our thoughts are more powerful than we can possibly imagine.

I so desperately wanted to manifest Sky into our reality. I knew she was already a fully conscious being existing on the Other Side. Heaven is not just the destination for souls leaving Earth. It's also where a soul departs from prior to being born. The spirit world is often called the afterlife, but in a technical sense it's also the *before*life. It's merely an airport of departures and arrivals with souls coming and souls going.

When a baby is born, the child appears to be helpless, clueless, and utterly vulnerable. Yet, babies are only babies in a physical sense. Just prior to birth, babies are wise and ageless souls, fully aware of their past lifetimes. They're also cognizant of the life they're about to enter. They've signed up to come back again, and are willing to accept the burdens and blessings of another lifetime. I hoped Sky was standing at the boarding gate of Heaven, suitcase in hand and eager to leave. I wished she would fly into our lives. We were ready for her, and we loved her despite not yet having met her.

There's some proof behind the notion that children are alive in Heaven before they're born, and that they have consciousness prior to being in the womb. I once met with a client named Meg. In 1999 she was still in high school and accidentally became pregnant. The pregnancy ended with a miscarriage. Years later, when she was married, she got pregnant again and delivered a healthy boy whom she named Nate. Meg explained that when Nate was around four years old, he would repeatedly ask her, "How old would I be right now if I were born in 1999?" Nate often reported he felt older than four years old.

Meg shrugged it off the first couple times Nate asked this question, assuming children are prone to saying odd things. However, she eventually realized what was happening. Nate must have been the same baby that was miscarried in 1999. On a subconscious level, he remembered nearly being born. After hearing this, I explained to Meg that often times when a miscarriage occurs, the child comes back to the same family when life's circumstances are more favorable. Nate had obviously selected Meg as his ideal mother for this lifetime. Yet, being a teenage mother would have been difficult for Meg, so Nate patiently waited and came back when the timing was better.

Being born is like jumping onto a spinning merry-go-round. It's all about timing. Jump a tad too early or too late, and a person is likely to lose grip and fall off. In a spiritual sense, this the equivalent of a miscarriage. To fulfill its destiny, a soul must hop into this world at just the right time. Nate was patient enough to wait several years before coming back into Meg's life. I wondered why Sky was taking so long to come into the world. *Was she not ready? Was I not ready? Was life's merry-go-round spinning too fast for her to hop on?*

As these thoughts floated through my mind, I glanced at the clock and noticed it was time to wrap up our discussion. I couldn't believe how long I'd gotten lost in the corn maze of my own thoughts. I politely interjected just as Fred was carrying on about hyper-drives and his theories about Area 51. I thanked everyone for coming and said I hoped to see them at the next metaphysical meeting.

As group members shuffled out the door, Kenzie helped me put away the chairs. "Hey, I wanted to run something by you."

"Sure. What's up?" Kenzie replied.

"While Fred was talking about aliens, I kind of spaced off for a while. I got to thinking about the law of attraction and was wondering if maybe you and I should do a little meditation together. We could focus our energies on Sky and maybe manifest her to be born sooner rather than later."

Kenzie folded the chair and propped it upright against the wall of the conference room. "Sure, we could let her know she's welcome any time now. But I've never done a meditation with another person before."

"Me neither, but maybe two heads are better than one. Anyway, what else are we gonna do on a day this cold?"

Looking at the frost on the conference room window, Kenzie proposed, "Maybe we could light some candles and take a hot bath together while we do this meditation."

"There might be too many distractions in the bathtub for me to focus on manifesting." I winked at her while grabbing my car keys from the counter. Kenzie playfully slapped the side of my arm.

"I hope there's soap in the tub so you can wash your dirty mind, mister."

Chapter 33

Once home, we got into the bathtub. Kenzie leaned back into me like I was a makeshift recliner. I wrapped my arms around her. We sat there in silence, watching the flame of the candle flicker back and forth. It caused me to think of the candle that shattered during Kenzie's psychic reading on the day I first met her. All along, we assumed it had been Henry and Sarah's way of getting our attention. Now, I was beginning to wonder if it had been Sky's way of saying, "Hi mom and dad. I'm glad you've finally found each other."

I closed my eyes, and suddenly my other senses were heightened. I focused on Kenzie's breathing and could hear her heartbeat. *In and out. In and out.* Our pulses matched beat for beat. We silently prayed, meditated, wished, and dreamed of Sky. We didn't want to pressure her into being born if she wasn't ready yet. We merely wanted her to know she was welcome anytime. I requested that our guardian angels help Sky arrive safely into our lives. I asked Dad, Grandma, and Boompa for assistance in ushering Sky's soul from Heaven to Earth.

In my head, I spoke to Sky, knowing with certainty she could hear me. I promised her the world, promised I would do everything it takes to become the best possible dad for her. I'd do everything in my power to grant her the life experiences she wished to have. I told her I missed her with all my heart and soul. Kenzie and I were grateful for all our blessings, but our lives weren't complete without Sky.

The emotions of the meditation spilled over. A tear fell from my eye and landed on Kenzie's shoulder. A moment later, she sniffled and rubbed wet mascara from her eyelids. I can't speak for Kenzie, but as for me, they weren't tears of sadness, per se. It was just a mental release, an emotional oil change of sorts. I'd never felt so close to someone while at the same time feeling like they were a billion miles away. During the meditation, it seemed like Sky was right there with us. Only, she wasn't.

I wondered what it would be like to see Sky grow up. I imagined hitting the fast-forward button on the remote control of my life. I envisioned the day Sky would be born. I imagined holding her in my arms and smelling the newborn baby scent from the top of her head. I pictured myself gazing into her soulful eyes for the first time as she opened her eyelids. I wondered if her eyes would allow me to see all the way back into Heaven itself. I imagined holding her gently to my chest and whispering into her ear, "Welcome home, sweetheart. I'm your dad."

These images were all part of the manifestation process. It was our request to the Universe. It's what we wanted our future to look like. The Universe is a giant mirror which reflects back to us our greatest hopes and dreams. This process works more efficiently when we cast aside doubt. Allowing ourselves to be vulnerable is the only way to truly believe in something with all our hearts. Doing so is like strapping a turbo-charger on the manifestation process.

I thought back to my soul-searching road trip years earlier – back when Grandma was still alive and my spiritual journey was in its infancy. I remembered the message given to me on that trip as I drove a loop around the Midwest. *Take care of everyone else and you will be taken care of.* It was a simple notion. And yet, ever since that moment, the Universe had upheld its part of the bargain.

Business was good. I was married to the love of all my lifetimes. I had my health, a beautiful home, great friends, and a supportive family. In exchange, all I was expected to do was offer people inspiration, validation, and direction through my intuitive readings. Everything had fallen into place. Taking this all into account, I suddenly felt there was no need to begin second guessing the Universe now.

The bath water was beginning to cool down, so we decided to finish our joint meditation. Kenzie stood to the floor and wrapped a towel around herself. She stared in the mirror and looked like she was lost in thought for a few seconds. "Will you still think I'm pretty if I get stretch marks when I'm pregnant?" It made me sad that she would ask such a question.

"Of course I will, honey. You're going to be a beautiful pregnant woman and you'll be just as beautiful afterward." She was silent. I could tell she was unconvinced. Still looking into the mirror, she turned sideways to view a profile of herself. She stuck out her belly as much as she could. "If you get stretch marks, just think of them like a medal of honor. Wear them proudly and know you earned them by pushing a human being out of yourself. That's pretty badass if you think about it."

"*Tolerating* stretch marks and being *proud* of them are two different things, dear." She turned from her right to her left and viewed herself in the mirror from the opposite side, again sticking out her belly.

I rose from the bathtub and placed a towel around my waist. Wrapping my arms around her midsection, I kissed her on the cheek. We stared at each other through the mirror as I rested my chin on her shoulder. "I promise honey, I'll love you no matter what. I'll think you're beautiful whether you have stretch marks or not, whether you're as skinny as a number two pencil or as big as a whale."

Kenzie grinned. She closed her eyes and leaned her head into mine, nuzzling me like a housecat who wanted affection. Her wet hair brushed my nose and it smelled like pomegranate. "If I become as big as a whale, will you at least feed me krill and splash water on me occasionally?" We both started cracking up. With my arms still around her midsection, I could feel her stomach vibrating and contracting with each laugh. It made me wonder what it would feel like to touch her stomach when a baby was kicking.

Our meditation was clearly over, so I attempted to keep the mood lighthearted. "Yes, honey, I'll feed you krill. And I'll splash water on you and teach you tricks just like that whale in *Free Willy*." We began making ridiculous whale sounds, mooing and bellowing with deep voices. We exited the bathroom and made our way to the dresser. Laughter filled the room. I pulled off my towel and playfully snapped Kenzie in the rear as she looked for socks in the top drawer. She hopped straight up like a bullfrog and screeched. There was so much love and laughter in our home the walls could hardly contain it. I wondered if the joy would act as a homing beacon, shining all the way to the heavens and showing Sky where to find us when she was ready.

Chapter 34

"Hot damn! Can you believe it, honey?" Kenzie shook her head. Her eyes were filled with tears of joy that looked like sparkling diamonds. We hugged each other tightly. As she exhaled, I could hear nine months worth of frustrations evaporate like dew in the midmorning sun. An egg had been fertilized. A tiny miracle resided inside of Kenzie. The moment had finally come, and it was nothing short of glorious. We paced around the house, not knowing quite what to do. *Who should we call first?*

I looked out the kitchen window. The sun appeared to shine more brightly. Colors were more vibrant. It was May, and the nature preserve was green and lush. My perspective on life was now entirely different. Everything was about to change. We were about to welcome new life into our family. By the time our baby was born, the leaves would be gone and the trees would be snow-covered. In my mind, I began to estimate the baby's due date. I held out my hands and started counting off the months on my fingers.

"What are you doing?" asked Kenzie.

"Let's see. It's May now. That puts us into . . . February."

She set the positive pregnancy test on the counter and took a seat at the kitchen table. "February . . . as in February *twenty-second? Two twenty-two?*"

"Oh my God. What if the baby is 'something blue' – as in a baby boy?"

She crossed her arms and smirked. "Well then we'll decorate the baby room in monster trucks instead of unicorns and we'll love him to pieces."

"I guess the doctor can give us a better idea of the due date, huh? And when is it possible to know the gender of the kid?"

"I'm new to all this, too. Just because I'm a nurse doesn't mean I'm an expert at being pregnant. We can ask my doctor all these questions." She grinned as she batted her eyelashes. Her look seemed to be a combination of *I love you* and *please chill out*. I kissed her on the forehead and continued to pace around the kitchen, too excited to sit.

I imagined Henry and Sarah nearby in spirit, sharing in our excitement. They must have known our patience would pay off. Our manifesting meditation worked! Of course it did. That's how it works. You drop a request in the Universe's inbox and before you know it, there's a reply. I imagined the spirit of my dad somewhere in the room with us. I bet he was delighted to become a grandpa, even if only from the perspective of the afterlife. And Grandma . . . she was surely in the kitchen with us also. It was a wondrous day.

We scurried over to my mom's house. She initially thought something was wrong since we were acting strange and dropped by on such short notice. She was relieved we had good news to share rather than bad news. My mom burst into happy tears as she congratulated us with a voice that was trembling with excitement. "Do you two think it's a girl?" My mom asked with hopeful anticipation. "I hope it's Sky."

I twiddled my fingers nervously and shrugged my shoulders. "We hope so, too," Kenzie and I said in unison.

The three of us got to talking about predictions involving the gender of babies. I reminded them of the time I had a client who was pregnant and I predicted she'd have a baby boy. She was only three months along at the time and not even the doctors knew yet if she was having a boy or a girl. The client was so confident in my prediction that soon after her psychic session, she went out and purchased enough items to furnish the entire nursery for a son, including a crib, blue bedsheets, dinosaur decorations, monster truck decals for the wall, and even a mobile with footballs to dangle above the child's crib. I was nervous leading up to her next ultrasound, knowing how inconvenienced she would be if my prediction turned out to be wrong. Thankfully, she ended up having a baby boy.

We laughed about that story in my mom's living room. She hugged us and congratulated us once more. She reminded us not to do anything drastic or get ahead of ourselves. "You guys don't go painting the nursery pink just yet, okay? Wait until you know for sure."

Chapter 35

My good friend Eddie has three daughters. I once asked him if he remembers the hard times of parenting when the girls were still very young. I wanted to know which one was the easiest baby to deal with and which of his daughters worried them most by getting hurt or getting into trouble. I suppose I was attempting to live vicariously through his stories of fatherhood since he was a dad three times over and it was an adventure I'd yet to experience.

He thought for a second and responded that he couldn't remember a great deal of difficult days from when his daughters were young. He assured me there were probably some sleepless nights. Surely there had been times when he was stressed beyond belief and struggling to keep up with the demands of having three daughters. Yet, he said he couldn't recall any specifics from the stressful times.

"I guess the not-so-fun moments fade away, and all you're left with are the highlights . . . memories of the good times and laughter. That's what I remember most from when the girls were young," he told me.

I let that sink in for a moment. To a certain extent, I agreed with him. Bad memories sometimes have a way of ending up in our mental waste basket, filed away into the shadowy corners and recesses of our long-term recollection. Perhaps it's because we don't want to remember. Maybe it's just too stressful or too painful.

I can't recall all the details from the day Kenzie had the miscarriage. It was in the month of May, but I don't recall the date. She'd only been pregnant for a couple weeks. I remember her saying something about spotting, that something didn't feel right, that she needed to check in with the doctor. And then we learned the sad news.

I don't remember the medical term for it. *A technical pregnancy? A chemical pregnancy?* Simply put, it just didn't take. She was barely even pregnant, and then . . . she wasn't. I remember feeling numb, and giving Kenzie some reassuring words as we sat there together on the living room couch. I can't remember what I said or how Kenzie reacted.

I remember feeling silly though – embarrassed that we'd gotten so carried away over something the size of a poppy seed inside of Kenzie. We were devastated. I wrestled with my thoughts, trying to make sense of it all. Was the timing *still* not right? *How could that be?*

After a few days, I got back to doing psychic sessions. Perhaps it was my way of coping with the grief of the miscarriage. However, I always made sure to be home from the office at a reasonable time. I realized that a successful career was not nearly as important as a healthy marriage. Adversity tends to rip couples apart or solidify their resolve. I was determined to learn something from the ordeal and grow together as a couple. To do that, we required plenty of quality time together. We made it a priority. We couldn't control what had happened, so we merely controlled how we responded to the situation. We cried a lot. And we prayed a lot. And we waited.

Chapter 36

A couple months passed. It was now August. My manuscript, *Flying Paint Rollers from Heaven*, was in the hands of the publishing company. Their office was located on Frances Street. It was a funny synchronicity since Grandma's name was Frances and the book's title was a nod to her antics with paint rollers. The book was a buffet of topics related to metaphysics, spirituality, and the paranormal. It wasn't yet complete, so I concentrated on writing the perfect ending to the book while my publishers edited what I had already written.

I was sitting at my desk inside my second-story home office. My laptop was open and I was staring at the last few pages of my manuscript. While searching for creativity and inspiration, I found myself gazing out the window to the line of trees below. The edge of the nature preserve was calling to me. I found the movement of the trees rhythmic and hypnotizing. The warm summer breezed caused them to sway to and fro, like a married couple slow dancing to their wedding song.

Occasionally the wind picked up and cause the trees to bend at a more acute angle. It amazed me how the trees were not only strong, but incredibly flexible. They were tall but not overly thick, so perhaps they were flexible and resilient out of sheer necessity. Had they been rigid, they would have splintered and toppled over long ago. Yet, they weren't about to fall. They didn't defy the breeze, they simply moved with it. They didn't resist the wind, they *danced* with it.

I envied those trees for their beautiful design. *How long had they been there? Thirty years? Forty?* There was no way to tell, but I assumed they predated the neighborhood itself and existed long before the nature preserve was labeled as such. Their method was tried and tested. Be flexible without breaking. Be still until something moves you. I wondered if Kenzie and I could operate in the same fashion. After all, the miscarriage had bent us, but we weren't broken.

I took my eyes off the trees and looked back at my computer screen. The curser was blinking like a flashing yellow stop light, inviting me to proceed with caution. I wasn't sure how to finish the book. It included many experiences Kenzie and I had been through – the candle that exploded in Kenzie's psychic reading, discovering Henry and Sarah, the serendipity of how we fell in love, Grandma's flying paint roller, the prediction of Kenzie's future daughter – it was all in my book.

Yet, the prediction of our future daughter didn't come true. It was a prophecy that hadn't played out, and it left me feeling unfulfilled. It seemed anticlimactic, like a rain-delayed baseball game in the bottom of the ninth inning, or like a firework show ending just before the grand finale. I hoped the readers of my book wouldn't feel the same way as they turned the last page.

My fingers rested idly on the computer keyboard as I pondered how to finish the book. At the risk of getting my dreams crushed again, I allowed images of my baby girl to dance around the stage of my imagination. Just as Kenzie and I had done during our meditation back in February, I imagined myself living a future where Sky was already here.

I pictured holding her fragile, newborn body wrapped inside a warm pink blanket. I basked in the euphoria and utter joy that moment would bring. I imagined how we would feel as first-time parents in the delivery room, observing the miracle of new life – the physical, tangible, end result of two people's love for one another. I was overcome with gratitude and joy. I could hardly discern between my imagination and reality. In my mind, it felt like I was already the proud new dad of a baby girl. The future would eventually become the present. I knew it was only a matter of time before Sky would arrive.

I held my face in my hands as a lump formed in my throat. Like presents spilling out of Santa's toy sack, joyous tears fell from my eyes and splashed down on my computer desk. Leaning back in my seat, I let out a big sigh. Just above me was a small dream catcher dangling from the pull chain of the ceiling fan. An idea came to me while staring at the dream catcher. It suddenly occurred to me how I would conclude my book. Sitting up straight, I placed my fingers on the keyboard.

The room was still and silent, but I was not alone. Two Native Americans stood behind me in spirit. Much like the wind, I could not see them, but I could *feel* them.

"Go ahead. Do it," they whispered. "Write it, and it will be so."

Looking at the computer screen, I could feel my eyes dilate like an eagle spotting a salmon in the stream. My fingers were no longer cemented in stone. The writer's block was gone. My fingers felt nimble and started twirling around the keyboard like an Olympic gymnast doing a floor routine. With a peaceful feeling in my heart, I confidently typed, "After submitting this book to WriteLife Publishing, Andy and Kenzie learned they were pregnant with their first child. It's a girl." I slam-dunked a period onto the end of the sentence, trusting that it would be a true statement in the near future. I was attempting to manifest Sky into reality by utilizing the law of attraction. I secured my wish to a boomerang and threw it into the Universe, knowing it would circle back to me soon enough.

Chapter 37

In the days that followed, I emailed my finished manuscript to the publishers. I felt relieved, relaxed, and care-free. Kenzie noticed an extra pep in my step but couldn't pinpoint the cause of my newfound optimism. I hadn't shared with her the prediction I wrote at the end of the book regarding her getting pregnant during the publishing process.

I was scheduled to do a psychic show in Chicago. However, with all we had been through in recent months, we thought a vacation sounded more appealing than a business trip. We hadn't advertised for the show or made tickets available yet, so we decided to cancel the show altogether and visit Chicago for leisure. The plane tickets were already purchased, so we just needed to pack our bags. At the time, my cousin lived in Chicago at the top of an apartment complex that overlooked the Navy Pier. From her living room, we had a spectacular view of Lake Michigan.

It was a short vacation, but it was just what we needed. My cousin acted as our tour guide. We rode the train to China Town where we ate puffed pastries inside a food mart. We snapped some pictures and purchased a few souvenirs. I loved the cultural diversity of Chicago. The city is an assault on the senses. Lake Michigan is so vast it looks like an ocean. The smell of hot dogs and fresh popcorn filled our nostrils as we traversed the busy streets. The sound of honking taxis buzzed in our ears. It was hard to take it all in, but we loved it.

It was mid-September and the temperature was still in the 90s. We booked a boat tour on the Chicago River. It snaked through the middle of the city, giving tourists a chance to admire Chicago's unparalleled architecture. The boat's canopy gave us a break from the sweltering sun.

While we were in Chicago, the United States men's soccer team played Mexico in a World Cup qualifying match. The game wasn't in Chicago, but the Windy City is known for its passionate soccer fans, and we got word there was a viewing party at a sports bar. We watched the game along with a hundred other soccer fans inside the jam-packed pub. It was situated within a hip little district known as Hyde Park.

The night reminded me why I generally stay away from loud bars. As an intuitive person, it's overwhelming to be in such a chaotic environment, especially when strangers around me are intoxicated. Booze has a way of taking the filter off people, for better or worse. It causes me to feel the full force of their personality, and it's overwhelming at times. Even when my psychic switch is set to *off*, it's still a bit much to handle.

Nevertheless, the U.S. defeated Mexico 2-0, which qualified them for the 2014 World Cup in Brazil. The adrenaline of the game ultimately overshadowed my anxieties of being in a crowded bar. We had a great time. We left the pub, proudly sporting our U.S.A. jerseys. We scheduled an Uber driver to give us a ride back to my cousin's apartment.

On the way back, Kenzie seemed unusually quiet. I asked what was wrong, and she said her stomach was a little upset. I reminded her that she shouldn't have ordered extra jalapeños on her chicken nachos. She regretfully agreed. I assured her my cousin probably had some antacids back at her place and we'd be there soon.

Just like that, our two-day trip was over. On September 12, 2013, our plane touched down at Eppley Airfield in Omaha. I had a busy week of psychic appointments ahead of me. Kenzie was gearing up for an eventful week at her nursing job. She worked at a group home with residents affected by physical and cognitive limitations. Just like my work, hers was immensely rewarding, albeit emotionally challenging at times.

"Well, I'm officially out of clean clothes," Kenzie said as she unpacked her suitcase in our bedroom. "I'm going to throw a load in the washer so I have something to wear for work. You need me to wash anything for you, babe?"

"Nah, I'm good," I replied. "I'll do a load later. Right now I'm gonna hop in the shower."

"Okay, sounds good. But first, can I get in there really quick to use the bathroom?"

I unpacked a few things from my suitcase as I waited for the bathroom to be available. Moments later, I was enjoying a hot shower to wash off the smells of the train and the airport. It was nice to feel the familiar water pressure, to use my own towels and shampoo. Returning from a trip makes a person thankful for all the familiar amenities home has to offer.

After my shower, I was rummaging through my top dresser drawer, searching for a matching pair of socks. Zico was lying on our bed, licking his paws. I glanced over my shoulder and asked Zico if he had fun at my mom's house while I was gone. She tends to spoil him when I'm out of town, and I could only imagine how many treats he'd been given.

Kenzie suddenly walked into the bedroom with a mischievous grin on her face. She'd been just a tad irritable on our flight home. I shrugged it off, assuming she was tired since we didn't get much sleep the night before. I was happy to see she was in a better mood now. I noticed that her arms were tucked behind her back as if she was holding a surprise. There was a playful twinkle in her eyes, as if she knew something I didn't.

Chapter 38

Without giving me a chance to ask what she was holding, Kenzie raised up both hands faster than Wild West gun slinger drawing a pistol. It happened in such a blur that it took me a second to realize what she was holding in front of my face. In each of her hands was a positive pregnancy test. With a playful tone, she asked, "So . . . do you want to be a dad?"

"Are you kidding me?" I shouted. She was silent and merely nodded. "For real? You're serious? Are you sure?" Again, she nodded. Kenzie's light brown eyes were watery. I'd never seen an individual so happy, so relieved, so joyful. Her smile would have been visible from the edge of space. We embraced each other and hugged so tightly I thought I was going to pull her soul directly into mine.

I turned my eyes to Zico, who was still lying on our bed. "Zico, you're going to be a big brother!" The words sounded nothing like 'treat' or 'walk', so he yawned and plopped his head back onto the comforter. I dropped to one knee and lifted Kenzie's shirt before kissing her stomach. "Hello little baby," I whispered with a trembling voice. "We've been waiting a long time for you."

As I rose to my feet, something occurred to me. I was completely naked. Kenzie had ambushed me with the wonderful news before I had time to get dressed. Clearly, she was too excited and couldn't wait. There I was, naked as the day I was born, standing before my wife and her little embryo.

The moment was perfectly *imperfect*. It was raw, real, and unrehearsed. Life's best moments seem to happen like that. They don't wait for the stars to align. They don't wait for perfect lighting or convenience.

Moments like these don't give us time to RSVP. They just . . . happen. They happen whether or not we're wearing clothes. They happen when we least expect it. They happen right when they're supposed to . . . when we've been flexible enough to bend without breaking, when we've held on to our faith when there was nothing left to hold on to.

Chapter 39

"Well, no, it wasn't true at the time I wrote that in my book, but it's true now. Yeah. She's definitely pregnant." I shifted the phone to my other ear as I handed Kenzie a glass of water. "How's it going? Ummmm, well . . ."

"Oh my God, I think I'm gonna be sick." Kenzie shoved me out of the way as she sprinted towards the bathroom and slammed the door. I muted the call with my publishers and spoke to Kenzie through the door.

"Can I get you anything, honey?" All I heard in return was silence. I grimaced and bit my bottom lip. Unmuting my phone, I continued, "Yeah, tomorrow would be great. I'll bring my best pen and sign all the paperwork. Yep, Frances Street. I know right where it's at. Okay. See you then."

Seconds later, the bathroom door opened. Kenzie was clammy and pale-faced. "False alarm," she mumbled as she moved past me. "I think I'm okay."

I suggested we step onto the back deck and get some fresh air. It was late September and starting to smell like fall. The sun was setting earlier each day. We took a seat in our deck chairs and looked to the west. I had a feeling the conditions were favorable for a gorgeous sunset. I've always had a knack for knowing when Mother Nature was in the mood to paint the sky orange. It's something I inherited from Grandma.

"So you meet with your publishers to sign the paperwork tomorrow?"

"Yep," I responded, still studying the clouds on the western horizon. "It's crazy, isn't it? The timing of it all?"

Kenzie extended her legs and propped her feet up on a metal side table. "I got pregnant as soon as you wrote that prediction in your book. Actually, maybe I was *already* pregnant and we just didn't know it yet."

I took my eyes off the sky and looked at Kenzie. She was wearing her caffeine molecule t-shirt. My gaze drifted from the molecule down to her midsection. "Does it feel weird? Having a living being growing inside of you?"

She looked down at her stomach and gently rubbed it counter-clockwise like she was waxing a show car. "Aside from the nausea, I don't feel a whole lot different. Not yet anyways."

I leaned forward, placing my elbows on my knees. "Don't be nervous about it happening again, okay."

"About *what* happening again?"

I inhaled deeply before taking Kenzie's hand in mine. "We're not going to lose her again. Everything's gonna be fine."

There was an awkward silence for a moment as Kenzie broke eye contact and looked at the trees. With misty eyes she turned back at me and forced a smile. "I know," she said, filling her inflection with as much confidence as she could muster. She squeezed my hand a little tighter.

A hawk silently glided over the nature preserve, temporarily blocking out the sun as it banked south. Crickets chirped. A slight breeze kissed our cheeks. Shadows were growing longer on the nature preserve. The walking path was flanked by long grass and reeds that swayed gently back and forth. Patches of wildflowers soaked up the remaining warmth from the sun. The two of us sat there, fingers interlaced, watching the sun go down. The night was still and quiet. Sometimes we conversed. Sometimes we sat in silence and admired the sunset. It was the color of a candle flame.

"Grandma Myers would have loved this one, wouldn't she?"

I raised my phone and took a photo. "It's a beauty."

Chapter 40

Kenzie and I needed to select a doctor to deliver our baby. Finding a qualified candidate wasn't exactly like searching the internet for a plumber or mechanic. We weren't dealing with faulty pipes or a tire alignment. We were dealing with a human being. We wanted our child ushered into this world by the hands of the most qualified doctor in the Western Hemisphere.

Finding the right doctor was like picking the perfect color from a paint deck. There were too many options. I wasn't sure if that was a good thing or a bad thing, but it was clear that Kenzie and I were starting to overthink the process. We decided to simplify our decision, relying more on intuition than endless research. Conveniently, many of the obstetricians in our area had short promotional videos online. The website depicted each doctor talking about his or her background and what led them to pursue a career in the baby-catching business.

We stumbled upon a video of a doctor whom I'll refer to as 'Dr. Kline' in order to preserve her privacy. She was relatively young as far as doctors go, but we reminded ourselves that *young* didn't necessarily mean inexperienced. In the video, she claimed that from a very young age, she knew she'd someday deliver babies. The words and phrases she used made it sound like she was talking about intuition and fate. She felt this career was her destiny. I had a good feeling about her. This lady spoke our language. Kenzie and I both agreed she was the one for us.

We called her office and filled out the necessary paperwork for Kenzie to become a new patient. I accompanied Kenzie to her first appointment. At the first visit with Dr. Kline, Kenzie was stripped down and only wearing a hospital gown. "I've never understood why those things open in the back rather than in the front like a bath robe," I said. "I mean, it would be a convenient gown for a proctologist who needs access to the trunk, but it doesn't make much sense for gynecologists who deal with the engine."

Kenzie smirked and rolled her eyes. "Are you going to be making bad jokes the *entire* time, babe?"

The mousy knock on the door misled us to assume Dr. Kline was quiet and reserved. As she stepped into the room, it was obvious that her personality was as captivating as a standup comedian. Her voice was loud and her handshake was firm. Her height matched her personality, and I wondered if she used to play basketball or maybe volleyball. She was serious enough to convey professionalism, yet casual enough to put us at ease. As the three of us made small talk and exchanged pleasantries, Dr. Kline swung the stirrups around and motioned for Kenzie to raise her legs up.

As she opened up Kenzie's gown, I quickly pivoted away from the stirrups and moved towards the head of the exam table. I averted my eyes, scanning the room for something, *anything* else to look at. I suddenly felt like I didn't belong in a room where such a personal examination was taking place. Dr. Kline must have sensed my sudden awkwardness. "You alright, Chief? We wouldn't be in this position if it weren't for you. Why so shy all of a sudden?"

I let out a nervous chuckle while fidgeting with a button on my shirt. I studied a pastel-colored landscape picture on the wall. Avoiding eye contact was my pathetic attempt at granting the two of them some privacy. "So, how does it . . . um . . . how long until we can know the gender?"

"About sixteen weeks along," Dr. Kline responded, as if she already knew what I was going to ask. "But getting insurance to approve another ultrasound before *twenty* weeks is almost unheard of unless there's complications . . . and we certainly don't want that." Kenzie and I remained silent, but we nervously looked at each other.

From seemingly out of nowhere, Dr. Kline pulled out a device that resembled a police officer's baton, and she explained she would now begin the ultrasound process. Kenzie appeared calm but I was growing more uncomfortable by the minute.

"Holy cow, Doc. How 'bout you put away your metal detector. We're looking for a baby, not pirate treasure." She was a good sport and humored me with a laugh. I couldn't help but wonder how many awkward husbands and bad jokes she dealt with on a weekly basis.

Kenzie mumbled under her breath, "I can't take you anywhere, can I?"

The standard checkup was over rather quickly. Everything appeared to be normal and Dr. Kline put our nerves at ease by fielding a few of our questions. She wished us well and reminded us to call her staff if we had any further questions or concerns. While walking to our car, Kenzie thanked me for going with her to the appointment. I reached for her hand and interlaced her fingers with mine. "Are you kidding me? I'm not gonna miss a single moment of any of this. Being my own boss means I have a flexible schedule and can come to every single appointment with you. It's one of the perks of the job."

As she buckled her seatbelt, she flirtatiously asked me, "What are some *other* perks of your job?"

I played along and responded, "Well, for starters, I get to kiss my secretary whenever I want."

She raised her eyebrows as she bit her lower lip. "Well, lay one on me, big guy." She puckered up and attempted to lean over the car's center console. However, rather than giving her slack, the seatbelt completely locked up. She couldn't quite reach my lips, and she resorted to extending her neck like a turtle trying to escape from its own shell. "Come on, lean in! I'm stuck here!" she hollered. The ridiculous hilarity of the moment overshadowed the romance, and we broke into laughter.

The part about kissing my secretary was technically a true statement. By that point in time, Kenzie had been assisting me with some office duties, business taxes, and coordinating my out-of-town events. Of course, her office duties were on a part-time basis, or 'PRN' as she called it. That means 'as needed' in nursing lingo.

During the initial checkup, Kenzie had admitted to Dr. Kline that she's a bit of a hypochondriac at times. It's the unfortunate byproduct of nursing school where she learned about rare diseases, birth defects, mutating viruses, and genetic deformities. During her pregnancy, I remember times where I'd have to convince Kenzie that the tickle in her throat was probably allergies, not walking pneumonia, and that her headache was just a headache and not the onset of West Nile Virus. Kenzie is tough and resilient, but sometimes her imagination joins forces with her fears and whirls around into a superstorm of anxiety. Perhaps we're *all* guilty of this from time to time.

I was hoping the pregnancy would be the most uneventful one in history with no complications. I knew if there *was* anything to worry about, Kenzie would definitely lose sleep over it. As we drove away from the medical facility, Kenzie was thumbing through some brochures she'd picked up in the lobby at the clinic. Without taking her eyes off the paperwork, she said, "Did you know that preeclampsia occurs in roughly five to eight percent of pregnancies even when the mom has no known health risks?"

I quietly shook my head, knowing exactly where this was headed. "Honey, don't sweat it. I'm sure you don't have preclampsinger."

She looked up from her brochure long enough to correct me. "It's called *pre-e-clamp-sia.*" She annunciated every syllable as though English wasn't my primary language. "It's a hypertensive disorder," she continued.

"Well don't make yourself *hyper tense* by worrying about those things," I replied. "You're going to be fine. You've got this."

She tried to assure me she wasn't worried about anything in particular, that she was just surprised by the percentage of women who experience pregnancy complications. "Pregnancy really throws the body for a loop. Pretty much any odd thing a woman experiences while pregnant can be chalked up to . . . *being pregnant!*"

As I turned from 192nd Street onto the Dodge Expressway, I silently pleaded for Sarah to use her guardian angel mojo in order to keep Kenzie from playing out worst case scenarios. Kenzie rambled on, "Iron deficiency, gestational diabetes, hyperemesis gravidarum, even bizarre dreams."

As we came to a stop at a red light, I gently pulled the pregnancy brochures away from Kenzie and set them in a cubby hole inside the center console. "We should go for a walk and take our minds off of pregnancy complications. I have an hour before I need to get back to the office, and some fresh air sounds nice."

Kenzie agreed that a walk was just what we needed to clear our minds. She informed me that she had some errands to run and would be unable to meet me at the office later that afternoon.

"I'll stop by the office tomorrow though, to check the answering machine and set up some appointments if you need me to."

"Thanks, I really appreciate that," I replied. "You deserve a raise."

"Tell me about it," she quipped as she flashed me a smile.

Our walk on the nature trail behind our house was utterly relaxing. Fresh air and a blue sky are the perfect cocktail to sooth the soul. Two red-tailed hawks circled overhead with the grace of ballerinas. I admired their uninhibited freedom. For reasons I can't quite explain, I've always felt drawn to hawks. I view them as my totem, my animal spirit guide. Seeing one hawk is enough to put a smile on my face. However, when I see *two* of them at the same time, I view it as a lucky sign from the Universe. I take it as a nod from the cosmos that all is well and I'm exactly where I need to be in life.

Some people find solace in seeing butterflies or dragonflies, viewing it as a message from a deceased loved one. Others see spiritual significance in finding feathers or pennies in the most unusual places. While I see the merit in such synchronicities and value them as meaningful, nothing speaks to me personally as much as seeing two hawks in the sky.

The two hawks above the nature preserve seemed like they knew each other. They were familiar with each other's moves. Red-tailed hawks often mate for life, and I imagined them as an older married couple. They'd likely danced that aerial dance a thousand times before. Perhaps they flew a little slower than in years past, but their experience and technique more than compensated for their decline in speed. I imagined Kenzie and I eventually following suit, walking that same trail in future decades, a little older and a little slower, but still as much in love as we were in that moment.

As we walked, I reached over and gently placed my hand on Kenzie's stomach. She smiled and placed her hand over mine, cradling her flat belly and imagining it was already round. I looked up, wondering if perhaps there was a juvenile hawk flying somewhere just beyond the two love birds. I couldn't spot one, so I figured Mom and Dad had their offspring long ago. Perhaps their kids had already flown the coop, so to speak.

Meanwhile, Kenzie and I were in a different stage of our marriage and on the verge of bringing new life into the world. We were mentally preparing for the changes and sacrifices to come as we eagerly awaiting the joys a baby would bring. We anticipated and accepted the challenges as well. Having a child must test a person's mental fortitude, and depending on the circumstances, can also challenge one's endurance, patience, and financial situation. As these thoughts circled around in my mind like the hawks overhead, I knew it was time to get back to the office for my next appointment. I planned on doing as many sessions as possible *before* the baby was born, because I'd scheduled myself three weeks off work once our little bundle of joy arrived.

I strolled back into my office with mental clarity, thanks in part to our nature walk. As I passed the front desk, a little red light was blinking on the telephone answering machine, indicating there were some messages that needed to be checked. I knew Kenzie would be in the next morning to return calls, and my client was set to arrive any minute, so I left the messages unchecked. Little did I know, there was one particular message on the answering machine which would leave us scratching our heads in bewilderment.

Chapter 41

"Oh my God!" I heard the surprise and urgency in Kenzie's tone, and I wondered what the problem was. She was at the front desk of my office and I was around the corner in the room where I deliver my psychic readings. It was nine o'clock the following morning and I was still putting my belongings into my desk and getting settled in.

"Oh my God, babe, come here!" I exited my room and walked towards Kenzie at the front desk. She motioned for me to join her by the answering machine. She studied the answering machine with a look of wonder on her face, like she was an entomologist who'd just discovered a new species of bug on the forest floor. "Listen to this," she exclaimed as she hit the 'play' button one more time. With hands on my hips, I leaned in and listened intently.

"Hi there. I was calling to make an appointment for a psychic reading with Andy. My name is Samantha Kline and I can be reached at . . ."

She proceeded to leave her phone number, but I'd stopped listening and reeled to face Kenzie. "Dr. Kline wants to see *me* for an appointment?"

Kenzie grinned and shrugged her shoulders. "I guess maybe after we left her office, she found out who you are and is curious to know what you do. Or, maybe she already knew who you were but didn't want to say so while we were in her office?" Kenzie playfully patted me on the chest and said, "Either way, you better knock her socks off and give her the best reading of your life, because we want to be on our doctor's good side."

I'd given psychic readings to doctors before. I'd done psychic sessions for lawyers, financial advisors, police officers, politicians, and other professionals who are trained to be critical thinkers. These folks are generally analytical by nature, and therefore require nothing less than substantial evidence to become a believer in psychic phenomena. I assumed Dr. Kline was a healthy skeptic. In other words, she was a person who *wanted* to believe but required definitive proof as she wasn't the least bit gullible.

Long gone are the days where a soothsayer's vague and generic predictions are enough to appease a paying customer. Modern day clients of psychic readers expect proof and evidence, most notably in the form of meaningful messages from deceased loved ones. Depending on the abilities of the psychic, this validation has the potential to be faith-affirming and even life-changing.

My reputation in the community was certainly a good one. Yet, an old sports adage came to mind. *A player is only as good as his most recent performance.* No doubt Dr. Kline had high expectations for me. My expectations for myself were equally lofty. I was determined to give her an experience she'd never forget, providing her with accurate, specific, and validating messages from her loved ones in Heaven. Regardless of how her psychic session turned out, I knew she was ethically obligated to perform her professional duties in terms of safely delivering our baby. Yet, I knew that giving her an amazing experience would mean she'd hold our family in high regard, and that certainly couldn't hurt.

"But what do I tell her?" asked Kenzie.

"What do you mean? Just tell her I'd be happy to meet with her and ask when she's available."

"No, I mean, *when* do you want to meet with her? You're booked solid for the next ten months. Our baby's gonna be here by then!"

My recent appearances on radio stations around the Midwest had allowed me to grow a larger client base. It was good in terms of having job security, but I couldn't help but feel a bit guilty for making people wait that long. We definitely wanted to get Dr. Kline in before the baby was born. Morally, there was no way I could justify bumping another person to make room for Dr. Kline, so I decided I'd meet with her the following week and we'd simply consider it an extra session on my schedule. That way, no one else had to lose their spot in the process.

Kenzie called her back and was surprised when she answered her phone right away. I could tell Kenzie felt uncomfortable calling her by her first name, because in her office we of course referred to her as Dr. Kline. She was thrilled when she learned her appointment would be the following week. After she found a time slot for Dr. Kline, Kenzie's tone became more casual. "Why didn't you say anything about wanting a psychic reading when we were in your office yesterday? This is too funny."

I was standing near Kenzie at the front desk, and although I couldn't hear Dr. Kline on the other end of the phone, it was apparent there was some confusion. After they ended the call, Kenzie explained to me what an odd synchronicity this was. Apparently, when we were in her office, Dr. Kline had no idea I was a psychic. She had been interested in having a psychic reading for a long time and kept putting it off. Weeks earlier, one of her friends at the office recommended me, and Dr. Kline was finally following through with setting up her own appointment. And as fate would have it, she just so happened to call at the same time Kenzie had become her new patient.

The following week, Dr. Kline arrived at my office for her appointment. She insisted I call her Samantha rather than Dr. Kline. I obliged, but it somehow felt wrong. It was like calling my first-grade teacher Julie rather than Mrs. Merriman. I tried to treat Samantha like any other client, assuming that if I put too much pressure on myself it would hinder the process. I settled into my intuitive rhythm, and in no time, we were communicating with her deceased grandparents. They prompted me to relay several messages which really hit home for Samantha. She enjoyed the experience so much that in the months to come, she referred several of her fellow nurses and doctors to come see me as well. I was honored. And a little relieved.

The two of us made small talk as I walked her to the lobby door. In a light-hearted tone, Dr. Kline asked me, "So, Mr. Psychic Man, do you have any predictions regarding the gender of your baby? Are you buying pink bedsheets or blue ones?"

I wasn't sure quite how to respond. After all, she'd just dipped her toes in the psychic waters by having her first psychic session. I certainly didn't want to overwhelm her with our super long story involving Sky. After pretending to think for a second or two, I responded, "My intuition tells me it's a girl." And I left it at that.

Chapter 42

We scheduled Kenzie for a sixteen-week ultrasound specifically to determine the gender. It wasn't at the doctor's office, but rather an independent, small business that specialized in ultrasounds. The building was sandwiched between other bays at a strip mall. It reminded me of a boutique. The place had storks on the window carrying little babies inside bundles of soft, white linen. "If only it were that easy," I thought to myself. The other window near the entryway displayed colorful cartoon-style images of baby animals. There was a zebra playing with blocks, a hippo sucking on a pacifier, and a lion wearing a cute little diaper.

I envied the warm-weather animals on the window. There, in the grasslands of the Serengeti, at least *they* weren't freezing. For us, it was mid-December. Kenzie and I were ankle deep in snow and slush making our way to the door. I suggested she hold onto my arm so she wouldn't slip on the ice. She grabbed my arm so tightly I felt like she was a prison guard and I was an inmate being transferred from one facility to another.

We entered the facility and filled out some basic paperwork. Compared to Dr. Kline's office, the paperwork was rather minimal. This visit was not picked up by our insurance as it wasn't a necessary appointment. It was just for fun. I assumed the place catered to people exactly like us – impatient, overzealous parents-to-be, delirious with joy, and all-too-eager to pay for overpriced baby supplies in the lobby.

As we took our seats, my phone chimed, alerting me to a new e-mail. As I checked it, Kenzie looked down and noticed it was my publishing company.

"Do you have them on standby?" she asked. I nervously bounced my foot up and down as though I were about to begin tap-dancing.

"Yep. They're trying not to be overbearing, but they know we find out today and they need to know as soon as possible."

The people at my publishing company were practically pacing the hallways awaiting the results of the gender-revealing ultrasound. My book, *Flying Paint Rollers from Heaven,* was one hundred percent edited. The manuscript had been formatted and the copyright was in place. All systems were *go,* aside from one little issue. Before officially sending the manuscript to the printing press and having the book mass produced, the publishers wanted to be sure that my prediction at the end of the book was, indeed, accurate.

If the avocado-sized human inside Kenzie's womb was, in fact, a girl, we were instructed to call our publishers so they could green-light the printing press to start making copies. If I was wrong and the baby turned out to be a boy, I wasn't entirely sure what would happen.

They say the gender of a child doesn't matter. Ask any pregnant lady for her opinion on what she hopes to have and you'll essentially get the same pre-programmed response. "Oh, we don't really care, as long as the child is healthy." It may be a common and generic response, but it's absolutely true. Penis or vagina. Blue pants or a pink dress. Name the kid Jack if it's a boy or Jackie if it's a girl. Same difference. Besides, some girls like blue, and some boys like pink. Some girls play football and some boys play with dolls.

As long as the child is healthy and loved, the rest is just details. That being said, there was a part of me that was nervous. *Were we naïve to believe in a Universe that grants wishes? Was this saga, spanning multiple lifetimes, nothing more than coincidence – a silly fantasy believed by two people searching for meaning in events that weren't even correlated?*

A staff member came into the lobby and informed us that it was our turn. We were escorted back to our room, which was warm and dimly lit, creating a relaxing ambience. Kenzie was instructed to lie down on the table. I sat beside her in a chair, nervously picking at my fingernail.

Overhead was an industrial size heating vent similar to the ones used in large, open offices. It kicked out a tremendous amount of heat. Our room couldn't have been more than 250 square feet. It was relatively small, and sitting underneath the vent made me feel like I was sticking my head over the rim of an active volcano. Due to a combination of my nerves and the heat, my shirt was sweat-soaked within minutes. As for Kenzie, she was as relaxed as a lizard sunning itself on a warm rock.

The lump in my throat left me feeling like I had swallowed a walnut, shell and all. My heart was beating faster than normal, and I imagined the adrenaline surge must have been comparable to an Olympic sprinter listening for the gunshot at the starting line. The technician spread lubricating jelly on Kenzie's abdomen. "Oh wow, that's cold!" she giggled. I sighed, wondering how anyone could be cold sitting inside a room that felt like a pottery kiln.

As the technician rolled the ultrasound wand around Kenzie's stomach, the image projected onto a large TV screen on the wall. We were essentially watching a movie and the little fetus was the main star. However, it seemed that our child was crossing his or her legs and wasn't positioned correctly to determine the gender. A process that usually takes five minutes had turned into ten. Ten turned into twenty. Just when the ultrasound technician thought she had a good angle, the baby squirmed into a new position, making it impossible to see what we needed to see. "Your little one seems to be a free spirit who doesn't want to follow the rules," the lady told us.

"The baby must take after you," Kenzie joked while patting me on the hand.

Suddenly, the technician informed us she'd finally spotted what she was looking for. "Are you guys ready to know what you're having?"

I looked deep into Kenzie's light-brown eyes. For a split second, I felt disconnected from the present moment, as though I was having an out of body experience.

A movie reel of highlights flashed through my mind at lightning speed. I mentally relived moments from the past, including images of the cold February day when I first met Kenzie. I recalled introducing her to Sarah, and the sound of the glass votive exploding while I spoke of Kenzie's future daughter.

I thought back to our first kiss and the moment she whispered *I love you* in my ear as we made love for the first time. I recalled cuddling in bed with Kenzie at the beach house in North Carolina, where we settled on the name Sky for our future daughter. I flashed back to Kenzie's past life regression and the morning I saw Henry and Sarah Cloud in Kenzie's family tree. I traveled back to the planetarium in Kansas City, the star map, and the engagement ring.

I thought of the miscarriage, the tears, the pain, the prayers, the joy, the laughter, the promises we'd made to one another. I thought of the text at the end of my book, and wondered if it were true. *Could it possibly be?* I wondered if the Universe was listening when I spoke. *Are fairy tales real or do they only take place in books and movies?*

As I focused my attention back to the ultrasound technician, I could hear my own heartbeat reverberating in my ears. It pounded fast and hard, reminding me of Native American drums at a pow wow. It was an echo that resonated from Kenzie's distant ancestors directly into my soul. I squeezed Kenzie's hand a little tighter and held my breath, for I knew the next few seconds would profoundly change the rest of our lives.

Chapter 43

"It's a girl." As the words left the lips of the ultrasound technician, I exhaled a shaky breath. Kenzie embraced me in a headlock of a hug. There was a symphony of euphoric emotions echoing through the concert hall of my heart. I heard a cacophony of voices from the spirit world, joyously yelling and hollering in unison. Surely, they already knew we were having a girl, but were sharing in our happiness nonetheless. I felt my dad there in spirit, smiling a smug grin and smacking on his spearmint gum. I could practically smell the minty scent. I knew he'd help Sky with her transition to Earth from the spirit world.

As the staff member wiped the lubricating jelly from Kenzie's stomach, I sensed the presence of Henry and Sarah Cloud nearby. I could hear Henry let out a high-pitched *whoop*, a celebratory holler belted out from atop his horse while he pumped the air with his fist.

Kenzie continued to hug me and was pulling my full body weight onto the exam table. I worried the table would topple over and crash to the floor. What a scene it would cause. I imagined the staff racing into the room after hearing a loud commotion and would find a smiling Native American girl atop a sweat-soaked man in a hat. No doubt they'd ask us to leave and never come back. Then again, the facility was probably used to such emotion-fueled moments.

I glanced back at the alien looking creature on the grainy television screen. I couldn't help but wonder what the odds were of the results being inaccurate. I didn't doubt the technician knew what she was doing, but there's always room for error. She printed out a low-resolution picture of our child that looked similar to an x-ray photo. She pointed to the reproductive organ and assured me that although the difference between male and female is subtle at this stage of development, she was ninety-nine percent sure we were having a daughter.

I had her double check and triple check. Thankfully, she was patient with me. She must have been used to dealing with dads who lack a certain sophistication when it comes to ultrasounds – like the fathers who point to their son's ultrasound picture and brag about the kid's "manhood" before learning it's merely a leg.

We walked out of the office. The cold December air felt good on my red flushed cheeks. Kenzie and I reached for our phones and began making calls to family members who eagerly awaited the news. Two similar conversations went on simultaneously.

"Hey mom, it's a girl, just like we thought," Kenzie said to her mom through chattering teeth.

Meanwhile, I spoke with my mom. "Yeah, of course I asked her to check again, but there's only so many times they can look, Mom."

Chapter 44

"**M**an, this thing really sucks. Literally, it *sucks*! Come touch it." Kenzie pulled the contraption off the display table and held it out towards me. She placed the palm of her hand against the funnel-shaped end of the device. I could hear a faint change in pitch as the contraption tried to inhale her hand. Feeling uneasy, I leaned away and scrunched my nose. It might as well have been a severed human finger. I wasn't going near it. "It's just a breast pump. Don't be such a baby," she insisted.

"I know what it is! I just . . . um . . . I just don't think it's for *guys* to play with . . . that's all."

I spun around to face another vendor's table and mumbled over my shoulder to Kenzie, "Hey, honey, check this out. It's like a futuristic garbage can or something. I bet we can use this as a recycling container in the kitchen. We've been looking for something like this!"

Kenzie set down the breast pump and walked over to join me. She cocked her head, and with sad, puppy dog eyes, looked upon me with pity. "Awwww babe, that's not a garbage can. That's a Diaper Genie." She gently patted me on the hand as if to say, "Good try." I felt sheepish and confused – like a toddler who'd just put his shoes on the wrong feet. "I know this is all overwhelming. Baby expos like this have all sorts of weird gizmos. But remember, we don't have to buy anything today, we're just getting ideas for when we go register for our baby shower."

As we walked away, I attempted to save a shred of credibility as I pointed back to the Diaper Genie and softly said, "But it looks like it *could* be a recycling container, right?"

She rubbed my back and consoled me. "I bet other dads were probably thinking the same exact thing." I knew she was lying, but it still made me feel better.

Walking through the gauntlet of vendors and baby supplies was enough to make our heads spin. The over-caffeinated vendors pulled us every which way, making us feel like we were at a carnival. Aisle after aisle of gadgets and whatchamacallits – butt paste, booger suckers, bottle warmers, bouncy chairs, and birth photographers. It made me wonder how humans managed to raise offspring ten thousand years ago – before the invention of the diaper-changing station and collapsible stroller combo, complete with iPad touchscreen, Bluetooth speakers, and a built-in pouch for hand sanitizer . . . gluten free and alcohol free, of course.

At the expo, we were shown car seats that looked more technologically advanced than the seats onboard a NASA space shuttle – fireproof, windproof, bulletproof, spit-up-proof, water-resistant, double-side-impact-tested, and complete with five-point harness buckles. Such contraptions allow parents to sleep well at night knowing their infants are safer than the gold inside Fort Knox. It made me wonder how kids from my generation or the baby boomers before me ever survived childhood at all.

As much as I sarcastically mocked some of the products at the expo, I was pleased to know we're taking such extensive measures to protect the youth of this world. The longer we can keep them happy, healthy, and free from danger, the better off they'll be. That being said, all of the cutting-edge baby supplies left me feeling a bit flustered. I had so much to learn and was overwhelmed by how many supplies are needed for babies. I was quickly realizing the smallest human in our house would require the most physical belongings. While I couldn't promise Kenzie I knew what every contraption was used for, I *could* promise her that I would be an amazing father.

My plan was simple, really. I'd be the dad who put in the most effort. The one who was there, the one who always showed up. By sheer relentless tenacity, it would eventually translate to me being a good dad. After all, the same tactic usually works in sports. You don't have to be the most talented athlete on the field, but if you give maximum effort and try harder than everyone else, you'll inevitably be at the right place and time to score some points.

I planned on being the dad whose kid *knew* how much she was loved. She would know because I would tell her a dozen times a day. I would *show* her with kisses, hugs, and acts of kindness. I would be the accessible dad, the one who wasn't afraid to get down on the floor and play with her. I'd be the kind of dad who would read to her every night before bed, sing her songs during bath time, and give her piggy-back rides up and down the stairs.

I planned on walking the tight rope in terms of being her friend when she needed a laugh, and being her father when she needed structure. I'd be the kind of dad who'd hold her all through the night when she was sick, and I would lay down the law when she was acting up. And later in life, the kind of dad she could call at 2:00 in the morning if she was in trouble. I'd be the dad who would move Heaven and Earth to make certain she knew she was loved unconditionally.

As we exited the expo and walked through the parking lot, Kenzie asked me what time it was. I pulled my cell phone from my pocket to check. I informed her it was 2:22.

"Oh that's funny," she said. "Last time I checked, it was 1:11. Today must be a day filled with synchronicity."

I was silent in thought for a moment before I replied, "Hey, do you remember that dream you had a while back? The one where you woke up with the words 'something blue on two twenty-two' stuck in your head?"

She shuffled through her purse looking for some lipstick, and gave a distracted response. "Oh yeah. I almost forgot about that. That never amounted to anything, did it?"

I shrugged my shoulders. "Guess not."

"You wanna grab some lunch?" she asked, as we got into the car and cranked up the heater.

I blew my warm breath into my hands and rubbed them together for heat. "Yeah, we could grab a quick bite, but I need to be home soon for that conference call with my publishers, remember?"

"Oh, yeah," she replied as she flipped down the visor mirror and began applying the lipstick. "Maybe we can just grab some fast food on the way home then."

"Sounds good to me," I said as I slowly backed the car out of the parking stall. A moment later, I pulled out onto 144th Street and headed north. Through the windshield, something caught my eye from above. Leaning forward and shielding my eyes from the sun glare, I saw two beautiful hawks overhead. They playfully went in circles like children enjoying a game of musical chairs. I smiled and silently nodded. I wasn't sure what the Universe had in store, but I knew it would be a good day.

Chapter 45

"Yeah, I'm getting my calendar pulled up right now, and um . . . no it looks like Saturday the eighth won't work for me. I've got something scheduled already."

It was my publishers on the line. We were trying to agree on a mutually convenient date for my book release event. "How about February fifteenth? Will that work on your end, Erin?"

"Let's . . . see . . . here," she said. I could hear her clicking away on her computer. "Nope. Sorry but February fifteenth is out for us. How about Saturday the twenty-second?"

We both chuckled, agreeing that we'd just take it week by week until we found a weekend that worked for us both. "Two twenty-two? Yeah, I'm completely free that day," I assured her. I switched the phone to my left side and held it to my ear with my shoulder. With two free hands, I added the book release party to my computer's online calendar. "I mean, I'll have to check with Kenzie to make sure I'm not overlooking something, but I think that will work for us."

"Okay, February twenty-second it is. See, I knew we'd get it eventually," she assured me.

"Hmmm," I mumbled under my breath as I slinked back into my chair and exhaled. Zico had been relaxing on the floor next to me. He stood to his feet quickly, suddenly concerned as to why my tone had changed. I gave him a gentle pat on his side to reassure him everything was fine. He twirled in a circle three times and plopped back to the ground once he'd found the perfect spot.

"What's wrong?" Erin asked. "Is the 22nd not going to work after all?"

"No, it's fine. It's just that a little over a year ago, Kenzie had a weird dream. She woke up with the words 'something blue on two twenty-two' stuck in her mind. We were never quite sure if it was an intuition of some kind. Anyway, do you think it could have been a premonition related to my book release event?"

"Oh boy, that seriously just gave me goose bumps," Erin whispered through the phone.

I picked up a pen from my computer desk and began to mindlessly twirl it in circles with my fingers like a baton. "Yeah, it's weird. But I can't figure out the 'something blue' part of Kenzie's dream. At the time, we wondered if it meant we'd have a boy rather than a Sky. But I'm glad . . ."

"You know what," she interrupted me, mid-sentence. I stopped twirling my pen and listened intently. "Andy, your book cover! It's almost *entirely* blue."

For a moment I was speechless. I quickly sifted through my emails, searching for an attachment Erin sent me weeks earlier. I finally located it, and doubled clicked the image preview. The picture of my book cover expanded on my computer screen. There it was, larger than life. A cover nearly entirely canvased in blue. It showed sun rays falling down from the heavens as puffy clouds dotted the sky. A blue paint roller cascaded down into the book's title at the bottom . . . *Flying Paint Rollers from Heaven*.

"Holyyyyy . . ." I trailed off into a barely audible whisper. Zico cocked his head and stared intently at me. He must have been wondering what all the excitement was about.

"Well, there you have it," Erin said, laughing to herself. "Kenzie is pretty intuitive herself, right? She'd *have* to be. This whole thing is too bizarre to be a coincidence."

"Yeah, she's prone to some psychic experiences from time to time," I assured Erin. "She's a little out of touch with the Native side of her family, but many of her Sioux relatives are apparently psychic as well."

"Well, let's take it as a sign that we've chosen the right date. I can't wait for the book signing. Bring your best pen."

I heard some soft footsteps behind me, and spun around in my computer chair to face Kenzie who was now standing in the doorway. She was holding up her cell phone and pointing to some small pictures. I couldn't quite make out what the photos were, but I could tell she needed to ask me a question.

"Okay, Erin, well I better let you go. We'll iron out some details as the event gets closer, but I'm glad we nailed down a date."

As we ended the call, Kenzie walked into my office staring at her phone and asking, "Sorry to interrupt. Hey, look at these bottle cleaners. Do you think we should register for two of them or do you think one will be enough?"

She glanced up from her phone and immediately noticed the coy smile on my face. She tilted her head in curiosity. "What's up? Did you two settle on a date for the book signing?"

"Yep," I said, still grinning, and purposefully withholding the punchline. I playfully dangled my little secret above her head like I was teasing a tiger with a raw steak.

"Well, tell me already," she insisted.

"Have a seat," I said. "You're not going to believe this."

Chapter 46

The morning of February 22nd was brisk and sunny. A few hundred people had registered to attend the book signing party. It was held at a hotel ballroom in Omaha. Prior to the event, my publishers informed me that *Flying Paint Rollers from Heaven* had already become an instant Amazon best-seller due to online orders and those who pre-ordered the book. It was a best-seller in the categories of angels, self-help, and psychology.

At the time, Kenzie was straddling the fence between her second and third trimester. Despite her aching feet, she was positively radiant. She was illuminated by an internal glow that only pregnant women are capable of emitting. With her petite frame, it looked like she'd tucked a size three soccer ball up the front of her shirt. Strangers carrying their freshly signed books approached Kenzie and rubbed her belly like it was a magic lamp. No genie ever appeared, but perhaps the real magic was that Kenzie remained accessible and so patient with these individuals, even though they ignored personal boundaries.

Kind-hearted belly rubs were a refreshing change of pace compared to the death threats we had recently received on social media from a local Christian extremist. He believed I was demonic since I talk to spirits, and he requested the help of his fellow churchgoers to harass me online. Compared to the police reports and restraining orders we had recently filed, the friendliness of attendees at my book signing was much appreciated.

At the midway point of the event, the security guard escorted me to the stage so I could deliver a brief speech. He was glued to my side and followed me like my own shadow. I hadn't been marked that well since my senior year when our soccer team played Bellevue West and their defenders were stuck to me like cellophane on leftover meatloaf. On stage, I was touched to see my closest friends and family members smiling at me from the front two rows – Kenzie, my mom, my sister, Aunt Terry, Grandma Smith, Jodi, Squirrelly Craig, UFO Fred, and so many others.

Even my brother, Dave, attended. He's not interested in psychic or spiritual phenomena, so I assumed my mom had guilted him into coming. Perhaps she reminded him of all the times he pummeled me in my youth. My brother had gotten a vasectomy in the months prior to my book signing, so I handed him a free copy with a signature that read, "You may be the older, tougher brother, but at least I still have my crystal balls." I'm not sure he ever read the book, but he at least appreciated the crude humor. Besides, I even wrote a little smiley face in there so he knew there were no hard feelings.

I turned on my microphone and took a deep breath. I looked down at Kenzie, hands folded and gently resting on her pregnant belly. She blew me a silent kiss from her ruby red lips. My mom looked at me with misty eyes and a proud smile. It had been a long journey, and she'd been with me the whole time. I thought back to when I first made the leap from social worker to psychic and how my mom helped me staple my business cards to coffee shop bulletin boards in hopes of gaining a new client or two. "We've come a long way," I said to her while fighting back happy tears of my own.

I introduced the audience to Henry and Sarah Cloud, and hinted that they'd learn more about those two while reading the book. I told the audience that Kenzie once dreamt of this very day. I thanked everyone for joining my family on what had been a wild and wonderful journey. I wondered if it would involve more spiritual twists and turns ahead.

The whole day was a blur, a surreal collage of countless names, faces, and signatures. Every face and every smile reminded me of a very personal journey I'd taken with each particular client – hearing intimate details of their lives, getting to know their families, both living and deceased, crying with them during grief-filled sessions, laughing with them and sharing in their joy. Through our psychic sessions, I'd been invited into their lives, into the top drawer of their soul's bedroom dresser where secrets, memories, and dreams reside.

I'd been with these people through deaths and births in their families. I'd seen these clients go through divorces, marriages, surgeries, career transitions, spiritual breakthroughs, legal matters, estate sales, adoptions, and moves across the country. I'd seen these people at their most vulnerable and I'd seen them at their very best.

I continued to sign books and the line of people kept coming. It finally dawned on me that my work as a psychic medium and life coach had allowed me to live vicariously through each and every one of those people. They'd given me the gift of feeling like I'd lived a thousand lifetimes within this one incarnation, riding shotgun with them and experiencing every turn, twist, and dip that life had to offer. As I handed each familiar face a signed copy of the book, I hoped it would suffice as a thank you.

As the ballroom emptied, I noticed Erin and the staff from the publishing company breaking down the empty boxes used to store my books. They picked through each box, fishing out one or two remaining copies and lumping them together into one pile, like siblings taking inventory of their trick-or-treat candy. "Not bad for your first book release party, Mr. Myers." Erin's smile was just like her – warm and sincere.

Kenzie and I gathered in the hallway for a photo opportunity with some immediate family members. The photographer snapped one last picture before we packed up the remaining supplies and headed towards the parking lot. The quiet after a big event is a strange sensation. It's like walking out of a concert into a soundproof booth. My ears were still ringing from the commotion of the audience, and suddenly we found ourselves in a space so quiet you could hear the hum of the hallway's fluorescent light bulbs. The day was perfect. A definite top ten in the photo album of my life.

In the parking lot, I dropped a small box of remaining books into the trunk of our car, right next to sample paint cans of colors such as sage, artichoke, and eucalyptus. They were potential colors for the nursery. Kenzie's always claimed I lack an eye for colors. What I call brown she calls beige. When I say it's white, she says it's pearl. We've carried on these lighthearted disagreements for years. She's a self-proclaimed Crayola color expert and holds it over my head that she won a kindergarten coloring contest in Mrs. Freeburg's class by staying between the lines on a picture of a drumming soldier.

As we got into the car, I suggested to Kenzie that we just leave Sky's bedroom purple. "It was painted that way when we moved into the house. I mean, what if it ends up being her favorite color anyway? All this work repainting will just be a waste of time."

By the look on Kenzie's face, you would have thought I asked her to stick her bare hand into a public toilet. "We're not going to leave her room *purple!*" Purple . . . she said it as if purple was the heel of the Crayola bread loaf.

"It's not really purple so much as violet," I said back to her with a smirk. Kenzie playfully smacked my leg with the back cover of my book. We pulled out of the hotel parking lot, debating the difference between violet and purple. Just like that, we stepped out of the public spotlight and back into the confines of our personal lives. Like anyone else, we had dishes to do, laundry to fold, and pets that needed some attention.

Life was good . . . *so* good it made me a little suspicious. I guess the only danger of feeling like you're on top of the world is how badly it will hurt to fall from such great heights. It's strange how life can be turned upside down in an instant. It's unfortunate how one mistake or moment in time can forever change a person's fate. Being at the wrong place at the wrong time can strip a person of everything they hold dear. *Poof* . . . and then it all disappears.

Chapter 47

It was a silver Ford F-150 with a broken side mirror. On any other day, it wasn't the kind of vehicle that would draw much attention. But on this particular day, an urgent voice inside my head compelled me to keep my eyes on the truck. *Watch it. Here it comes.* We were in the left-hand turn lane of 156th and Maple Street. *Easy. Careful.* The green turn arrow prompted me to proceed. As I accelerated, the driver of the silver truck roared through his red light in the oncoming lane. *Brake! Now!*

The tires squealed as I decelerated. The seat belts locked up, pushing the air from our lungs. Loose papers and a bag of nursing supplies flew over the center console and crashed into the dashboard.

"Shit!" Kenzie hollered. She shielded her face and leaned away from the passenger side window, bracing for impact. I smashed my right palm into the steering wheel, blaring the horn. The truck roared past us, just inches from the front bumper of our vehicle. He never attempted to slow down.

Other vehicles honked, too. Our hearts pounded. For a few seconds, we sat there in the middle of the intersection, shocked and flustered. I collected my thoughts enough to finish turning left onto 156th Street. By this time, our turn arrow had changed to red, and all the cars behind us were left stranded, waiting for another green light.

"*Jesus Christ,*" whispered Kenzie. The incident had robbed her face of color and she looked like she might vomit.

In hindsight, I'm not sure how fast the truck had been traveling. I didn't know if the driver was drunk, in a hurry, or simply not paying attention. It all happened too fast. Had the silver truck 't-boned' our vehicle, it would have plowed right through Kenzie's passenger side door by a foot or two, maybe three. There might not have been much left of the right side of our vehicle. My brain flooded with images of shattered windows, tangled heaps of fiberglass, and broken dreams. I wondered how an unborn child in the womb might fare in such an impact. I couldn't bring myself to dwell on such thoughts as they made me nauseated.

The close call left us both in stunned silence. We continued driving toward home. I suddenly felt compelled to change the radio station. The notion seemed like a silly one. After all, music isn't generally what comes to mind immediately following a scary incident. My heart was still racing and my palms were sweaty. The intuitive nudge to change the radio station was strong and insistent. It was coming from something or *someone* outside myself. It originated from the same voice that warned me about the silver truck.

I flipped the station to 99.9 FM. Norman Greenbaum's *Spirit in the Sky* poured through our car speakers. Kenzie's expression changed immediately. She looked like a child who was just told she was getting a new puppy. "Oh my God!" she shouted. "It's your dad's song!" I reached my hand over and gently touched her pregnant belly as I exhaled a sigh of relief.

"I'm just glad we're safe," I said with a shaky voice. We mouthed the words to the song as the hairs on the back of our necks stood on end. I knew it was my dad who caused me to change the radio station. He must have known *Spirit in the Sky* was playing, and he knew it would put a smile on our faces. He was the voice in my head that prevented us from being in the car accident.

My dad, Steve, was a nervous driver. He didn't like to be behind the wheel. I'd nearly forgotten about his driving hesitancies until Aunt Terry reminded me in recent years. Terry is my dad's sister. She said he always insisted that my mom drive, whether it be on road trips or taking us kids to soccer practice. I'm not entirely sure why my dad didn't like driving. I suppose it had to do with incidents like these – close calls that remind us how fragile life truly is.

I was grateful to have channeled my dad's defensive driving skills that day. The experience validated a notion I'd been having – a suspicion that he would be a guardian angel for Sky (one of a handful of guardian angels she'd have upon being born). It's a special arrangement for a person to have a blood relative as a guardian angel. It's not unheard of, just rare. I've seen it happen before, most often when a family member passes away when a child is still very young, or in cases like ours, when a grandparent passes away and never had a chance to meet the grandchild on Earth. Just because a grandparent and grandchild never met on Earth doesn't mean they haven't met elsewhere.

I've heard countless stories from my clients that leave me with goosebumps. Each account is different but they have similar elements. It might begin with a young child flipping through an old family photo album with Grandma. When they come upon a picture of Grandpa, the child gets excited and says, "That's Grandpa Bob, but his friends called him Bubba. He always wore a green hat when I saw him before I was born."

The record scratches, jaws hang open in disbelief, eyes get misty. Grandma says something to the effect of, "Yes sweetie, people called him Bubba. And I got him that green hat for our 30th wedding anniversary. He wore it all the time, but you wouldn't know that because he passed away before you were born."

The child shrugs her shoulders and loses interest as she gets up from the couch and skips down the hallway. These incidents happen frequently. They offer proof that children cross paths with their departed loved ones in Heaven before they're even born. When circumstances permit, it's possible for a deceased parent or grandparent to perform the role of guardian angel for a child who is about to enter our world.

Kenzie and I finally made it home. Our garage door lifted and we pulled to a stop. I said a silent prayer of thanks as I shifted the car into park. I'd never felt so happy to be home and step outside of a vehicle. The emotions of the day left us a bit fatigued that evening. I suppose that's how it is when we experience a close call. We replay the incident in our minds over and over again until we feel like we've lived through the event a hundred times. In the end, it leaves a person utterly exhausted.

Kenzie and I went to bed early that night. She nestled into her spot, lying on her left side. Months prior, she'd begrudgingly trained herself to sleep on her side. She'd been a stomach sleeper her whole life, and the habit was hard to break once pregnant. Maybe it was the fresh bedsheets or maybe it was the excitement of the day, but I knew we'd both be asleep within minutes. I tried to quiet my mind, tried to escape images of car accidents. The thought of Sky being taken from us was too much to bear.

Yet, as Kenzie drifted off to sleep that evening, she had a dream that would put our minds at ease. Sky would not be taken from us, not by car accident, not by miscarriage or other means. Rather, she was in the process of coming *towards* us. In a way, Sky was about to make her grand entrance into our lives, and Kenzie's dream rolled out the red carpet for her unexpected arrival.

Chapter 48

Kenzie rested her head on her own hand as she propped herself up with her elbow. Using her free hand, she gently caressed her stomach and glanced down at the bump with a smile on her face. As her eyes looked back to me, I was surprised by how clear they were, how bright and alert. There was a glow about her. Kenzie's eyes shimmered in a way I hadn't seen the night before. I asked how long she'd been awake.

"Only a few minutes," she claimed. She continued to touch her pregnant belly, gently rubbing it in circles like she cleaning a window.

"Is everything alright?" I asked. "Is Sky kicking in there?"

"No, she's been pretty still in there and hasn't really kicked me much since yesterday afternoon."

I reached over to touch her stomach. It was 8:00, a typical time for us to wake up. I knew that lazy mornings like this were a luxury we'd soon forfeit. In two months or less, we'd be new parents, at which time 8:00 would be considered sleeping in. It was a sobering notion for a night owl like me.

"Do you feel anything?" Kenzie asked, as my hand rested on her stomach.

"I mean, I feel a little hungry, I guess. Should I make us some breakfast?"

With a half-smile, she sighed at my lack of awareness. "No, I mean right *here*." She pulled my hand firm against her stomach. "Do you feel anything *in here*?"

"Intuitively, you mean?" I studied her abdomen a little closer and squinted my eyes to focus. "Well . . . I'm not really sure." I was surprised she had put my psychic senses to the test so early. She knows that until I have my first cup of coffee, I'm about as intuitive as a door stop.

"Never mind," she said as she got out of bed and stood to her feet. "You're gonna think this is weird."

I gently took her by the hand, asking her to sit back down and talk with me. I wondered why she'd leave me with a cliffhanger and then change the subject.

"Well, when I woke up this morning, I felt a lot closer to Sky. It's like we bonded overnight or something. I can suddenly feel her little soul and even her personality inside me."

Kenzie bent down to pick up a sock, giving me a moment to respond. Propping her left foot onto her right knee, she began to put it on. Her socks contained pictures of whimsical little garden gnomes with pointy hats. I stared blankly at the garden gnomes as I contemplated what she'd just said.

"Maybe she's finally in there," I replied. "Maybe Sky's soul finally merged with her physical body. Like she's locked and loaded and finally ready to blast into the world."

"She's not a bullet, dear," Kenzie replied.

"I know, but you know what I mean."

Kenzie stood from putting on her socks. Shrugging her shoulders, she said. "Yeah, that's kind of what I figured, too. It's the strangest feeling . . . I've always felt connected to her and everything because we love her so much already. But this morning, it's different. It's like she's *really* in there, like I can feel her energy or something."

I thought back to some of the concepts I'd taught in my lectures – that it's generally accepted that humans are comprised of a body, a mind, and a soul. Each component can operate independently, so it's entirely possible for our body to be in one place while our soul is in another. This is often referred to as an 'out of body experience' or OBE. The separation of the body and soul explains how Grandma Myers was able to fast forward the clock in her hospital room just seconds after they unhooked her from the ventilator. Her soul had already crossed over even though her physical body didn't expire for several more hours.

In our everyday lives, we don't give much thought to notions like this. After all, the vast majority of the time, our body, mind, and soul are conveniently located in the same place, right inside us. Things get a little more complex when a person is transitioning between dimensions. Being born or crossing back into the afterlife includes so many factors and variables that the body, mind, and soul aren't always bundled together in a neat little package. A baby's soul can enter its physical body at any point during a pregnancy. It can happen at eight weeks, four months, or in Sky's case, during the third trimester. It's just a matter of timing and personal preference.

For example, my brother generally arrives early to events. On the other hand, when I meet my friend Eddie at the movies, I know he'll be there ten minutes late. It's just how each of them are known to operate. Every person has different habits when it comes to time and schedules.

Inside the womb, Sky's soul had just merged with her physical body. Why had she waited so long? I suppose once a baby's body, mind, and soul are fully inside the womb, it's pretty tight quarters. Plus, there's not much to do. I wonder what it was like for my brother as he cooked inside our mom's oven. I bet his soul arrived *really* early, and there probably wasn't much to do in there besides suck his thumb and kick Mom's uterus. Maybe that's why he's always been such a fantastic soccer player.

I've spoken with enough parents to conclude that a pregnancy can be a very good indicator of what a child's personality will be like. If a child's soul enters the womb early, the kid is likely to be a very punctual person. Children who are born prematurely often grow into adults who rush around a lot, always in a hurry. Alternately, if a child 'arrives' in the womb rather late in the game, he or she will tend to have a laid-back concept of time as an adult.

Kenzie was well into her third trimester. Although Sky wasn't technically late to the party, she was cutting it pretty close in terms of her soul merging with her body. It made me wonder if she would grow up to be a procrastinator. Maybe she'd be the type of kid who assembles her science project the night before it's due, or the kind of person who files her taxes on April 14th.

Chapter 49

The Ruby-throated Hummingbird is scientifically known as Archilochus colubris. It's a name that's difficult to say, but not nearly as difficult as constructing one of its homes. Ruby-throated Hummingbirds build knot-like nests, and then anchor their nests to the branches of trees using spider silk. Yes, *spider silk*! The nests themselves are made using bark, silk fibers, and leaf strands, which make the structures incredibly strong, yet flexible. The insides of the nests are cushioned with hair and feathers, while the outside of the nests are covered with lichen, providing necessary camouflage. Simply put, these nests are a superior feat of engineering, appearance, and comfort.

Kenzie and I were preparing for a baby birdie of our own. We were 'nesting', as they call it. The term makes me feel like a bird. It makes me think of collecting twigs and straw and . . . spider silk, apparently. In human terms, nesting meant we were getting ready for our baby to arrive. We were determined to give our daughter the coziest home possible. There was no way to tell if it would live up to the standards of a Ruby-throated Hummingbird, but we did our best. Between decorating the nursery, organizing closets, and putting safety measures in place, we may have gone a little overboard. Perhaps, other first-time parents can relate.

We hired a company to clean our carpets. It was one of the trendy new companies who claim they don't use harsh chemicals. Rumor has it they only use water collected by steams high up in the Himalayas where it's blessed by Buddhist monks and quadruple filtrated . . . or so the legend goes. By the time they steam the carpets, a homeowner feels like they've had holy water infused into the very fibers they walk on.

In hindsight, the carpets weren't that dirty to begin with. Looking back, I marvel at how much free time we had to worry about such frivolous notions. I suppose it helped Kenzie and I to sleep better at night knowing we did everything possible to make the house more sterile for our child. Yet, we failed to realize that by the time Sky was ready to crawl, the carpets would once again be covered with dirt, dust, and dog hair.

We continued to nest. Kenzie won the epic paint color debate of 2014. I painted the nursery in a color of her choosing. I can't remember if it was called *sage, aspen bark,* or *honey pine,* but it was right there in the range of muted earthy colors. Kenzie liked it better than the existing purple walls. I was determined to get the job done in one coat, but the purple still showed through and made *honey pine* look more like *honey plum.* I had no choice but to apply a second coat.

No paint rollers flew on their own accord this time, nor did I expect them to. I hadn't sensed my grandma's presence for quite some time. I didn't fret about it. Our loved ones in Heaven might give us several signs or messages in a short period of time. Then, they pull back for months or years at a time. It's their way of granting us space so we can live our lives without obsessing over them. I missed Grandma, but I didn't have time to stew about it because I was simply too busy. After all, we were nesting.

We bought baby bottles, sterilized the nipples, and placed them in the cabinets. A couple weeks later, we got them out and sterilized them all again, just for good measure. We dusted, vacuumed, and dusted again. The carpets still smelled like Himalayan holy water. We gave Zico a bath and took him outside for a good brushing so he would shed less in the house. We made sure he was up to date with his flea and tick medication. Those types of medications can contain harsh chemicals, so we discussed switching him to an all-natural flea and tick medication once the B-A-B-Y was born.

Oh yes, we started spelling words rather than saying them. Soon, we'd have tender, impressionable ears in our home, listening and absorbing every sound in her environment. B-A-B-Y wasn't the four-letter word that worried us . . . it was the others. We didn't exactly cuss like sailors around our house, but we wanted to be more conscientious about it nonetheless. One slip up and our daughter's first word might rhyme with *truck*.

"How much S-H-I-T can a size one diaper actually hold?" Kenzie wondered.

"How in the H-E-double-hockey-sticks does this Nose Frida work?" I'd ask.

The Nose Frida, otherwise known as a pediatrician endorsed baby nasal aspirator. It kind of looks like a turkey baster. The general idea is to stick the open end of a plastic tube up the little human's nose before using one's mouth to suck on the other end of a straw-looking thing. Like magic, out come the boogers. Mind you, they don't go into the parent's mouth, but are caught in a filter midway up the straw. Ingenious really, considering kids of generations past found less sophisticated methods for disposing of mucus.

I was quickly learning that every aspect of caring for a baby in today's world is more complicated than one would presume. I discovered apps which synch to sensors in the baby crib, allowing parents to monitor a child's heartbeat while the baby sleeps. The contraptions were expensive as H-E-L-L, but still, the blending of technology and parenting was quite remarkable.

In the weeks leading up to Sky's birth, it felt like the calm before the storm. Our evenings were spent daydreaming and wondering what she would be like. I painted Kenzie's toenails one night because she'd become too jolly around the midsection to comfortably paint them herself. Luckily for Kenzie, my steady hand with a paintbrush translated to applying fingernail polish. It wasn't the Sistine Chapel by any stretch, but my handiwork wasn't too shabby.

Kenzie became frustrated that her maternity clothes were no longer fitting very well. One day, she wore a bright, pastel top that contained several colors, and she asked for assurance that it looked okay. Giving her a good look up and down, I encouraged her by saying it was beautiful. I said she looked like a beautiful supernova exploding with color. I could tell by the shock on her face that I'd chosen the wrong metaphor. Comparing my very pregnant wife to a large, celestial explosion was not one of my wisest moments. I'd somehow managed to put my size 10 ½ foot in my mouth. Thankfully, Kenzie laughed it off, knowing I meant well.

The anticipation was palpable, and we were ready. The dishes were done. The laundry was caught up. The crib was assembled and the bedsheets were on. The car seat was installed. Our hospital bags were packed. Our house was immaculate. I suppose that's how it goes with first time parents. They have more free time to make all the preparations.

Parents of multiple kids will tell you it's quite a different game by the time baby number two or three comes along. They're no longer concerned with the nursery looking like a home décor magazine cover. As long as there's no blood on the carpet and everyone has on clean underwear, they consider all systems "go" for welcoming a new baby into the home.

In retrospect, it seemed like we spent just as much time at the hospital as we did in our own home. Kenzie was afflicted with a condition known as placenta previa. Only about one in 200 women deal with this condition in the later stages of pregnancy. It has to do with part of the cervix being covered by the placenta. It's easy to lose sleep (and your mind) reading online articles about the potential risk factors of the condition. The scary part was the occasional bleeding, which caused us to fear the worst. It seemed like we were at the doctor's office or the hospital twice a week, sometimes more.

One night, Kenzie was having contractions and we rushed in to the hospital thinking it was code pink, the real deal. After finding out it was a false alarm and not actual labor pains, we were cleared to leave. However, a severe thunderstorm had formed while we were inside, and cloud-to-ground lightning strikes were slamming down all around the hospital.

I pulled my flat cap tight onto my head and dashed through the parking lot as fast as my thirty-three-year-old legs would carry me. Rain pellets stabbed at me while I said a silent prayer, asking Henry to keep me safe. The lighting was intense, and as much as I didn't want to admit it, I was scared as S-H-I-T. Being lit up by one billion volts probably wasn't the best way to prepare for being a new dad. Had my car window been down,

I would likely have jumped in feet first, *Dukes of Hazzard* style. Once safely in my car, I pulled up to the front doors of the hospital. I quickly escorted Kenzie into the passenger seat while thunder rumbled and shook the very ground we stood on.

We continued to discuss potential middle names for Sky on the way home that evening. Aubrielle, Aurelia, Lennon, and Lanea were all in the running. We had agreed the middle name was up to Kenzie since I'd selected Sky's first name.

As much as I tried to keep my opinions to myself and defer to Kenzie, I was partial to the name Aurelia. It's a word that means 'gold' or 'golden', so when combined with Sky, it would translate to *golden sky* – the kind of sky I've always loved, and the type of sunset Grandma Myers used to chase up and down the hilly streets of Benson all those decades ago.

On the morning Sky was to be born, I stepped out our front door to let Zico do his business. There, in our front yard was a peculiar sight. Two golden birds sat side by side in the tree. They cocked their heads, studying me with curiosity. The two birds hopped from one branch to another as if they were performing a routine. They looked like they'd practiced this one before. Their agility impressed me. Their golden feathers shone brightly in the morning sunshine and they were truly beautiful.

They flew off faster than my eyes could follow. I was left wondering if there was a reason for their timely visit. I'd never seen a goldfinch in our tree before. *Gold* made me think of the name Aurelia. *Perhaps it was the most fitting middle name for our daughter after all.* I looked to the sky with a smile on my face, wondering why those birds had visited me on that particular morning. I called for Zico to come back inside, and I entered the house to see Kenzie standing in the kitchen.

"Alright honey, I know it's your decision and everything, so feel free to say no, but I'm voting for Aurelia as the middle name."

She was packing some items into her overnight bag for the hospital. "Oh yeah. What makes you say that?"

"I was just letting Zico outside and a little birdie told me so."

Chapter 50

After seeing the beautiful golden birds in our front yard, I drove Zico to my sister's house. Elizabeth would babysit him throughout the day while we were at the hospital 'hatching' Sky. That's what Kenzie called it. *Hatching* . . . as though Sky was a baby ostrich on the verge of breaking through its shell.

It was Monday, May 19, 2014. It was delivery day. For a whole host of reasons, Kenzie was scheduled to be induced. I liked the thought of our daughter being born on a Monday. It made it feel like she was clocking in for work at the right time, so to speak. After all, most new employees begin on a Monday. It's the start of the week, a fresh beginning, a new chapter. People born on Mondays must live more productive lives. At least that's what I told myself. We were asked to arrive at the hospital at 7:00 in the morning. Although Kenzie generally has a relaxed concept of time, we were actually early and walked through the doors at 6:55. We were eager and ready, hoping to score some bonus points for enthusiasm with the nursing staff.

As we soon learned, the day became more like a marathon and less like a sprint. For such a memorable day in one's life, it sure required a lot of patience. Everything seemed to move in slow motion. Minutes seemed like hours. Hours seemed like days. Not much was happening. Nursing staff came into our room and took some vitals every few hours. That was about the extent of our excitement for a good portion of the day.

Kenzie was a real champ. If she was nervous at all, she didn't show it. She was calm and tranquil like the surface of a pond on a windless day. Her strength throughout was quite astonishing. As for me, I was a little on edge. I bit my nails a lot and picked at them. It's a regretful habit I inherited from my mom. I've never been able to break it. I rapidly bounced my foot up and down on the floor as we spoke in hushed tones and sent occasional text messages to family members who wanted a status update.

The nurses suggested Kenzie get up and walk around, claiming it could help speed up the process. We slowly shuffled up and down the hallways together. Kenzie held her portable IV stand with one hand and clasped her gown shut with the other. She stepped gingerly, as though the floor was wet and her feet were made of ice cubes. Baby steps we walked, up one hallway and down another. Passing by other rooms, we saw other husbands biting their nails and bouncing their feet rapidly. *Clearly, first-timers just like me.* Some moms were sleeping. Others were watching TV. Some were texting updates to family members. Same story, different people.

Of course, some of them had done this before. Little Noahs and Emmas, ages two, three, or five were in some of the other rooms, sitting on Dad's lap or playing a game on electronic devices. It was a comforting sight, these small kids. They reminded me that children are born all the time. It's the most natural thing in the world and humans have been doing it for eons. Doctors must know what they're doing or else the world's population wouldn't continue to grow. I kept trying to remind myself that we were in good hands.

Throughout the afternoon, Kenzie was in and out of sleep. To say she was relaxed was an understatement. I thumbed through a sports magazine. It was a special edition focused on the upcoming World Cup. I imagined watching countless soccer games on TV later that summer while a newborn Sky slept on my chest. It would be the perfect summer, truly my idea of Heaven. I'd already tweaked my work schedule, giving myself nearly a month of paternity leave. Of course, this meant conducting an insane number of psychic readings in prior weeks to compensate for having so much time off work. Kenzie worried that I'd burn myself out and get sick leading up to Sky's birth. In years past, getting sick was the price I often paid for doing too many sessions and not resting my intuition enough. Thankfully, that didn't happen leading up to delivery day.

By 4:00 Kenzie was nearly five centimeters dilated. As the evening progressed, family started to arrive in the lobby. My mom arrived first, followed by my brother, Dave, and his wife, Megan. Then came my sister, Elizabeth, and her then-husband, Nate. I felt like a middle-man that evening, a liaison between the birthing situation and our family in the lobby.

"Six centimeters," I'd text the group. "Now seven!" All the excitement had caused me to work up an appetite, so Nate met me in the lobby and handed me a burrito. I figured I'd have plenty of time to eat since things were still progressing so slowly. I felt guilty snacking on the burrito in the lobby because poor Kenzie hadn't been permitted to eat anything all day long. With a mouthful of beans and salsa, I received a text message from Kenzie which simply read, "Get in here. I'm pushing."

I tossed my burrito back to Nate like it was a game of *hot potato*. I dashed down the hallway towards the delivery room. Once inside, the nurse insisted I help with the pushing process. "Grab her left knee and hold it back like this, out and away from her hips. I'll get the right knee," said the nurse. No prior conversations had taken place regarding the holding of the knees. However, it didn't seem like the place or time to argue, so I did as I was told. There was a part of me that wondered if the mechanics of the whole process worked like a rubber band. I wondered what would happen if the nurse and I let go of Kenzie's retracted knees at the same time. *Would the baby come flying out like a rock released from a slingshot?*

Admittedly, it was a silly notion. But I was willing to let my mind wander because it distracted me from feeling like I was going to pass out. The blood, fluids, and raw reality of the situation were leaving me extremely woozy. The nurse must have seen the color drain from my face because I remember her asking if I was okay. Just hearing the question left me feeling embarrassed. I certainly didn't want to take any attention away from the health of Kenzie and the baby. I figured that if I passed out, they could just leave me on the floor indefinitely and tend to me later.

In the midst of all the pushing, our doctor finally arrived. Dr. Kline burst into the room with the confidence of a motivational speaker taking the stage. A few feet beyond the doorway, she squatted down and held out her hands like a quarterback waiting for the football. "Okay, Kenzie, HIKE!" Everyone in the room erupted into laughter, including Kenzie.

Dr. Kline gave me a nod and smile. "Okay, Chief, are you sticking with your prior prediction? Seven pounds, four ounces?" Months earlier, she'd forced me into making a prediction on how much Sky would weigh at birth. Putting my psychic senses to the test was one of Dr. Kline's guilty pleasures. For her, it was a win-win. If I was right, she'd brag to the hospital staff that the psychic was right all along, like I was a winning horse she'd bet on. On the other hand, if I was wrong, she'd take pleasure in playfully busting my chops about it.

I assured Dr. Kline that I was sticking with my previous prediction of seven pounds, four ounces. Everyone in the room exchanged a few more jokes and pleasantries before a quiet hush took over and the tone became more serious. Kenzie continued to push. The nurses cheered her on. I remained alert but lightheaded. Dr. Kline kept giving instructions. Her voice calm but assertive. "You're doing good Kenzie, give me another push. Goooood."

The birthing process is a messy one. It's uncomfortable yet wonderful, painful yet joyous, scary yet beautiful. It's the ultimate thrill ride. I guess that's fitting, considering life itself is much the same. Unlike a movie, there was no soundtrack playing in the background. Without music, there were no clues or hints regarding the outcome of the birth. *Was everything going to be okay?* I just heard silence between labored breaths from Kenzie and instructions from the doctor. It was tense.

Suddenly, I heard a gush of fluids that surprised me and scared me at the same time. I was just about to ask what happened, when suddenly . . . I saw her. Cradled in the hands of Dr. Kline was a tiny human, her skin wrinkled and pink. Sky was wide-eyed and surprisingly alert. She glanced at me for just a moment and we made eye contact. I wondered if I looked hard enough, deep enough into her soulful eyes, I would see all the way back into Heaven itself.

While choking back tears of joy, I had the wherewithal to grab my camera and snap a quick photo of the very first moment Sky ever saw my face. Switching my camera over to video mode, I began recording. I struggled to hold the camera still between my trembling hands as the doctor gently handed Sky to Kenzie. She cradled our newborn daughter on her chest and the world stood still.

Never in all my lifetimes will I forget the look on Kenzie's face as she embraced Sky for the first time. It was the look of someone who was experiencing the single most joyous moment of her entire life. It was embodiment of Heaven on Earth, a flashpoint that signified all that is pure and miraculous about our existence – the ageless, timeless wonder of bringing forth new life into the world.

I reached out and touched my daughter, gently gliding the back side of my index finger down the length of her forearm. Her skin felt like silk.

"She's so beautiful, isn't she?" Kenzie said as she sniffled and wiped away a tear.

"She really is. She looks like her mom," I whispered.

Sky's tiny toes and delicate little fingers reminded me how fragile and vulnerable our physical bodies are. Yet, looking into her eyes reminded me that our souls are ancient and wise. It's the most ironic of all pairings, how something so precious and irreplaceable can be stored inside something so fragile – a heart, brain, spirit, and essence, all housed inside a frail body that hardly serves as a protective barrier. It's the equivalent of wrapping the *Mona Lisa* in a thin layer of paper towels and shipping the painting across the country. The vulnerability is enough to make one shudder.

The nursing staff lifted Sky from Kenzie's chest and took her to a little area on the other side of the room. They cleaned Sky and weighed her. Next, they wrapped her in a white blanket and placed a little stocking hat on her head. In a light-hearted tone, Dr. Kline informed me that I was wrong about the weight. I had predicted seven pounds, four ounces, but Sky actually weighed seven pounds and *five* ounces. I was wrong by a single ounce. I shrugged my shoulders and smiled. "I hope you didn't have any money riding on me, Doc."

Moments later, I found myself holding Sky for the first time. It was unlike anything I'd ever experienced. I had no reference point for something so surreal, so pure and wonderful. I thought back to the meditations Kenzie and I did in the months leading up to conceiving Sky. We'd imagined this very day and bargained, prayed, pleaded with the Universe to grant us this wish.

The meditations were delightful, but they paled in comparison to the real thing. For there in my arms was a tiny little human who I'd known for all of ten minutes. And in that short time, I'd grown to love her more than any person I'd ever loved before. It was a different kind of love. It was a love without equal, a love without conditions, restrictions, measure, or expectations.

The seven pounds and change felt so light in my arms as I held Sky. I studied her every feature. I noticed the nearly microscopic bumps on the surface of her nose, the fuzz on her skin that reminded me of a peach, the wrinkles on the bottom of her feet, the lines of the palm of her hand, her itsy-bitsy fingernails. I was mesmerized and couldn't take my eyes away from her.

As much as I wanted to stare at Sky for all of eternity, I knew our family was still out in the lobby waiting for some good news. I handed Sky back to Kenzie very slowly, as though I was trying not to trip the motion sensors inside a bank vault. The staff assured me holding and handling a baby becomes more natural with practice. I assumed they were right, but until I felt more comfortable with transfers, I was planning to move as slowly as a three-toed sloth.

I walked back into the lobby flashing the smile of a proud new dad. My mom hugged me first, letting go only to take off her glasses and blot the joyous tears in her eyes. By this time, it was nearing half past 8:00. Light reflected through the windows, bathing the lobby in a shade of yellowish-orange. I glanced out the window and was met by a golden sunset that made the sky look like a giant tangerine. It was the kind of sunset Grandma Myers would have chased. As I snapped a quick photo of the sky, my mom asked, "So have you guys chosen a middle name yet or is Kenzie still thinking about it?"

I couldn't help but grin. I took one final look at the sunset before turning around and informing family members that Kenzie had chosen the name Aurelia as the middle name. "It means gold or golden," I explained.

"Golden Sky!" said my sister Elizabeth, as she pointed curiously to the light coming in from the windows.

"Yeah, I think it's very fitting," I agreed.

My mom asked me to repeat it. "Uhrayleus?" she asked, hoping she hadn't butchered the name too much.

"Australia?" asked my brother, completely kidding, and doing his best to be a smart-ass.

I pronounced it once more for everyone, enunciating each syllable. Neither Sky nor Aurelia were common names. I doubt my family was surprised by our choices, considering both Kenzie and I are known to color outside the lines. My mom's side of the family is more reserved with members sporting names like Ed, Joan, Barb, Pat, and Karen. I expected them to raise an eyebrow when catching word of Sky's name, even if they were too polite to comment on it. "*Wait until they find out Sky was coincidentally Kenzie's name in our Native American past lifetime,*" I thought to myself.

Two by two, my family took turns stepping out from the orange glow of the lobby and into the delivery room to meet Sky. "She looks like an old soul," said my sister, Elizabeth. My brother, Dave, dialed down his obnoxious meter and melted like butter as he held his niece. He's a wonderful dad and I knew he'd be a fantastic uncle as well. When it was my mom's turn to hold her granddaughter, it was enough to take her breath away. She gently stroked Sky's head, and agreed that she looked a lot like Kenzie.

"What time was she actually born?" my mom wanted to know.

"8:08," I proudly said, as if it was the best possible time to be born. They are, in fact, very symmetrical numbers. If you flip the numbers and stack them vertically, it looks like a perfect circle sandwiched between two infinity symbols. I've noticed that before while resting in bed and seeing 8:08 on the clock from my horizontal vantage point.

Was 8:08 on May 19th truly a good time to be born? I assumed it was. Perhaps an astrologer could dive deeper into the subject. Personally, I don't know much about astrology since it's not an aspect I incorporate into my psychic sessions. However, I *was* aware that Sky was born under the sign of Taurus, which is apparently an earth sign. I wondered if that would someday translate to her collecting rocks like Kenzie had in her youth; like Grandma Myers had done throughout her life.

As night fell, my family took their cue to leave. It was obvious that Kenzie needed her rest. We gathered our belongings and went to another room on the upper floor where we stayed for the next two nights. Once settled into the new room, we continued to look at Sky, staring at her like she was a lottery ticket containing the winning numbers. And that's how lucky we felt. Sky had chosen *us* . . . the nurse and the psychic. Out of all the other potential parents on Earth, we were the ones she picked. That thought alone was enough to give me goosebumps.

As we settled into our new room, I found my mind wandering. I thought back to Sky's birth weight of seven pounds, five ounces. She was one ounce heavier than I'd initially predicted. I wondered what Sky would do with that extra ounce. *What might reside within it?* Perhaps that one ounce contained enough potential for Sky to change the world, to spruce up her own little corner of this planet, leaving it in better shape than it was when she arrived here. I wondered if that one extra ounce contained remnants of Heaven or memories of lives before this one. I wondered if my daughter and I had ever crossed paths before.

I hoped that extra ounce was heavy enough to keep her grounded when life gets more complex. Yet, I hoped she'd remain light enough to fly, to soar, to spread her wings and venture far enough from home to have some adventures. She could do a lot with that one extra ounce. Contained inside there was raw, limitless, potential. There was wisdom from her eternal soul, and a glowing ember that contained a spark of the Divine. I knew that spark would make this child glow. Nobody would extinguish her light, not now, not ever. This bond between Kenzie, Sky, and me was something that transcended space, time, reason, and circumstance. As I looked into her ancient eyes, I saw an ocean of wonder, a treasure trove of intelligent thoughts. I saw the reflection of a proud new dad looking at his beautiful new daughter.

We watched her sleep. We watched her scrunch her face when she was upset and blink her eyes when she was alert and curious. We watched her move her arms about like she was trying to figure out what they were actually used for. After we'd been in the room for a while, we heard a faint knock at the door, and without taking our eyes away from Sky, we both said in unison, "Come in." There had been so many hospital staff in and out, it was becoming common place for visitors to walk in. From my peripheral, I noticed a lady approaching our bed. She was tall and wore scrubs. Before we had a chance to look up, she spoke to us.

"I've been waiting a very long time to meet this child. Is this Miss Sky?"

Andy with Sky in the delivery room

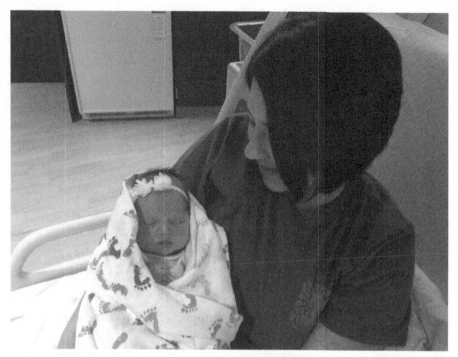

Kenzie with Sky at the hospital

Chapter 51

The woman in scrubs looked vaguely familiar but I couldn't quite place her. She bent over and reached down to adjust Sky's swaddle blanket. "Oh, she's just *precious*, isn't she?"

Kenzie and I exchanged looks. I felt like I somehow knew this woman but wasn't sure how. I assumed Kenzie was thinking the same thing. The woman stood to her feet and extended her arm for a handshake. "Hi, Andy. I'm Nora. I've been to some of your events and I loved your book. I feel like I already know your whole family."

Shaking her hand, I attempted to introduce her to Kenzie, but she beat me to it. "Hey, Kenzie," she said, as if they were longtime friends merely catching up. "Let me know if you need anything, okay. I'm going to be your overnight nurse, so rest assured, you're in good hands."

I smiled and let out a sigh of relief. *What were the odds?* Out of all the nurses in all the hospitals, we were assigned a nurse who already knew us. It quickly became apparent that Nora was not the only hospital employee who was familiar with our story. Passing by the front desk in the lobby, two receptionists waved and said hello to me. They said they followed me on social media. It was a good feeling to know we were surrounded by kind and supportive people. On the way to the vending machines, I even bumped into a past client who was at the hospital anticipating the birth of her second grandchild. The place was teeming with familiar faces.

The announcement of Sky's birth on my social media pages created quite a frenzy and we were blown away by the thousands of congratulations that poured forth from clients, past and present. Kenzie wanted me to double-check and make sure the online announcement didn't include any information as to our hospital location or room number. The religious extremists and skeptics hadn't bothered us in a while, but we weren't about to take any risks in terms of having strangers show up at our door. I assured Kenzie that my social media post didn't include any details relevant to our location. Besides, I figured we were safe anyway since the hallway doors were locked and guarded with cameras.

My main concern was that Kenzie kept claiming she wasn't tired. Our hospital stay was nearing its end, and soon we'd be headed home. I kept insisting she get some rest while we had multiple people helping out with Sky. It would be much harder to get rest once back at home, because we wouldn't have so much additional assistance. She kept assuring me she wasn't all that tired. I knew it was just the adrenaline speaking and she'd eventually crash. Sky was in and out of our room as the staff occasionally took her to run routine tests.

Nora frequently stopped by, giving Kenzie some breast-feeding pointers, answering our questions, and making sure we had everything we needed. She stayed in our room longer than protocol required. She told us stories of how her departed relatives visit her in dreams, and how she would find pennies in the most unusual places, taking it as a sign from her deceased grandma. We didn't mind one bit. We loved her company and appreciated her stories. We even shared some stories of our own, reaching into the invisible bins labeled *ghost stories*, *miracles*, or *synchronicity*.

On the morning we were scheduled to leave, one of the nurses brought Sky back to our room after they'd run some standard tests. We held out our arms and welcomed her back like she was a lost puppy who'd been missing for weeks. We missed her every time she was out of sight. Sky was a bit fussy from all the commotion, but we decided to give her a diaper change. It was a risky idea considering her cry was comparable to the howl of a banshee and we didn't want to provoke her to the point of a full-blown meltdown.

During the diaper change, we noticed some discoloration on her bottom, a bluish-brown hue that resembled a bruise. Upon further inspection, we were horrified to realize the discoloration extended half way up her back in splotchy patches. "What the hell is this?" I exclaimed. "Where the hell did she get all these bruises from?"

Kenzie's eyes grew wide, and the look of terror on her face matched what I was feeling inside. We pushed the red button on the side of Kenzie's bed as worst-case scenarios ran through our minds. Within seconds, a nurse answered the call button and was talking through the speakers. "Yes, do you guys need something in there?"

In a fiery tone, Kenzie replied, "Yeah, can you please get someone in here immediately? We have some questions."

Chapter 52

The hospital staff informed us that Mongolian spots are completely harmless. It's a discoloration of the skin that often fades with time. It's sometimes seen in newborn babies who have Native American genes, but can also be seen on babies of Asian heritage, hence the name Mongolian spots. Apparently, Kenzie's Native American genetics had infiltrated Sky's skin tone.

"Mongolian spots? That's so weird! Have you ever heard of such a thing?" I asked Kenzie. I tend to mistakenly assume she's aware of every medical condition on Earth simply because she's a nurse. I suppose it's an unfair assumption, similar to strangers believing I can read their minds just because I'm a psychic.

She shook her head. "Nope. Never." Sky was now sound asleep, but all five of her digits were wrapped around Kenzie's index finger. I couldn't believe how tiny her little fingers were.

"You had Mongolian spots when you were born," interjected Kenzie's mom, Amber. She'd stopped by for a visit to meet her granddaughter.

"I did?" Kenzie gasped. Her tone was one of utter shock, as if her mom had just divulged that Kenzie was raised by a clan of wild hyenas. "Why didn't you ever tell me that?"

"I don't know," Amber responded. "I distinctly remember it though, because I thought the same thing as you guys. I thought they were bruises, like someone had dropped you or something."

Kenzie suggested we better list Sky as part Native American on her birth certificate. That way, in the years to come, doctors wouldn't be so alarmed when they noticed discoloration on Sky's bottom and back. In many cases, the spots fade with time, and even if they didn't, we hoped Sky wouldn't be too self-conscious about it as she got older.

However, her toes might be another matter. She may have gotten her mother's beautiful, tan skin, but she got her daddy's toes. And that means she's bound to be a good swimmer. I was born with webbed toes. Not all of them. Just the two little piggies closest to my big toe. There's skin between the toes that joins them together just like a scuba diver's flippers. It's never really bothered me, and besides, people don't notice it unless I pull my sock off and spread my toes apart. It was a party trick I used a time or two in college.

In recent years, retailers invented toe socks. They're like cotton hand gloves, but for feet. Unless I alter the socks with a pair of scissors, it's biologically impossible for me to wear them. I've accepted this truth, but I've never much wanted to own a pair of toe socks anyways. As for swimming, I do believe my webbed toes make me a faster swimmer, perhaps just by a fraction of a second.

I inherited this genetic knock-knock joke from my dad, Steve. His toes were also webbed. I was secretly hoping to pass this along to Sky. Perhaps she could use her toes to gross out her friends at a sleepover or gain some laughs at a college party someday. But now that she actually *has* webbed toes, I feel slightly guilty, like I manifested it into reality. I can't help but wonder if she'll embrace it or feel embarrassed. While I have webbed toes on both feet, Sky only has it on her left foot.

It makes me wonder if it will make her an unbalanced swimmer – like her left leg will be highly effective and her right foot will be lame. I picture her bumping into the walls of the pool at swim meets, or worse yet, just swimming in circles like some confused tadpole. Like most things in life, I suppose it won't be as bad as I imagine. Unless, that is, she wants to wear those toe socks when she's older.

Chapter 53

We continued to study Sky's body for other anomalies. The doctors assured us she was a very healthy child. A couple days after she was born, we were permitted to leave the hospital. On the way out, nurses, doctors, the receptionist, and even a janitor waved goodbye to us and wished us well. "See you later!" they hollered. "Godspeed!" So many familiar faces, so many friendly smiles. It made us feel like we were Disney characters embarking on a journey far from home and the entire village had gathered to send us off.

Sky was the main attraction in this little parade, and her combination car seat/stroller served as her float. Had she been able to, I'm sure she would have sat up and given a refined hand wave, like Miss Nebraska perched atop a convertible while wearing a glittering sash. The elevator dinged and the doors opened. We waved goodbye as we hit the button with the star on it and made our way down to the lobby.

It's hospital protocol to ensure the parents have a properly installed car seat before leaving, so one of the workers accompanied us to the car and watched us get Sky inside. Little did they know how much research and time Kenzie had already spent ensuring our car seat was properly installed. She was nothing short of a car seat whisperer.

I lifted our seven-pound, five-ounce bundle of joy into the Toyota Camry and clicked the car seat into its base. Technically, our bundle of joy had dropped a couple ounces since birth and weighed a bit less by this time. The weight loss was completely normal and expected, they assured us. I walked around the car and sat down in the driver's seat. Our car was clean and washed, but I couldn't help but imagine a future where Sky was three or four and the car was no longer so tidy. I imagined our car smelling like stale French fries, the back seat littered with toys, the floor a graveyard of Cheerios, stickers, and sippy cups. I welcomed such messes, assuming they'd be accompanied by amazing memories.

I was ready. Ready for this adventure to begin in earnest. Ready for the messes, the sleepless nights, the spit-ups, the diaper changes, and the dance classes. I'd been told that parenting isn't so much about planning as it is improvising and adapting to the unexpected. I assumed it would be the hardest thing we'd ever do. Perhaps it would be the equivalent of a one-armed juggling act in a three-ring circus. I hoped Kenzie and I wouldn't end up being the clowns in our own little circus, but I figured mistakes were to be expected. Besides, we'd have each other and we made a good team.

Meanwhile, the drive home from the hospital was an anxious one. I'd never driven so slowly or cautiously in my entire life. Then again, I'd never before transported cargo so precious. Sky looked so tiny and fragile in her car seat. Kenzie sat in the back seat with Sky, glaring at nearby cars who dared to come within fifty feet of our vehicle. She groaned and mumbled under her breath, reprimanding the behavior of other drivers. In their defense, I don't think the other drivers were actually doing anything wrong.

"Look at that this guy over here," Kenzie said. "Look at him driving like a bat out of hell . . . what, with his hands at ten and two and everything. *What a maniac!* And look at *that* lady – blowing through a yellow light!"

"Um, I think it was green, dear."

"Yeah, but it was *about* to turn yellow in just a few seconds. What a speed demon!"

"Honey, the lady looked eighty years old," I assured her. "And she was only going twenty-five miles per hour."

With a huff, Kenzie turned her attention back to Sky. From the sounds of it, I couldn't tell if the drive had put her to sleep or not, but she was quiet and content. As for Kenzie's anxiety, I could hardly blame her. I found myself wishing there was a magical, baby-transporting bubble, an impenetrable force field that ensured safety while in transit. I held my breath as we crossed the intersection where months earlier, the silver truck had almost changed our fate.

We finally arrived home safely. We brought Sky inside to meet her two older brothers. Zico trotted up to us with the confidence of a show dog who'd just won first place. His tail was wagging and he was eager to inspect the new guest. He sniffed Sky, inhaling her unfamiliar scent. From the very moment he met Sky, Zico seemed protective over her. Now and forever more, he was determined to be her bodyguard. As for Darwin, our male tabby cat, I'm not sure if he even realized we'd been gone in the first place. It was business as usual for him. Thanks to automatic feeders, his food and water status had remained unchanged. He didn't care who came or went.

Kenzie, Zico, and I just stared at Sky for what felt like hours, wondering, "Okay, *now* what do we do?" It was like our whole world had changed, and yet everything remained the same. Our house was still and silent. Sky would occasionally wake up from napping. She would blink, yawn, and stare back at us. It seemed like she was asking herself the same question. "Okay, so *now* what?" It felt like we'd spent years building a boat and studying how to sail, and now that we were out at sea in calm waters, we were left wondering, "Can it really be this easy?"

As it turns out, it wasn't. Sky was a good sleeper for about the first week and then things quickly became more challenging. She had lured us into a false sense of security and set a snare that we stepped directly into. We maintained a disciplined daily routine with Sky. Yet, she seemed to take after me in that she'd rather question the established system than do as expected.

Family came in town from lands near and far to visit our little web-toed banshee. It was nice to see everyone, but as any new parents will attest, it can also be overwhelming. With low energy and little sleep, it's hard to muster up enthusiasm to entertain. It can be even harder for new mothers experiencing baby blues due to the hormonal corkscrew that ensues after birth. That being said, we couldn't in good conscience deny anyone the chance to meet Sky. So, we put on our smiles, opened the door and said, "Come on in. You came at a good time."

Truth be told, there *was* no good time. Sky was starting to show signs of being introverted. That's a nice way of saying she *hated* everyone but her mom and me. Kenzie was the food source, so she was always in Sky's good graces. As for me, I resorted to humor, hoping my silly faces and bizarre noises would continue to keep me on Sky's good side. At the very least, my shenanigans would keep her confused enough to prevent a meltdown. As for everyone else, they were essentially playing with fire each time they interacted with Sky.

"Can we hold her?" guests would ask with outstretched arms, grinning the smiles of village idiots. They knew not what they asked for. Kenzie and I would shudder as we cautiously handed Sky over to family members and friends. Within seconds, the air raid siren would sound. Baby was passed back to Mom, and the whole process was repeated indefinitely until we politely asked everyone to leave.

As time went by, Sky began cluster feeding. It was a term I'd never heard before. Apparently, in breast feeding language, it means she was using Kenzie as her own personal vending machine. Sky would grab a snack here, a snack there, constantly requiring small meals. This obviously makes it difficult for a new mother to get any sort of rest.

I continuously offered help when Sky would wake in the middle of the night. Kenzie's response was always the same. She was grateful for the offer, but since I was not lactating, I was useless. On one particularly stressful night, Kenzie came back in our bedroom around midnight. She had tended to Sky for what seemed like the tenth time in less than an hour. On the verge of tears, she collapsed in a heap on our bed and said aloud, "Okay Grandpa Steve, if you really are one of Sky's guardian angels, can you *please* help her stay asleep until 2:00 so I can get a quick nap."

We had resorted to begging spirits for help just so she could get two whole hours of sleep. As the clock rolled over to 12:01, Kenzie sighed and pulled the comforter up so high it nearly covered her head. I pulled it down just enough to kiss her on the cheek. She'd already fallen asleep. The static hum of the baby monitor filled our room with white noise. I rolled over onto my left side and silently dropped the same request into my dad's inbox, asking him to keep Sky asleep so Kenzie could get some rest.

Guardian angels and loved ones in Heaven aren't permitted to help with every little challenge in our lives. Depending on the circumstances, some requests are granted and others are not. They tend to help at their discretion, often allowing us to solve our own problems. I suppose they have faith we're usually stronger than we think we are. That being said, I prayed my dad would keep Sky asleep until 2:00 like we'd requested. They say it takes a village to raise a child. I prayed our village included spirits who were willing to help.

Chapter 54

A whimper came through the baby monitor and escalated into a full-blown cry. Kenzie startled awake and I could tell she was a tad disoriented, likely due from the exhaustion. I swore that her ears had already adjusted to motherhood. Earthquakes, thunder, or barking dogs couldn't wake Kenzie from her slumber, but the slightest squeak on the baby monitor would cause her to spring out of bed like a live rattlesnake was in our sheets. As the sound of cries came through the monitor, I cringed, expecting to roll over and see the clock read 12:20 or maybe 12:45 if we were lucky. *How long had we actually been asleep?*

When I noticed the clock read 2:00, I nearly started laughing. Grandpa Steve had answered our request . . . right down to the *minute*. It was a validating moment, truly faith-affirming. For us, it proved that my dad was, in fact, one of Sky's guardian angels. It may feel like a one-way conversation when we speak to our departed loved ones. Yet, there are times when they find creative ways to speak back to us. Sometimes, this comes in the form of answered prayers.

Kenzie wasn't exactly skipping into Sky's bedroom with the enthusiasm of a jazzercise instructor, but she *was* finally alert. The two solid hours of sleep did her wonders, and I could tell she felt much better. The cluster feedings continued. Our daily routine was repeated again. And again. And again. The days all blurred together. They were a mix of diaper changes, spit ups, doing laundry, and catching a few minutes of sleep whenever we could. It was exhausting, yet truly wonderful.

Around this same time, when Sky was two weeks old, she smiled for the first time. I was pretending to eat her toes and I guess she found it comical. Initially, I wondered if she was merely gassy, but her smiling became a regular occurrence, and she'd only smile when she was happy or when she found us entertaining. I knew it was a bit unusual for a two-week-old to be smiling. After doing some research, I learned it's more common to occur when a baby is six to eight weeks old. Perhaps she was slightly ahead of schedule because Kenzie and I were so silly and our house was filled with laughter.

I was blown away at how alert Sky was. Children at that age are essentially unaware of their surroundings. They don't generally pay attention to what's going on. And unless they're gassy, hungry, or tired, they aren't very expressive.

Sky was different. She was curious. She paid attention. She tracked our movements and studied her environment. Sky seemed older than she actually was. There was wisdom in her eyes. They contained intelligent thoughts which she couldn't yet articulate. It seemed like she was bored of being a little baby. Perhaps she was growing impatient. Her little body wasn't yet able to crawl or walk, let alone kick a ball, solve a puzzle, or play with blocks. I knew she'd enjoy such things, but her little body wasn't ready yet.

At five weeks old, Sky began cooing and babbling on a regular basis. Again, this was ahead of schedule according to research I did. A couple weeks later, she said her first word. Kenzie prompted her by saying, "Hi, Sky. Can you say hi? You can do it. *Hi.*"

With a voice so high pitched it hardly sounded human, she replied, "Hi." She even enunciated the "y" sound at the end of the word. "Hiyyy." She was able to repeat this trick on a daily basis, but would only do it after we prompted her first. Family members didn't initially believe us, and I couldn't blame them. It sounded absurd, but it was true. We texted them video evidence of Sky's new trick.

I certainly didn't claim to be an expert on babies in terms of their developmental milestones. I figured Sky might be ahead of the curve, but I also know that most parents view their children as geniuses. I guess we love our babies so much we tend to be biased. I did plenty of research, and the articles stated that most children will speak their first word sometime between the ages of ten and fourteen months. Sky was only seven weeks old.

For reasons scientists can't quite explain, some children simply develop language skills much earlier. There was a story which made international news in 2015. A mother in Northern Ireland captured video of her son saying, "Hello," at just seven weeks old. More recently, parents Caroline and Nick of Cheshire, England caught video of their son, Charlie, uttering the same word at the tender age of *eight* weeks old. The story was published on countless news outlets in August of 2020.

If a child is an old soul, he or she may reach developmental milestones earlier than expected. An 'old soul' refers to a person who has lived a great deal of previous lifetimes. With each incarnation, a soul acquires traits such as wisdom, intelligence, depth of character, empathy, and a wide array of talents. Usually, we come into each new lifetime with a 'blank slate', learning everything from scratch all over again. However, if a child has lived enough lifetimes (or lived a very *recent* lifetime), some of the developmental skill sets are already present within the child's brain and body. In other words, it can be a matter of *remembering* a skill rather than *learning* a skill. This includes speech, walking, throwing a ball, playing the piano, and so on.

Thus, if a professional baseball pitcher died and came into another life rather quickly, I wouldn't be surprised if the child had a rocket for an arm, even at the age of two. If a child has lived many past lifetimes with an aptitude for math, it would be possible for the little one to demonstrate off-the-chart mathematical skills from a very young age.

As for children hitting their developmental milestones earlier than expected, we can certainly make a case for these instances being related to topics such as past lives and old souls. However, speaking early is not a prerequisite for intelligence. Take Albert Einstein for example. He was one of most brilliant minds in human history, but it's said he didn't speak his first word until the age of four. Therefore, we can't assume every child who talks earlier will be a genius, nor can we conclude that a child with a speech delay will be low functioning. Every person develops uniquely.

As for Sky, she was certainly intent on making her voice heard. Kenzie and I had no plans to contact the local news stations regarding her first word. Yet, she was on par with the kiddos from England and Northern Ireland in terms of youngest documented child to utter a first word. *Could she have been a famous speaker in a past lifetime? A long-winded politician, perhaps?* George Washington lost all his teeth by the age of thirty, and Sky didn't have any yet. I bent down to see if there was a resemblance. For some reason, I couldn't quite picture it.

Sky at seven weeks old

Sky at seven weeks old

Chapter 55

Kenzie's biological dad was the link to her Native American side of the family tree. She hadn't known his whereabouts for many years. Despite this, Kenzie got in touch with her dad's grandmother. She was Kenzie's great-grandmother, and she went by Flossie. She was full-blooded Yankton Sioux and resided on the reservation in South Dakota. Kenzie had never met her before. Flossie insisted on making up for lost time and asked us to pay her a visit. Kenzie was nervous but excited. Both of us were delighted for Sky to meet her great, great, grandmother.

Sky was no stranger to road trips. She was only five months old at the time, but had already traveled with us to five different states. A few of the trips were for my work events, and a couple were for leisure. After a five-hour drive that included many stops, we arrived at the Yankton Sioux reservation. It was October, and the drive allowed us to see some colorful foliage on the way.

Flossie welcomed us into her quaint home. It was decorated with authentic Native American artwork, and her home contained so many family photos I thought the walls would buckle under the weight of the frames. Kenzie and I have met some celebrities over the years, but meeting Flossie for the first time made us feel star struck in a way we'd never experienced before.

She was revered among the Yankton Sioux community and was the matriarch of a *very* large family. She was ninety-three years old when we met her, but mentally she was very nimble. She rattled off countless names of uncles, grandparents, cousins, and second cousins of Kenzie's. The names were vaguely familiar to Kenzie through second hand stories. If that weren't enough, she knew each family member's birthday, where they lived, and a story or two of what they'd been up to in recent years. Her memory and recall were quite impressive. She was sharper than the arrowheads her own ancestors had chiseled in generations past.

Winyan Numpa was her given name. It means "Two Women" in the Dakota language. I'm not sure how she got the name Flossie, but I was willing to call her whatever she wanted. She'd lived all over the country, and had so many amazing stories from her travels. She'd crammed three lifetimes' worth of experiences into this one life. She was an accomplished star quilter. In fact, she was world-famous. Some of her Native American quilts are on display at the Smithsonian Museum in Washington D.C. and also at the Vatican.

We placed Sky on Flossie's lap, giving her the chance to meet her great, great grandmother. It was a rare photo opportunity that not many people in this world get to experience. Despite Sky's 'stranger danger' aversion to anyone besides her mom and me, she seemed quite content to sit on Flossie's lap. She never cried. In fact, she was smiling and laughing much of the afternoon.

Flossie excused herself from the couch and walked to the back bedroom without the assistance of a walker or cane. She returned with a pink quilt she'd made just for Sky. We graciously accepted the beautifully crafted blanket. I touched it with reverence and awe, like I was holding a Congressional Medal of Honor or the Dead Sea Scrolls. The quilt was new, but in our minds, it had already been grandfathered in as a family heirloom. It would remain in our family for the rest of time . . . an item that would be passed down to Sky's children and grandchildren and great grandchildren.

We spent the afternoon listening to Flossie speak of Sun Dancers, relatives of Kenzie's who were known to possess intuition. They were individuals prone to psychic visions and spiritual visitors. "It runs in the family, dear," Flossie assured Kenzie. We hung on her every word, and took notes as if there was a test afterward. She showed us pictures of family, past and present. She had countless bins, drawers, and shoeboxes full of documentation. She presented family trees, lineage charts, old birthday cards, and obituary pages. She was a packrat when it came to family memorabilia. We were immensely grateful for the history lessons. Kenzie asked if she could snap some photos of the documentation, and Flossie granted permission.

We asked if Flossie ever heard of ancestors named Henry and Sarah Cloud.

"Oh, of course I have." Her casual tone made it seem as though she'd bumped into them at the post office earlier in the week. Our hearts fluttered with anticipation. We hoped she could divulge some information to us about Henry and Sarah. *Did her parents personally know them? Had she heard second hand stories about Henry and Sarah?* Kenzie and I also wondered if Flossie might know who Henry and Sarah's best friends were, as that would provide us with information about who *we* were in that past lifetime.

Our hearts sank a bit when she confessed she didn't know much about them. Nevertheless, she *did* have some documentation containing Henry and Sarah's names, and Kenzie snapped some photos of these documents on her phone. Flossie had heard their names come up many times while discussing the trunk of the family tree. She mentioned a place in Minnesota where Henry and Sarah might be buried. I wondered if our next road trip might be to Minnesota in order to visit the grave sites of our guardian angels.

To be in the presence of someone so wise and talented was nothing short of awe-inspiring. I took a picture of Flossie, Kenzie, and Sky together. It showed three women who spanned *five* generations within the family. As we exited her house, I couldn't help but wonder if that was the last time we'd ever have the pleasure of visiting with Flossie. At ninety-three years old, you just never know.

A year or two later, we caught word that she'd passed away. We asked what she passed from. They told us it was old age. When she died, the family found a quilt in the back bedroom that was in the process of being made. It's one she'd been working on just days earlier. Nobody knew for sure who it was intended for.

I stayed home and tended to Sky, giving Kenzie the chance to drive up and reconnect with her long-lost relatives at the funeral. She said it was more of a celebration of life than a sad occasion. It was an event for the ages. People drove and flew in from all over the country – hundreds of people, perhaps *thousands*. They mourned. They swapped stories of Flossie. They shed tears of sadness and tears of joy.

Reconnecting with her relatives left Kenzie feeling curious about her lineage and family ancestry. In line with that, we both ordered a couple of DNA home testing kits. The company uses saliva samples to trace lineage as far back as modern technology allows.

My test results showed that one percent of my genetic makeup can be traced to unknown parts of Asia. I found this especially interesting because the Sioux (and all Native Americans, for that matter) are descendants of nomadic Asians who crossed the Bering Land Bridge and settled into the midwestern plains around 12,000 years ago. This caused me to wonder if Grandma Myers was technically correct all along. Maybe I really *was* one percent Native American. It was a stretch, but it made me excited nonetheless. Kenzie humored me with a pitiful smile as she allowed me to retain the title of Honorary Chief.

As for Kenzie, the bulk of her genetics were similar to mine, containing good helpings of Scottish and English with a dash of Swedish. It's not surprising considering most of us are genetic mutts. Of course, nearly a quarter of her blood is Native American – passed down from her father, his parents, and ultimately back to Flossie.

Winyan Numpa would be remembered. She'd live on in our hearts and minds. Her blood still runs in the veins of Kenzie and Sky. They are the descendants of Sun Dancers, which means the spirit world is never too far away.

Flossie with Sky and Kenzie

Quilt that Flossie made for Sky

Chapter 56

We'd been co-sleeping with Sky for a few months. One afternoon, I was attempting to put her down for a nap in Kenzie's and my bed. Her eyes looked like two cups of dark roast coffee. They were dark brown, soulful, and kind. She hadn't inherited her mother's light brown eyes and she didn't get my hazel shade either. Sky was her own person, unique and different.

Her left eye displays something known as segmental heterochromia. It's a completely harmless condition where the iris of the eye contains a section that's a different shade. It's literally a twinkle in her left eye that's amber in color. It shimmers when light reflects off it. Most people don't notice her "lucky fleck", as I call it. In bed with her, it was obvious to me since we were nose to nose. As we stared into each other's eyes, I wondered what she was thinking. Perhaps she was doing the same thing.

Her eyes were heavy. She was calm, silent, and still. Sky looked inquisitive as she studied me, reaching over to touch my cheeks, eyebrows, and lips with her tiny index finger. She studied me like I was a pile of puzzle pieces. *Was she trying to figure out how I fit together?* She grinned a half smile and blinked slowly at me, as though she'd figured it out.

She was resting on her side. I gently rubbed her back, hoping it would make her sleepier. I began to trace letters on her back and doodle shapes with my index finger. I wondered if she could feel the difference between a square and a triangle. She shifted her head and looked at me from a slightly different angle. She was tranquil and calm, emanating a feeling of complete serenity I wasn't quite accustomed to. Her gaze shifted from left to right as she studied each of my eyes. Our heads were only inches apart and I could see her pupils focusing. *What was she thinking about?* The look on her face made it seem like Sky was remembering something she'd nearly forgotten, like she was reaching into the basement of her memory and searching for a recollection of where she'd come from. She was an ageless old soul who'd come into our world as a spirit wanting a human experience. *Was she finally realizing this truth?*

I listened to her breathe in and out. She suddenly seemed familiar to me in a way I'd never noticed before. I wasn't just looking into the eyes of my daughter. I was looking into the eyes of my friend. I studied her face – her full red lips, her long eyelashes, her brown hair, her cute little button nose. We stared at each other for what felt like a very long time. I peered deep into her eyes and it felt like we were communicating on a soul level, her eyes feeling like a portal which allowed me to see her past, present, and future.

As our hearts and minds intertwined, a great irony occurred to me. Sky's soul was ageless and eternal. Yet, against the infinite backdrop of time, her existence here on Earth as my daughter would feel brief . . . just a fleeting pit stop along her endless journey through a never-ending succession of lifetimes. I wondered if we'd crossed paths before. I wondered if she'd been a friend of mine in the past. Or maybe a relative. Perhaps she was *my* parent once upon a time . . . in a story I can't quite remember, an adventure lost in the diaries of our souls.

It occurred to me that the terms and definition we humans place on one another are merely labels we use to make us feel more in control. I suddenly realized that Sky didn't *belong* to me any more than I *belonged* to *my* dad. We *choose* to spend our time with certain people – walking side by side with them through brief moments in time, never quite sharing the same lane and all the while fooling ourselves into believing we're walking the same exact path as another person.

Sky doesn't belong to me. She belongs to the Universe, to a Higher Power, to the nebulous and indefinable energy that connects us all. We might share a last name, but in the grand scheme of the cosmos, I am merely leasing her. I am borrowing her from the Universe for a brief moment in history. I am the fortunate recipient of a gift so special, a soul *so* precious that no single individual can claim ownership.

Maybe I wasn't discovering these truths. Perhaps I was simply *remembering* them . . . remembering that we belong to one another, not as pieces of property, not as possessions, and not even as mothers and sons, fathers and daughters. We humans only belong to each other in a grander sense of the word; in a sense that we *choose* to be together, fluttering in and out of each other's lives, voluntarily crossing paths, promising nothing but a unique and painfully brief intersection – a juncture where we overlap at just the right place and time to have some shared experiences; just long enough to remember what it feels like to love and to *be* loved in return.

Up and down the Ferris wheel of infinity we go, swinging out of one life and into another. And each time we pass near the bottom, a familiar face or two will hop into our car for a couple trips around the circle, knowing that the journey will be a brief, unique, amazing ride that no two people will experience in quite the same way, despite riding in such close proximity to one another.

I drew circles on Sky's back as her eyes grew heavier. I wondered why she chose to ride this ride with me. I wondered what her destiny entailed. I imagined where she'd been, what she'd done, and how many scars she'd acquired in rides she'd taken without me. I pondered her future and how I could help her become the person she wanted to be. *What could I say to her, what could I teach her, what could I show her that would be of most value during our brief time here together?*

I imagined what her first memory might turn out to be. I thought of her future and all the life events she'd partake in as a spirit who was now having a human experience. *Would she someday fall in love? Would she feel the pain of a broken heart? Would she achieve her dreams? Would she encounter unforeseen obstacles along the way?* I winced at the thought of not being able to protect her from the inevitable pain we humans sometimes feel as we stumble through life. Despite the obvious risks, I hoped Sky would take the scenic route through life. I hoped she would take a chance on herself and be brave enough to wander into uncharted territory. Along the way, she might lose herself, find herself, reinvent herself, and discover her true calling.

I reached out and held her hand. Her silky-smooth palm felt like baby powder against my dry skin. She continued to gaze at me curiously, her eyes growing misty, as though a tear might roll out at any moment. *Was she sad? Was she happy? Was she feeling nostalgic?* The corner of her lip raised ever so slightly, giving the hint of a smile without offering up the real thing. I felt a bond with Sky that could not be rationalized or described with adjectives. The feeling was a bit too much, and I found a tear rolling down my nose from the corner of my eye. Sky slid her hand out from my palm and wiped the tear from my face like she'd done it before, like she still remembered how to be a caretaker although she was still confined inside the body of a five-month-old.

I leaned in and kissed her on the forehead before gently brushing her cheek with the outside of my index finger. She was clearly growing sleepier, and I took it as my cue to leave. Before sitting up, I smiled and winked at her, as if to say, "Thanks for sharing that moment with me."

I gently reached across the bed, attempting to grab my phone. It had been playing a random playlist of New Age songs from a music app. I didn't own any of the songs, so when hearing one I really liked, I'd always check to see what it was called in case I decided to purchase it.

The song that was playing was quite beautiful, so I turned on my screen in hopes of learning what it was called. My heart skipped a beat when I read it was titled *Sky (Friends)* by an artist named Corciolli. *What were the odds?* Although it was a small synchronicity, I viewed it as significant and meaningful. Moments like these are the Universe's way of proving there's some order among life's chaos. There's a deeper meaning underneath the reality we're living in.

I wanted a 'souvenir' from this special moment. So, with the song and its title still visible on my screen, I snapped a screen shot of the image and saved it to the photo album on my phone. "Kenzie is going to think this is so cool," I thought to myself. And right then, as I looked closer at the screen, it occurred to me that I'd snapped the screen shot at precisely five minutes and nineteen seconds into the song. 5:19 reminded me of Sky's May 19th birthday.

The whole experience was a double-decker synchronicity sandwich covered in coincidence and served up with serendipity sauce. I'd grown accustomed to such happenings, and yet, moments like those never seemed to get old. I'm constantly amazed by the way the Universe works. From the outside looking in, our world appears to be a pinball machine of random cause and effect . . . chance encounters that often seem chaotic and unrehearsed. But, when we're right in the thick of it all, there are special little moments when time slows down just long enough for us to see the gears of the Universe perfectly synchronizing. It allows us to realize we're each a cog in a perfectly designed machine that runs on miracles and is maintained by our belief in its very existence.

When life looks through its scope and has us between the crosshairs of fate and destiny, it allows us to find meaning in places that others find none. Moments like the one I shared with Sky remind me that sometimes the biggest love resides in the smallest places. When we quiet our minds and open our hearts to notice the little miracles right in front of our faces, the Universe has a way of giving us a smile and a nod. It's a little reminder that all is well. That life is good. That everything in Heaven and Earth is as it should be.

Chapter 57

*N*othing was where it should be. It felt like a giant had picked up our house and shook it around like a Christmas package, causing our physical belongings to end up in places they didn't belong. It was often hard to find what we were looking for. *Are the spare diapers in her closet or did we leave them in the car? Where was the binky last seen? Is her checkup on the 4ᵗʰ or the 14ᵗʰ?*

We were merely cast members in a tragic comedy. It was a play where the script had changed at the last minute and the main characters had resorted to improvising the entire plot. All our planning, researching, organizing, and sterilizing leading up to Sky's birth was the equivalent of putting beautiful new shutters on the windows prior to an EF-5 tornado rolling through the neighborhood. In theory, it was a cute idea, but it proved to be pointless when the storm hit.

Despite our best efforts, it was sometimes hard to stay caught up on household chores. There were times I'd eat a snack on a Tupperware lid because all the plates were dirty and I'd forgotten to start the dishwasher. Diapers piled up, stacking vertically inside a plastic sleeve within the Diaper Genie. It was my husbandly duty to empty it, and when extracting the long sleeve of diapers, it looked like a three-foot caterpillar (a poop caterpillar, if you will). I'd plug my nose, haul it down the stairs and outside to the garbage can, holding it away from my body like it was a savage boa constrictor from the Amazon rainforest. I'd slam dunk it into the garbage can before washing my hands and racing back upstairs to tell Sky bedtime stories. Our home was a blend of interesting smells, sounds, and emotions. We lived in a cement mixer of activity that tumbled around in circles.

At five months, Sky cut her first teeth. She was teething, and constantly craved something to gnaw on, something to put in her mouth. One day while we were lying on the floor together, Sky began trying to suck on my forehead and cut me with her sharp, little teeth. Drool ran down my temple and into my eyes, and I was laughing uncontrollably by the time I was able to pry her off of me. Kenzie was no help as she just stood nearby and took video.

By sixth months, Sky was regularly saying nearly a dozen words. Her pediatrician was astonished. She said in twenty years of practicing, she'd never known a child to talk so early, let alone possess such an extensive vocabulary at such a young age. I knew exactly which words Sky said at which points in time because I'd kept an ongoing journal which started before she was even born. I wrote down how her mom and I met, how we chose her name, the details of the day she was born, and which milestones she was hitting as she developed. The whole journaling thing was an old habit. It started when I was seven years old, and I suppose I picked it up from Grandma Myers.

She'd kept journals her whole life too. They were beautiful, handwritten diaries documenting details of her and Boompa's travels. Since Grandma has been gone, I've traded those journals back and forth with Aunt Terry. I'll bring them out occasionally to read about road trips Grandma and Boompa had – which rocks and fossils they'd found on which trips, how much they paid for a motel room in Billings, Montana in 1973, or how they'd gotten lost in Utah because their map was outdated.

I've always figured journaling was a harmless habit, and finally someone other than myself could benefit from it. I assume that later down the road when Sky's a bit older, she might enjoy reading some details of how she came about and what happened on the day she was born. They're details that tend to get lost in the flea market of our minds as the years go by.

It wasn't just Sky's vocabulary that was impressive. Her ability to identify objects in her surroundings was quite remarkable. We'd hold Sky and walk around the house, asking her if she could point to various objects such as the dishwasher, a fan, a banana, the window, a light switch, or the kitchen table. Without hesitation, she'd immediately locate and point to each object. She couldn't say some of these words yet, and we couldn't even fathom how she was able to identify them. Yet, her awareness of her surroundings was nothing short of astonishing. Again, we asked the pediatrician if this was normal for a six-month-old. For a child so young, she said it was completely and utterly unheard of.

Being new parents meant that Kenzie and I were exhausted most of the time. Despite our fatigue, life never slowed down. My business continued to grow and evolve. I continued writing and working towards publishing my next book. I was still delivering psychic readings and giving lectures in multiple cities. Some days, while watching Sky from home, Kenzie would be setting up appointments for me while simultaneously nursing Sky. The balance, focus, and coordination used to accomplish such a feat was nothing short of impressive. Holding the phone up to her ear using her shoulder, she'd feed Sky with one arm and use her other hand to enter the client's contact information into the computer.

In January of 2015, when Sky was eight months old, I was scheduled to do a psychic show in Minneapolis, and we opted to fly instead of drive the six hours. I often travel alone but I think Kenzie was experiencing some cabin fever since it was winter time and she'd been a stay-at-home mom since Sky was born. I couldn't blame her for wanting to get out of town for a bit. The real problem was that Sky hadn't pooped in the four days leading up to the trip. We were terrified to get on the plane with her for obvious reasons. If she exploded at 30,000 feet, it would be bad news for us and every soul on board the aircraft. We weren't sure TSA would let us through security, because, given the circumstances, Sky was essentially a loaded weapon.

I don't think I ever admitted it to Kenzie, but I honestly said a silent prayer, asking my dad to work his heavenly magic and make Sky poop before we left for the airport. In the world of prayers, it was surely a ridiculous plea for help. Yet, as new parents, that's what our lives had come to. I thought back to the time when I was around ten, and I was standing in the kitchen with my dad and sister as a thunderstorm rolled through the city. After a big clap of thunder shook the house, my sister bolted into the bathroom. I think she was just trying to hide because she was only six and she was scared, but my dad joked that the thunder must have scared the poop out of her.

For us, it was winter time and no thunderstorms were in the forecast. Whether it was my dad or just nature taking its course, our prayers were finally answered. Less than an hour before we headed to the airport, Sky required a diaper change.

The trip itself was a tiring one. Our flight got delayed, our car rental situation was a nightmare, and snow was coming down in Minneapolis by the time we arrived. We didn't get much sleep at the hotel due to Sky crying most of the night. I was exhausted come morning and had to wake up by 5:00. I was scheduled to make a live appearance on a morning radio show. I took questions from callers and promoted my event which took place that same evening.

Sky didn't accompany me to the radio station in Minneapolis, but she was no stranger to the radio station in Omaha. I took her into the Sweet 98 radio station to meet the disc jockeys, Pat and J.T. From inside her stroller, she looked around the studio, wondering what all the lights, buttons, and microphones were. She was contained inside her stroller but I could tell by the look in her eyes that she would chew on cords and smash all the blinking buttons if given the chance.

After all, she was crawling by this time, and her mobility gave her the freedom to explore anything she wanted when she wasn't contained by a stroller or car seat. Unfortunately for us, Sky gravitated towards anything hot, sharp, or remotely dangerous. Corners we buffered with baby-proofing hardware. Cups of coffee were no longer safe on side tables. TV cords, the fireplace, the register vents . . . nothing was safe. She was drawn to every area that presented potential hazards. If I sat her in a room filled with a thousand new toys and one rocket launcher, she would have found the rocket launcher immediately and ignored all the toys. It seemed like this kid was either completely fearless or just plain nuts. I wasn't entirely sure.

Some days, when she was feeling especially adventurous, my only option was to barricade the perimeter of the living room with pillows and couch cushions. It was a bubble of safety. No pillows were spared. I pulled them from every room in the house and lined the living room to block her from getting out of my sight. I'd collapse on the couch in a heap of exhaustion, and just when my guard was down, she'd make her escape. She'd gravitate towards the rug by the door where she'd find pebbles or twigs that had been carried in by our shoes. She'd put these things in her mouth and gum them like a savory chocolate treat.

Lucky for me, Sky never got away too quickly because her style of crawling was rather inefficient. You see, she only used her right leg to push off while crawling. Her left leg just dragged behind her like the lifeless limb of a zombie who was pulling herself across the floor. It looked like a scene from *The Walking Dead*, and I couldn't decide if it was cute or creepy. It allowed me enough time to run over and scoop her up before she pried the safety plugs from the electrical sockets. We later consulted with our pediatrician to make sure this leg dragging thing wasn't a concern, and when they assured us Sky was fine, we found it rather comical.

Sky was putting together short sentences such as, "Hi Dad," and, "No Momma." She could even string together three-word and four-word sentences when she was feeling chatty. The doctor insisted this doesn't usually occur until a child is closer to two years old. Sky was only nine months old.

According to my journals, by ten months old, Sky could point to and identify all of her own body parts including toes, feet, legs, knees, tummy, elbows, arms, hands, fingers, lips, teeth, cheeks, head, hair, and ears. I hated to use her for our own amusement, but I figured it was a win-win. She kept us entertained, and in the process, she was learning so many new things. We couldn't take much credit for her cognitive milestones. All we did is talk to her constantly. Sky simply had an uncanny ability to remember things and was hyper-aware of her surroundings.

Her brain was shaping up to be a remarkable instrument. In March of 2015, an incident occurred that jeopardized Sky's precious little noggin.

Kenzie took Sky for a walk in her stroller while she held Zico on his leash. A dog walker passed by with two huskies, and whether it was Zico being overly protective of Sky or the huskies being a tad aggressive, the dogs got into a minor scuffle. The leashes got tangled and through the chaos, Sky's stroller got knocked on its side. Her cheek hit the pavement and there was blood. Through the screams and crying, the man offered Kenzie a flurry of apologies as he pulled his dogs back. Kenzie scurried home and cleaned the wound. We monitored Sky for symptoms of a concussion, but the only aftereffects were a small scrape and some minor bruising.

The trauma of it all was probably worse for Kenzie and me than it was for Sky. I think that's how it goes when you're a parent. The worst kind of pain is not your own, but the pain you feel when your *child* is injured. I thought back to times in my youth when my mom would take me to the doctor when I had the flu or to the hospital when I needed stitches. Still to this day, I can remember the look on her face. It contained helplessness, worry, and unconditional love. I'm sure it was the same expression on *our* faces as we stared at Sky after the incident. Any parent will admit they'd gladly trade places with their child if it means sparing them some pain.

We also dealt with the ear infections, the fevers, and croup, which is a cold that settles in a child's upper airway, making her larynx and trachea swollen. It causes a cough that sounds hoarse and painful, like the bark of a seal. I can't count the number of sleepless nights we had. There were nights when we didn't get one single minute of sleep. Sky would be up six, ten, twelve times, crying and hysterical from fevers, teething, or upset stomachs. Four o'clock was usually the point where fighting the battle was futile. I'd carry her downstairs to the living room, hoping that a change of scenery would calm her down.

We'd sit there together in my recliner and the living room would be dark except for the glow of the TV screen. We'd watch documentaries about UFOs, Bigfoot, or other world mysteries – subjects Grandma Myers got me hooked on so many years ago. I'd dry Sky's tears and hold her as we'd snuggle in a blanket and wait for the sun to rise. Eventually she'd fall asleep and so would I. Kenzie would come down to find infomercials playing on a muted TV. Hot coffee was brewed but untouched in the coffee pot. Pillows and cushions lined the perimeter of the living room.

It wasn't always me that pulled all-nighters with Sky. Kenzie did so just as often. It really depended on my work schedule and whether or not I had clients scheduled for the next morning. If I didn't have sessions the next day, I'd stay up all night with Sky, knowing I could catch a nap once Kenzie relieved me in the morning.

Times weren't always easy. Sky was a terrible sleeper. "Let her cry it out," people would suggest. "Crying isn't going to hurt her. Besides, if you go in there every time she makes a peep, you're giving her exactly what she wants." I wanted to grab these people by the shirt collars and shake them. I knew they meant well, but they had no idea what we were up against. I wanted to stare at them with bulging, blood shot eyes, and scream, "You don't understand. You don't know what it's like. She has more stamina than *we* do. Resistance is futile!"

The stamina part was absolutely true. Sky could go longer than we could without sleep, and she wasn't very good at self-soothing when she was upset. We tried the 'let her cry it out' method. Three hours, four hours, five hours later . . . she was still going with a set of lungs that would make an opera singer jealous. At less than a year old, she stayed awake for more than twenty straight hours – nearly a *full day* without a nap or shut-eye of any kind. Sometimes I wondered if she'd ever wear out, and I wondered what we could do differently to help her sleep better.

If we could do it all over again, one thing we would do differently is we wouldn't have put her to bed with a binky in her mouth. Pacifiers were good in terms of getting Sky sleepy, but the problem was that when they fell out of her mouth in the middle of the night, she'd wake up and become hysterical. Eventually, we got to the point where we'd throw a handful of pacifiers in her crib. We'd use two, four, six, however many we could find throughout the house. We'd toss them in, hoping there was strength in numbers. It increased the chances of her finding another binky should one fall out of her mouth. It was the equivalent of fishing with multiple lines in the water, and it reminded me of how my dad would fish with two, sometimes three poles at the same time. Only, instead of trying to catch a fish, we were trying to catch some sleep.

Some nights it worked and other nights it didn't. Come morning time, I'd carry Sky down the stairs. At ten months old, she'd point to the coffee maker and say, "Coffeeee!" She'd 'help' me make a fresh pot as she'd reach out and press the 'brew' button after I'd filled the water and coffee grounds. Out of sheer exhaustion, I'd often use a lot of grounds. The coffee was stronger than Hercules in his prime.

By the time her first birthday rolled around, Sky had developed a taste for coffee, insisting that she needed a sample from each pot we'd brew together. When the coffee was finally room temperature, I'd dip my finger into my cup and place a single drop or two onto her tongue. She always responded with a satisfied, "Mmmm." I asked the pediatrician if one drop of coffee could be the reason Sky wasn't sleeping well. *Was she riding a caffeine high?* Our pediatrician assured us that a single drop of coffee was not enough to have an effect on Sky whatsoever.

I was surprised Sky could handle the bitterness of my plain black coffee. Had it been watered down with creamer the way Grandma Myers used to drink it, I could have understood the fascination. But a baby liking medium roast with no cream or sugar? I found it odd.

I was still facilitating the Omaha Metaphysical Network meetings once a month, and attendees were always interested to hear what new things Sky had done or said. Sometimes we'd even bring her to the meetings and she'd sit on our laps as the group discussed spirituality or world mysteries. She got the chance to meet our regulars such as Squirrelly Craig, UFO Fred, Brandon "The Sho" Shostak, Jodi, the two Dans, and so on. Sometimes Sky would fall asleep during our meetings, but more often than not, she'd get fussy. Kenzie would take her out of the conference room and calm her down in the room where I delivered my psychic readings.

Group members found it heartwarming that Sky was now attending our spiritual discussion group. It felt like only yesterday that group members shared dreams they were having of Sky. And now, she was actually *attending* the meetings.

Sky was such an affectionate baby, and much of the time she loved being held and snuggled. Kenzie and I gladly obliged, and this meant we often carried her when she was perfectly capable of using her legs. In hindsight, this probably delayed her ability to walk on her own, but she finally mastered it around thirteen months old. Not long after that, we figured it was time to give potty training a whirl. I kept documenting her milestones in my journal, and figured she was so smart that potty training would be a breeze. *How hard could it be?*

September 22, 2015: Went potty on the potty chair on the very first try! Looks like it's gonna be an easy process! Yay!

September 24, 2015: Dropped her pants in the living room and peed on the drapes by the window. Never mind.

I wondered how it was anatomically possible for a female to urinate on the vertical hanging curtains. I assumed 'writing one's name in the snow' and other urine-related tricks were only conducted by boys. I'm no physicist, so I didn't bother overanalyzing the mechanics of it. I just cleaned up the mess and washed my hands.

In October of 2015, there was an entry detailing the time we found Sky with a cheek full of dog food. She was pouching it in her mouth like a hamster and saving it for later, apparently. How this had transpired in the few seconds that it took Kenzie to place a cup in the dishwasher was a complete mystery. Surely, instances like that were helping Sky build her immune system. At least that's what we told ourselves to sleep better at night. Besides, we'd heard equally horrific stories from fellow parents whose children were still alive and well despite some questionable parenting moments.

My good friend Eddie told me of a time when his oldest daughter was a baby and she fell off the bathroom vanity and smacked her head on the porcelain toilet before hitting the floor. She's now in college and is a straight-A student, so I suppose the incident didn't scramble her eggs too badly. From what I've gathered, it's like opening up Pandora's Box to ask other parents about the odd and unusual ways their children have gotten dirty, injured, or covered in bodily fluids. Each story is topped by one that's even more remarkable. Truly, it's a miracle any of us survive childhood at all.

At one point in time, there was a video circulating around social media that was a compilation of clips referred to as 'dad saves.' Essentially, it consisted of moments where fathers used instincts and quick reflexes to save the day. It showed dads diving to catch a birthday cake that was falling off the table, snatching a child up before a bicycle ran them over, or catching a kid who tumbled off a trampoline like rag doll. Ironically, not long after seeing one of these compilation videos, I had my own 'dad save' experience.

Sky was standing on my recliner (something I'd told her a thousand times not to do). She lost her balance and tripped backwards on the arm rest. It looked like slow motion as she free-fell from the chair with a terrified look on her face. Her arms flailed uselessly at her sides, and she was unable to brace for impact. I was several feet away, folding laundry on the couch, but was paying attention and saw it happening. I mentally flashed back to playing baseball in my youth, and thought of all the times I'd leap to make a diving catch just before the ball hit the ground.

I leapt towards Sky, horizontal and airborne, arms outstretched like I was trying to catch a fly ball to win the World Series. I cradled the back of her head just in time to cushion the impact, and our bodies slammed down on the ground simultaneously. The impact knocked the wind out of her, but I'd gotten there just in time to save her noggin from the crushing blow. Kenzie came thundering down the stairs to see what had happened, her footsteps heavy and panicked like a stampede of bison.

Sky was crying and the ordeal had clearly frightened her, but she was uninjured. As for me, I was groaning in pain on the floor because the impact had jammed my shoulder. Sky was playing and laughing five minutes later, but I was in quite a bit of discomfort for the next two weeks.

Despite evidence to the contrary, we really were attentive parents when Sky was a baby. In fact, most of the time we fit the description of 'helicopter parents.' We often hovered over Sky and following her every move like a police chopper circling above a high-speed chase. And even though we had her outnumbered two to one, Sky was so sneaky and mobile that it was simply impossible to track her movement every second.

There was one incident where Kenzie found Sky chewing on something that resembled a pen or thermometer. She rushed over to Sky and gasped in horror to find out she was actually chewing on a used pregnancy test. Sky had apparently snuck into the bathroom and fished it out of the trashcan like a five-dollar DVD from the bargain bin at the store. Kenzie shuddered in disgust. I assured her that urine is sterile. I wasn't entirely sure it was true, but I thought I heard it on the Discovery Channel years ago. If I was wrong, at least Sky was building her immune system . . . yet again.

As for the pregnancy test, it was negative. We were back and forth on the idea of a second child. Sometimes we felt guilty that Sky didn't have a brother or sister to play with. On the other hand, we really enjoyed the amount of attention and affection we could devote to her as an only child. Taking into account these two opposing factors, we were torn on the decision.

What ultimately tipped the scales in terms of *not* having another child were the blood clots Kenzie experienced during child birth. In the moments after Sky was born, Dr. Kline and the nursing staff were extremely alarmed. They anticipated Kenzie would require an emergency procedure. Thankfully, they got the situation under control before it came to that. Dr. Kline cautioned it could happen again if Kenzie were to have another child in the future. She was frank in saying it could be life-threatening.

At her eighteen-month checkup, the doctor was once again impressed with the things Sky had been doing and saying in recent months. We agreed that Sky was certainly sharp, but conceded that she also liked to eat Purina dog food and pee on the drapes. The doctor shared with us all the hilarious mishaps she had with her own daughters when they were young, and gave us peace of mind we were doing a good job. It was nice to feel like we weren't being judged for our parenting imperfections. Besides, we figured we weren't doing a terrible job since Sky was happy and healthy.

The potty training continued and Sky proceeded to grow and develop. The weeks were a blur. It's true what they say about parenting. The days are long but the years are short. I continued to write in Sky's journal and I took a *lot* of pictures and videos. I managed to capture all of her firsts, such as her first diaper change, her first smile, her first word, first bath, first steps. *All* of it was saved in my camera and on my computer.

Since I was a teenager, video editing has been a hobby of mine. I've become familiar with movie making software, allowing me to splice together compilations and short documentaries from several videos I've captured. Although it takes countless hours, I put together these montages from all the footage we had of Sky. I overlaid some appropriate music into the project, and these mini-movies documented Sky's entire life, moment by moment.

Kenzie and I would have unofficial viewing parties in our living room as I showed her the finished product. I felt like George Lucas at the premier screening of Star Wars, hoping she'd appreciate the hours of work that went into the videos. During the first year of Sky's life, I made one every four months. Since then, I create one per year, finishing the project right around her birthday. They usually run about forty-five minutes, but take closer to forty *hours* to create. It's a labor of love, a true passion I've developed.

These video projects have always been a way for me to reminisce, to pause and appreciate what's happened in previous months. It's fun to see how Sky has grown and changed. It's fun to relive each moment as I watch the old videos and extract the best segments for the final cut. I guess making those little movies is the digital equivalent of the journals I keep for Sky. When she's older, maybe she'll appreciate them and will understand why her old man was always hitting the record button.

Eventually, I started to include Sky in our little viewing parties. When she was as young as eighteen months, it kept her attention far longer than I imagined it would. She'd squeal with delight as she watched herself on the video, reliving fun and hilarious moments. Our house was always filled with laughter and love. Even on the most stressful days when nerves were fried and the bills were adding up, there was still an element of hope and optimism. We felt a sense that the next day would be better and that everything would be alright.

No matter what the day was like, Kenzie and I always showed affection towards each other. We never parted without a kiss, a hug, and an "I love you." I never felt like the affection was something that needed to be hidden from our daughter. I wanted Sky to observe the way Kenzie and I treated each other. I hope that someday Sky will have a very high standard when it comes to selecting a partner or spouse. We wanted to set a good example so she knows what a healthy relationship looks like.

One morning, I was getting ready to leave for work. Sky watched as I leaned in and kissed Kenzie on the lips. I never kiss Sky on the lips, so I squatted down to kiss her cheek and forehead just as I always did. She looked at me with a dissatisfied expression and appeared frustrated. She then furrowed eyebrows, grabbed my cheeks between her hands, and said, "No! Lips!" Then, she planted a wet one right on my mouth. The kiss was slobbery, containing plenty of drool and even some mushy bits from the cereal she'd been eating. I laughed hysterically, and although we didn't capture video of the moment, it will be seared into my memory for years to come.

I know she won't be young for very long. Precious moments are fleeting. I'll keep recording footage for her yearly videos. It's the best way to preserve the twinkle in her eyes while she still believes in magic. The best part of being a parent is seeing pure, uninhibited joy on Sky's face as she experiences life's wonders for the very first time . . . the first time in *this* lifetime, anyways. The second-best part of being a parent is *sharing* in that joy and remembering what it felt like to be a child myself.

Chapter 58

In January of 2016, Sky was eighteen months old. Eighteen months. I sometimes wondered what was the cut-off for measuring her age in months was. When she went off to college, would we say she's 216 months old? At eighteen months, she still wasn't a good sleeper. We decided to do away with afternoon naps altogether since it helped her sleep better at night. However, one particular evening proved to be problematic.

As the minutes turned into hours, I was still having no luck getting her to fall asleep. I broke out all the tricks such as softly drawing letters on her back, singing her songs, and gently stroking her hair. When none of these tactics worked, I simply placed her in the crib and walked out of the room. She screamed non-stop for over an hour. I gave her time to self-sooth, but she was unable to. I went back in to calm her down, and we began the process all over again.

I couldn't call for backup as Kenzie was not home. She'd recently taken a part time job at a local indoor soccer center. It was the same place I'd played soccer for the past twenty years. We knew the owner, and they desperately needed someone willing to work until midnight one day a week. Kenzie had been a stay-at-home mom since Sky was born, so she jumped at the chance to socialize while making a few extra bucks. More than anything, it was good for her mental health to have some time away from mom duties. I totally understood that and was supportive of her. On this particular night, though, I found myself frantically texting Kenzie, asking for help or suggestions to get Sky to sleep. Everything I tried had failed.

Yes, I know the purple binky is her favorite.
Yeah, I gave her the pink one too.
No, she doesn't need the gas drops. She's not gassy.
Yes, her diaper is dry. That's the first thing I checked.
Wait...
Never mind, NOW she needs a diaper change.

As midnight arrived, I'd already conceded the fact that Sky wasn't going to sleep for me. I doubted Kenzie could get her to sleep either, but figured she might have a better chance than I. Mentally, I had given up on trying to get her sleepy. Sky looked up at me with her big brown eyes, and she smiled a victorious smile. I think she knew I was frustrated, and the smile was the equivalent of a pat on the back. She must have been thinking, "Nice try, Dad. You never really had a chance."

Suddenly, her eyes darted away from me and focused on the open doorway to her bedroom. Through it, I could see the upstairs hallway, which was dimly lit. She studied the entryway, and seemed to be looking at something which I could not see. She pointed to the doorway and said, "Guy!"

Her eyes turned back to me and she had a curious smile on her face. She seemed like she was thoroughly entertained. *Was she playing peek-a-boo with an invisible presence near the doorway? Had someone dropped by for a visit?* Whoever it was, they clearly had Sky's attention. Suddenly, she did it again. She pointed to the entryway and shouted, "Guy!" She giggled with delight before looking back at me for reassurance. She wanted to know if I could see him too.

Chapter 59

Goosebumps formed on my arms and the hair stood up on the back of my neck. Again, Sky giggled with joy as she pointed toward her open bedroom door and said, "Guy! Guy!" One of the feathers on her dream catcher shifted just a bit. Part of me wondered if it was caused by the air coming from the register vent on her ceiling. Part of me contemplated if we were being visited by a spirit. I wondered if it was a mustached man in a flannel shirt making silly faces at Sky.

Moments later, Kenzie arrived home from the indoor soccer center. Sky was upbeat and wide-eyed, looking like she'd just gotten up from a refreshing nap. She practically leapt into her mom's arms.

"I hear there's a little girl in here who won't go to sleep."

"It's meeeeeee," Sky squealed with pride.

Kenzie finally spotted my face via the glow of the night light.

"What's wrong?"

"She keeps saying there's a guy in the doorway," I whispered. "I don't see anyone there, but I can sense a presence."

"Did Grandpa Steve make a visit?" Kenzie thought aloud.

"Grandpa Steeeeeeve," Sky shouted before chuckling to herself.

"Do you see Grandpa Steve, Sky?" Kenzie asked.

"Where is he now?" I pondered aloud.

Without hesitation, she whipped her head around to the far corner of the bedroom and pointed in that direction. It was the opposite part of the bedroom, away from the doorway. I locked eyes with Kenzie and we were silent. The air in the room was now completely still. The pressure change inside the room was palpable. It reminded me of hot July days when the temperature suddenly drops and the wind picks up just before the tornado sirens sound. I glanced in the direction Sky was pointing to, holding my breath and looking for any signs of movement.

Just then, something occurred to Kenzie. She looked as though she'd found the missing piece to a puzzle she'd been working on. She reminded me of something that happened weeks earlier. The two of us had been lounging around one evening when we'd heard something odd on Sky's baby monitor that sounded like an adult's voice. It was too muffled to make out any words, but it was unmistakably an adult's voice.

We'd held the baby monitor close to our ears and heard some commotion. It sounded as though Sky was shifting around in her bed. We turned on the video screen just in time to see Sky sit up in her crib. She looked over to the corner of her bedroom and raised her hand to give a little wave as she said, "Hi." And just like that, she placed her head back down and went to sleep. The casual nature of her interaction with this 'visitor' made it seem commonplace, like it was an everyday occurrence. *Oh, hey there. It's you again.*

I thought back to all the times we'd heard *Spirit in the Sky*. I remembered the car accident we narrowly avoided and the night my dad answered our prayer to help Sky sleep. Add to that, the baby monitor incident and now the presence in her doorway. Guardian angels are known to make themselves known in a variety of ways. They are persistent enough to get our attention when we need some support. Once we've noticed their presence, they'll pull back for a period of time, allowing us to live our lives without distractions.

Kenzie insisted she could take it from here, so I passed the bedtime duties on to her. I kissed my daughter on her forehead. "Get some rest, Sky."

"Night night, Dadda," said Sky.

"I'll be down in a bit," said Kenzie.

I walked into the dark upstairs hallway, and made my way downstairs. I knew my dad would pay another visit in the weeks or months to come. My heart was full. Yet, I secretly hoped he would bring Grandma with him next time he paid us a visit. It had been a long time since I'd sensed her presence. I figured she was busy chasing sunsets and collecting rocks in Heaven. The thought made me happy. Still, there was a part of me that missed her terribly.

Chapter 60

Winter slowly morphed into springtime, but not without a good fight. In Nebraska, the overlapping of winter and spring is like watching an arm-wrestling match that teeters back and forth, neither opponent wanting to concede. It was 2016. When late March came around, it dawned on me that it had been nine years since we'd celebrated Easter with Grandma Myers. When she was alive, we'd often take her out for a nice breakfast on Easter morning.

After eating, my mom would give Grandma some potted plants or hanging baskets of flowers as a gift. As the years went by and Grandma's health declined, my mom would hang, plant, and water the gifted plants herself. My mom has always been abundantly generous with her time and energy. To say 'acts of service' is her love language would be a profound understatement. After breakfast, Grandma would give me and my two siblings a plastic Easter egg with some cash tucked inside. "Use it for gas money," she'd say. "Don't push your luck and travel too far on an empty tank like Boompa and I did."

I couldn't believe how we'd taken nearly ten trips around the sun since Grandma had been gone. *How did it go by so quickly?* Traditions had changed over the years. Nowadays, Easter brunch is held at my mom's house rather than at a breakfast buffet. In 2016, my siblings and I were conducting Easter egg hunts with our own respective families before heading over to our mom's house later in the morning.

At the time, Sky was going through a phase where she was obsessed with the Disney movie *Frozen*. The Easter Bunny must have caught wind of this, because her basket was filled with a *Frozen* sippy cup, *Frozen* socks, and even a pair of *Frozen* sunglasses. Kenzie and I woke up Sky and walked her down to the kitchen so she could find her Easter basket. She was a couple months shy of two years old, and looked adorable in her yellow footie pajamas as she sucked on a pink pacifier.

As always, I had my phone ready and planned on capturing video as she dug into her basket. Sky walked into the kitchen, and immediately noticed the basket as something that was out of place, something that didn't belong. She approached it and studied it for a few seconds before squatting down to inspect it more closely. It was quickly apparent that she was most interested in the sunglasses, so she pulled them out and looked at them for a moment before dropping them and moving on to other objects.

By late morning, we were having brunch at my mom's house. Easter egg hunts ensued. The kids ate malted milk balls and fun-sized candy bars. My siblings and I, along with our spouses, stood around debating whether marshmallow Peeps are delicious or disgusting. We debated other subtleties of the holiday itself.

"If Jesus rose from the dead, doesn't that qualify him as a zombie?" my brother theorized.

"I don't know, but bunnies don't even lay eggs, so shouldn't there be an Easter Chicken instead?" added my sister, Elizabeth.

We all nodded silently as we contemplated and shoved more quiche into our mouths.

As is always the case, the holiday went by in a blur. Sky fell asleep that night without much trouble. Apparently, all the festivities had worn her out. Kenzie was upstairs taking a bath as I collapsed into my recliner in the living room. I'd taken several pictures and videos throughout the day, and decided to scroll through the photo album on my phone. During the action, it's often hard to gauge whether a particular video or picture had turned out okay. *Was it blurry? Does it need to be deleted?* I love weeding out the bad photos from the keepers.

I came across the first video of the day. It was the one where Sky squatted down to take toys out of her Easter basket on the kitchen floor. While watching it, I chuckled to myself thinking that I couldn't believe how curly Sky's hair had become. Just months earlier, it had been flat and straight. And *poof.* Just like that, her brown hair was beginning to swirl around into little curls and ringlets.

Suddenly, I noticed something very odd in the video. I scrolled back to the beginning of the video and hit play as I held the phone closer to my eyes for a better look. "*What in the heck . . .*" I noticed an anomaly that was so peculiar it appeared to defy the laws of physics. I watched the video again. And again. And again. Each time, I was more baffled by what I saw. My mouth hung open in disbelief. I figured Kenzie had her phone within arm's reach as she soaked in the bathtub upstairs, so I texted her the video along with words that read, "It looks like Sky had a little visitor this morning . . ."

Chapter 61

"Oh my God, it just . . . *flies out of her hands.* That's insane!" Kenzie was holding her phone right up to her nose, watching the video over and over again. She studied the footage so closely, she looked like an NFL referee reviewing a slow-motion replay to determine the correct call.

"I know," I replied. "I've watched the video ten times already. It looks like a practical joke. Like the *Frozen* glasses were attached to fishing string and someone yanked it away from her."

We stood there together, analyzing the footage frame by frame. It was nothing short of astonishing, and it was hands down the best piece of paranormal footage I've ever captured on video. The object was propelled out of her hands with velocity. They flew horizontally through the air for about twelve inches, skidding slightly as they crashed to the floor.

"I didn't even notice it when it happened. Did you?" Kenzie asked.

"No, I was standing right there with you, just a couple feet away and I didn't see it either. When the glasses hit the floor, I just assumed she'd dropped them."

I later uploaded the raw footage into my video editing program, which allowed me to slow the video down. Watching it at one-tenth the normal speed, I saw the glasses actually spin 180 degrees in mid-air as they flew away from Sky, solidifying our notion that they were pulled or batted out of her hands by an intelligent presence. It was clear she hadn't merely dropped them.

In the days that followed, I uploaded the video to my *psychicandymyers* YouTube channel under the title "Undeniable Ghost Evidence – Wow." The video is still on YouTube for those interested in viewing it. The video made the rounds on social media, and caused quite a frenzy as people theorized possible explanations. What we had captured was clearly unusual, even by Kenzie's and my standards. *Who was the culprit? Why would a ghost or spirit steal glasses from a child? Was their significance in it happening on Easter?* People on social media had so many questions.

In lectures, I've explained to audiences that spirits like to show off during holidays and special occasions. That's when we miss our departed loved ones even more than usual. They're fully aware of this, so spirits tend to use any methods available to give us a smile during holidays, birthdays, weddings, anniversaries, and family reunions. They might do this by opening or closing cabinet doors in the kitchen, moving a picture frame on the dresser, or causing the bedroom lights to flicker. It's their little way of dropping by to assure us they're present and haven't missed the party.

The first Christmas after Grandma Myers died, we took a family photo on Christmas morning just as we always did. When we looked at the picture, we noticed an orb resting against my left cheek. It was a translucent bubble the size of a golf ball. *A kiss from Grandma?* I like to think so.

As for the Easter morning sunglasses thief, Grandma wasn't my prime suspect. I doubted she needed a pair of sunglasses so badly she'd snatch one from a toddler. Given all that had recently transpired in our home, I thought the culprit might be a male, standing 5'8" with a handlebar mustache. My mind flashed back to the late 1980s and I thought of times when Dad would take my sister's pink sunglasses and try them on just to make her laugh. She would have been four or five at the time.

It takes a lot of *umph* for a Heavenly visitor to move items in our surroundings. It requires tremendous energy for a non-physical entity to move a physical object. Ounce for ounce, sunglasses aren't as hefty as flying paint rollers, yet my dad's feat was no less impressive. When Dad was in a good mood, he could be quite the jokester. Dads can be like that sometimes. Grandpas too. There's a prankster in every family, whether it be a crazy uncle or a hilarious cousin that's the life of the party.

A few weeks after the Easter incident, I was at the office and received a call from Kenzie. I could tell from her voice that something unusual had occurred because she was flustered and lost for words. She told me she'd been sitting on the floor with Sky, who was fidgeting with some building blocks. A cartoon was playing in the background. Suddenly, the TV changed stations all on its own and landed on a channel that was airing a movie called *Superstar*. It's a goofy comedy from 1999 starring Will Farrell and Molly Shannon of *Saturday Night Live* fame. When the TV mysteriously switched over to the movie, Kenzie's first reaction was to make sure Sky wasn't sitting on one of the remote controls. She ruled out that explanation as no remotes were nearby. They were resting on the side table several feet away.

Seconds later, the movie cut to a cheesy scene where Will Farrell is playing the role of Jesus and the song *Spirit in the Sky* is playing in the background. Kenzie says she practically laughed out loud, and she immediately knew who the mystery channel surfer was. I suppose for my dad, it really wasn't that difficult to push a button on a remote control. Surely, he knew what channel the movie was playing on, and was probably giggling like a school boy as he changed the station just in time for Kenzie to hear the familiar song.

Compared to moving physical objects, it's rather easy for spirits to manipulate electronics. Anything with a button, cord, wire, battery, or power source is easy for spirits to manipulate. The reason is that battery-operated toys, TVs, radios, phones, and lights already have a power source within them. Therefore, it's just a matter of the spirits manipulating the energy that's already present. Even electronic potty chairs are fair game.

On Memorial Day weekend, Kenzie and I asked my dad to drop by for a visit. We weren't sure what method he'd use to make his presence known, so we remained patient and attentive to our surroundings. Within the hour, we heard a little melody chiming from the bathroom. It was Sky's battery-operated potty chair she'd been using for potty training. The sensors are triggered by moisture, so anytime Sky tinkled in the basin, it played a cute song.

Sky had been using the potty chair for several months, and not once had it malfunctioned. To rule out common-sense explanations, I went in there and lifted the lid to see if maybe Sky had pottied when we weren't looking, or maybe we'd forgotten to fully wipe out the moisture from last time she went. But when I checked, the bowl and the sensors were completely bone dry.

Later that night, Kenzie and I were resting in bed together when we heard the unmistakable sound of rocks and crystals clinking against one another. It was obvious where the sound was coming from. On Kenzie's nightstand, there's a little waterfall decoration. The bottom reservoir of the contraption is filled with rocks, crystals, and gemstones. We heard the rocks moving around as if someone was sticking a finger in there and swirling them around. "Someone is in here," Kenzie whispered in a tense voice.

Wanting to catch our mischievous cat in the act, I grabbed my cell phone and turned on the flashlight feature. My heart began to beat faster when we realized Darwin *wasn't* playing with the rocks. He was on the floor sleeping with Zico in the dog bed. I turned off the flashlight and we lay there in silence for a few moments. Then it happened again. The rocks and crystals loudly clinked together by the hands of an intelligent presence. Kenzie rolled over and snuggled into me as she nervously said, "Okay, Grandpa Steve . . . thanks for the sign, but we need to sleep now. You can visit us again tomorrow, okay."

That's how it goes when communicating with the spirit world. We humans are always asking for Heavenly signs, but when we receive them, the experience can feel a little unnerving. I suppose it's the shock factor that catches us off guard – the fact that signs can come when we least expect it. Inanimate objects like sunglasses, potty chairs, and rocks are supposed to behave in a predictable manner, only moving or making noise when we want them to. Yet, these rules don't apply when we're dealing with spirits. Signs can come in a variety of ways, and it's true that everything seems scarier at night, even when it's merely a sweet relative dropping by from Heaven.

In my dad's defense, we never specified visiting hours. He was surely playing with the decorative waterfall just to make absolutely certain we knew he was around. Spirits are persistent like that. They won't go away until they know we've sensed their presence. Usually, there's no specific message attached to their visit. It's not to give advice or offer urgent warnings. They just want us to know we're loved and we're not alone.

If one is prone to spiritual visitors in the home, I would suggest the person set some boundaries. A person who scares easily might not appreciate a sign that's startling or loud. A fatigued individual might prefer signs from Heaven to occur during the day in order to get restful sleep at night. Generally speaking, spirits try their best to accommodate our requests. Speaking to them out loud or silently through our prayers is a good way set some guidelines with the spirit world.

Chapter 62

L ife's conveyor belt continued to propel us forward. We felt protected by my dad and knew Sky was in good hands since he was one of her guardian angels. Although we were in constant communication with the spirit world, we stayed grounded by doing what any other family does. We played games. We went swimming. We took Sky to carnivals and had play dates with her cousins. We did laundry, cleaned the house, and watched movies together.

She was still amazing us daily with her cognitive development. This was consistent with my initial psychic predictions of Sky. Yet, part of me was amazed at how intelligent she was and how quickly she caught onto things. I say this because school didn't always come easily for me. I always passed my classes, but had to work twice as hard as my peers to get the same grade. It was already apparent that Sky wouldn't have that problem. She was as sharp as a surgical knife and highly attentive. She studied her environment with a keen eye. It seemed like she was *remembering* how everything worked as opposed to *learning* it for the very first time.

As for her balance and coordination, that was another matter. To say she was clumsy would be an understatement. I inherited a good deal of athleticism from my dad, but those genes must have been lost in the DNA cement mixer because they certainly weren't passed on to Sky. She often stumbled around like a newborn giraffe, unsure of how her legs worked. We consulted with her pediatrician several times to see if her poor balance was related to an inner ear problem. The doctor kept assuring us that Sky was healthy.

I told Kenzie it must be Sky's first time on Earth, and that all her previous lifetimes must have taken place on planets where gravity works much differently. I was merely joking, but Sky's falls and tumbles were very real. Thankfully, she'd gotten accustomed to picking herself back up and dusting herself off.

One tumble that wasn't entirely her fault was the time she fell into a flower bed. It was at a family party in Albion, Nebraska, where Kenzie's mom and aunts grew up. There was a boy there named Oliver. He wasn't a cousin, so I presumed his parents were friends of the family. He was flirting with Sky and chasing her around the yard in circles like a greyhound trying to catch a bunny. I swore at one point he'd tried to kiss her. Content to let them sort it out themselves, I kept my distance and observed their shenanigans. Moments later, the little Romeo mustered up the gumption to wrap his arms around Sky and plant a kiss right on her lips. Not knowing he'd chosen the girl with the wobbly legs, his momentum caused them both to topple over a tractor tire and into the flower bed.

I rushed down the hill to make sure the two kids were okay. Sky rose to her feet but tripped on the tractor tire again and fell to the ground once more. I couldn't help but notice the grin on her face. She looked exhilarated and terrified, like she'd just gotten off a rollercoaster. If nothing else, Oliver was bold. I should have seen it coming. He was wearing a Lightning McQueen sticker from the Disney movie *Cars* – a sure sign of a bad boy who plays it fast and loose. He'd attacked Sky's lips like a barracuda going after a school of anchovies.

Sky was just shy of three years old. I was *thirteen* when I experienced my first kiss. Her name was Mary and it took place on the baseball bleachers one Friday after school. I don't reckon I was the world's best kisser back then, but at least I didn't push Mary into a flower bed.

I walked up to Oliver and said, "State your intentions, young man." This tongue-in-cheek interrogation fell on deaf ears as the kid simply roared at me like a lion before running off and summersaulting in the grass. Sky found this hilarious. I assume someday she'll go for a man with a sense of humor. And that's fine by me. She joined Oliver for a roll in the yard, staining her clothes and kicking up a cloud of dust. She looked like

Pig Pen from the *Peanuts* gang. She rose to her feet and shook herself off, dust and twigs falling from her ringlets of curly hair.

She enjoyed getting dirty, catching bugs, going fishing, and wrestling with her cousins (all of whom are boys). Yet, she has a softer and more delicate side as well. She likes to play with stuffed animals and enjoys dressing up in princess costumes. There were many times we found her applying makeup she'd gotten from Kenzie's purse. We laughed and took a picture, figuring it was a rite of passage for any little girl – an inevitable photo opportunity that no scrapbook is complete without.

Most days, Sky was a big goofball and her sense of humor was second to none. I suppose this balanced out her propensity for the paranormal and helped keep her grounded. Besides, when odd or unusual instances occur, Kenzie and I didn't make a big deal out of it. Fear is a learned behavior. If a parent shows fear towards the paranormal, a child is likely to pick up on that and become anxious herself.

Around our house, we often kept the mood light. We made silly noises and sang silly songs. I'd drag Sky around the house on blankets like it was a makeshift sled. I gave Sky 'tatanka rides' up the stairs each night at bedtime. Tatanka is the Lakota/Dakota word for buffalo. It's our own equivalent of a piggyback ride, and I don't claim to remember how piggyback rides ever became tatanka rides, but it became a mainstay in our bedtime routine. She'd hop onto my back and yell, "Giddy up, tatanka!" I'd gallop up the stairs and towards her bedroom with Sky giggling uncontrollably in my ear.

Sky would build blanket forts throughout the house. Kenzie and I referred to them as 'beaver dams.' They were epic engineering feats where Sky would gather every blanket, couch cushion, and pillow from the main floor of our home and construct elaborate monuments that were often taller than she was. They were the Taj Mahal of blanket forts. Sometimes, Kenzie and I were allowed to enter, but other times, she preferred Zico's company. From inside the fort, they peeked their little heads out. Sky laughed hysterically and shouted to us, "Go away, monsters!" Zico was like an actor taking part in a play for which he didn't know the script. He had no idea what to expect and merely went along with whatever Sky had in mind.

As a toddler, Sky used Zico as her jungle gym. He exhibited patience with the gentle disposition of a therapy dog. He was her play buddy, her snuggle companion, her best friend. When I looked at the two of them, I saw a beauty and her beast. Zico and Sky. Sky and Zico. He was no longer my dog. He belonged to Sky. As for Darwin, Sky claimed I could have him. She was indifferent. And so was Darwin. After all, he's a cat. When Kenzie would feel left out, asking which pet belonged to her, Sky would grant her ownership of Milwaukee. He was a blue beta fish we had at the time. Why Sky chose the name Milwaukee, I'll never know.

Sky's love of animals was apparent from the very beginning. By the age of two, she was regularly touching, riding, holding, and interacting with animals. She'd pet goats, llamas, donkeys, horses, bunnies, and countless other critters. While getting a behind the scenes tour of the Omaha zoo, there was even a giraffe that stuck its head inside her baby stroller when she was six months old. I managed to snap a photo just in time. When she was a bit older, I tried to convince Sky that her belly button was a scar from the time a giraffe bit her. Eventually, she called my bluff and didn't believe me.

I can't count how many stray, injured, or lost animals Sky and Kenzie attempted to save when Sky was a toddler. There was the injured duck we found at the park that had been abandoned by its mom. There was the baby bunny they rescued, and the sparrow that was stuck inside the garage. One time, we drove back to Omaha from Minneapolis with a car full of guinea pigs. While I was doing a psychic show there, Kenzie and Sky spent the afternoon attending a guinea pig expo (yes, that's a real thing). The two of them swooned over the little fur balls in the back seat while I drove the six hours home. Kenzie named one of the guinea pigs Elvis on account of his stylish hairdo. Sky named one Daisy, as in Daisy Duck.

One time, Kenzie and Sky found an abandoned baby opossum hobbling through our back yard. The little guy was tiny and his eyes weren't even open yet. He was bound to make a nice snack for the hawks that fly above our nature preserve. Despite her best efforts, Kenzie was unable to find the opossum's siblings or mom. So, she gently wrangled him up and brought him inside.

My job was always the same. I was the shoebox fetcher. The warm lamp retriever. The go-getter of the heating pad, the dish of water, and the old towels. I was never certain exactly which creature Kenzie and Sky had brought into the house. I'd just see them hovering over some helpless, furry lump in Kenzie's palm as they spoke in hushed, high pitch tones. I didn't bother asking questions. I just assumed they'd found a little bird. Or bunny. Or squirrel. Or feral cat.

As for the opossum, it would have finished last place in a beauty contest. Bless its heart. We took pity on it . . . like we were looking at a coyote with mange, or a three-legged bulldog with an underbite. The more we stared at it, the more we found it cute. Kenzie phoned a local wildlife rehab group that operates on a volunteer basis. The only unfortunate part of having a child who's fearless around animals is keeping her *away* from the ones that are wild and possibly infected with diseases. Uncertain as to the health of the opossum, we wouldn't let Sky touch it, despite her begging.

Two ladies from the rescue organization finally arrived at 10:30 PM to pick up the opossum. Sky was still awake, as she refused to sleep with all the excitement of having a wild creature in the house. Kenzie handed over the shoebox to the rescue volunteer. The opossum was not happy and hissed at her, sounding like a king cobra. The lady was wearing an embroidered sweater with a cat on it. She accepted the shoebox with outstretched arms and a big smile as she said, "Oh look, he really likes me!"

We closed the front door and Sky jumped onto my back, demanding a tatanka ride up the stairs. Once in her room, she flopped into bed and we gave her a 'love sandwich.' Kenzie got one cheek and I got the other. We peppered her with kisses as though Sky was the turkey and we were the bread. "Here comes the mustard." *Kiss.* "Here come the pickles." *Kiss. Kiss.*

I figured other families had similar routines and bedtime rituals. Every kid should be so lucky as to receive the equivalent of a love sandwich before bed. I always tried to seer those moments into my memory . . . those moments when the laughter couldn't be contained and there was so much love in the room, I thought the house's foundation might crack beneath the weight of it all.

We took Sky for walks on the trail behind our house, just like I had imagined we would years earlier when Sky was nothing more than a dream. She'd hold Zico's leash and he would drag her along like a tin can dangling from the back of a newlywed's car. She'd squat down to count the dots on a lady bug, and giggled as bunnies crisscrossed the trail. Her wild hair danced in the breeze. She shielded her beautiful brown eyes from the sun as she flashed a smile brighter than a 100 watt light bulb.

We walked together, hand in hand. I asked what she wants to be when she grows up, and her response was always the same. "I want to be a betwanawian." Given her exposure to animals, a veterinarian sounded right on the money. Down the trail we went. She'd fall. She'd get up. And she'd fall again. Sometimes she'd grab both of our hands with me on one side and Kenzie on the other, and she'd leap into the air, propelling her legs outward and pretending to fly.

It made me think of our metaphysical meeting years earlier, when someone shared her dream of that exact moment. It was now real. We were *living* the dream. Things weren't always perfect. There were moments filled with tears. There were temper tantrums. There were sleepless nights, spills, and constant messes to clean up. Yet, amid the chaos, there were those occasional moments of tranquility and unspeakable joy.

One particular morning, Sky was unusually calm. We were having a lazy morning together, and were snuggled underneath a hand-knitted, red blanket that Grandma Myers gave me many years ago. Sky wasn't particularly interested in the cartoon that was on TV. She just sat quietly, resting her head against my chest and sticking her tiny fingers through the holes of the knitted blanket.

Suddenly, she looked up at me and planted a kiss on my left cheek. It caught me off guard as it was completely unprompted. I smiled at her. She smiled at me. I took a sip of my coffee, which was now lukewarm. She insisted she needed a taste, so I dunked my finger into the cup and placed a single drop on her tongue. "Mmmmmmm," she mumbled.

She ran her index finger along the exterior of my coffee mug, studying the picture with curiosity. It was a coffee mug I'd bought in New York City. A year earlier, I'd traveled there to receive an award for my *Flying Paint Rollers from Heaven* book. The mug displayed a picture of Times Square, complete with tall buildings, taxis, billboards, and pedestrians walking along the sidewalk.

"Do you know where this is?" I asked Sky.

"Where's dat, Dadda?"

"That's New York City. I went there last year. It's a *really* big city. That's where I got your little snow globe, remember?"

"Mmmm hmmm," she mumbled, still studying the coffee mug as though she was interested.

"Would you like to see more pictures of New York City?" I asked her.

"Mmmm hmmm."

I used my cell phone and did an internet search for 'New York City.' One by one, I swiped through the pictures, pausing for a few seconds to let Sky study each one. We looked at photos of Central Park. I showed her pictures of the endless lights and advertisements inside Times Square. We gazed at photos of taxis and the Empire State Building.

I pulled up a photo of the Twin Towers, pre-September 11th, of course. The buildings stood tall and resolute in the sky on a clear sunny day. There was a lens flare in the photo caused by the sun. It was a little halo accompanied by a few glowing bubbles or orbs. They reminded me of the orb that appeared on my left cheek in the Christmas photo after my grandma died. The thought made me smile, and I reached up to touch that spot on my cheek. It was the same spot that Sky had kissed me moments earlier.

Still touching my cheek and feeling nostalgic, I looked down at Sky and kissed the top of her head. She didn't notice. Her gaze was solely focused on the picture of the Twin Towers. Her facial expression was one of intense consternation. She looked perplexed, worried even. I couldn't fathom what was going on inside her head. As far as any child would know, it was merely a picture of two tall buildings under a clear, blue sky. The silence was broken as she pointed to the buildings and said, "Airplanes."

Chapter 63

I flipped on the microphone and was about to begin my lecture. It was a presentation on past lives and reincarnation. A cacophony of background noise gave way to muted whispers as the audience saw I was about to begin. While walking to the front of the room, Kenzie grabbed me by the hand and gently tugged me back. I held the microphone away from my mouth and asked what the problem was. She ripped something sticky from the back of my shirt. Holding it up to my face, she asked, "Is Elsa going to help you with your presentation tonight?"

"Tonight's presentation is brought to you by *Frozen*," I joked back with a sarcastic grin.

I wasn't entirely surprised. Our lives had been overtaken with stickers for quite some time. I suppose that's just how it goes when you have a young daughter. We'd find stickers everywhere. They were on the wall, on the floor, on the kitchen table, even stuck to our clothes and the bottoms of our shoes. Checking ourselves for stickers was like checking ourselves for ticks after a mid-summer hike.

Stickers were only the half of it. Months earlier, I'd sat down with clients to begin a psychic reading and felt something uncomfortable jammed in my back pocket. I couldn't imagine what it could be, so I rose to my feet and discovered it was a Minnie Mouse comb Sky must have placed in there sometime that morning as I was rushing to leave for work. I simply tossed the comb into my desk drawer and explained to my clients that I had a young daughter.

"Say no more," said the husband. "Last week, I found a pacifier lodged in my briefcase."

"I found goldfish crackers crumbled in the pocket of my jacket yesterday," said the wife.

Kenzie patted me on the butt and said, "Go get 'em, babe. You'll do great." She scooted me towards the front of the audience. The lecture on past lives is admittedly my favorite. I've enjoyed lecturing about guardian angels, psychic children, and sharing ghost stories. However, the past lives presentation comes with so much factual information, so many case studies, that the concept itself is very compelling, if not completely undeniable.

As always, I fielded a number of questions from the audience. One lady wanted to know how much of an individual's personality is shaped by past lifetimes as opposed to influences from this current life. I said it's about a 75/25 split, meaning that seventy-five percent of who we are is shaped by our *present* life experiences since birth. The remaining twenty-five percent of a person is molded by *past* life experiences. This can include our likes, dislikes, fears, quirks, talents, and overall demeanor. Although much of the past life information remains dormant inside our subconscious, it still influences us in subtle ways.

The brain doesn't always remember past lives, but the soul never forgets. It's common for people to gravitate towards professions they've done countless times in previous lifetimes. Additionally, past lives can certainly account for a person's fascination with a particular country, time period, or historical event.

Some members of the audience asked me for specific examples from my readings. This was difficult because there are simply too many examples to choose from. That's like asking a musician to choose a favorite song. Similarly for me, each past life reading I deliver is memorable and special in its own right, so it's hard to choose just one.

I once met with a client and described to him in great detail a past lifetime where he'd traveled all over Europe. Yet, every time he was passing through Florence, Italy, it was truly his favorite place to be. Simply put, it felt like home. He'd have a glass of red wine and lounge around a patio area as the locals would pass by, walking up and down the cobblestone streets.

After relaying this information to my client, he chuckled and said that in his 20s, he spent a year or two traveling all over Europe. And, just like the previous lifetime I described, he was most fond of Florence, Italy.

"I've been there a half dozen times and have even thought about moving there," he told me. "I know that city like the back of my hand and it's always seemed familiar to me – even back when I visited there for the very first time."

I relayed to the audience another example of a time I met with a woman who was curious to explore her past lifetimes. I described one that took place in the 1800s in a sleepy town. It reminded me of a cowboy western movie. She was a southern belle and married a man who loved to drink whiskey. He was emotionally abusive and enjoyed playing poker far more than spending time with her. After describing the details of that lifetime, she offered some feedback and informed me that she can't stand the smell of whiskey nowadays. She has a *major* aversion to it.

Additionally, she divulged that her ex-husband was emotionally abusive. To boot, he was practically addicted to playing poker, often staying out all night and losing large quantities of money. My client admitted that anything having to do with cowboys or the Old West really puts her off. Apparently, her father is a big John Wayne fan, but every time he turns on one of the movies, she leaves the room immediately. Given her recent past lifetime, who could blame her?

As I shared these examples with the audience, one lady raised her hand asking about irrational fears as they relate to past lives. "I've been terrified of horses my whole life," she claimed.

"Did you grow up on a farm?" I asked. "Did you get bucked off a horse?"

"No, that's why it's so weird," she continued, throwing her hands up in confusion. "I've never even been on a horse. I'm just afraid of them for some reason."

In terms of fears spilling into our current life from the past, one session in particular came to mind. I shared it with the audience. I was meeting with a client and saw images of a past life she lived in Thailand.

She was a small boy who went fishing with his father. I explained that she didn't enjoy fishing, because there were catfish in the water that were actually bigger than her. She (the small boy) was afraid to fall in the water lest she be eaten. After describing this to her, she divulged that she's always been afraid of catfish for as long as she remembers – big ones, small ones, even ones on television give her the creeps.

She even claims to have had nightmares about catfish. Additionally, she said she's always been fascinated with Thailand. She loves the history, the culture, and the language. She's a Caucasian lady, but said her best friend is actually from Thailand, and she's starting to pick up on the language because it's always seemed familiar to her.

Then there was the mom I spoke with who wanted to know some information about her young son's past lifetimes. He was around eight years old at the time of the session. I informed the lady that her son has been in the military in several of his past lifetimes. Additionally, I said he was an inventor in many previous incarnations, creating countless gizmos and contraptions that were rather ingenious. She laughed as she reported back to me that her son still has the heart of an inventor.

In recent months he'd actually invented a new board game that has to do with soldiers, war, and military strategies. She said he's currently working on some prototypes for the board game and planned to submit the idea to Milton Bradley or Parker Brothers once it was complete. So in that case, his love for the military *and* inventions is still prevalent today.

The examples are truly endless, and it's sometimes astonishing how history can repeat itself. There was the time I read a nice Caucasian lady and described a past life where she was a dark-skinned tribal warrior in Tanzania, Africa. She was the youngest of four brothers and her significant other always cheated on her in that past lifetime. I was completely shocked to hear her feedback. She said in this current lifetime, she actually married a man from Tanzania . . . a man who is the youngest of four brothers . . . a man she eventually divorced because he cheated on her.

"What about hobbies?" It was a no-nonsense guy towards the back of the room who was wearing a Harley Davidson bandana. He had braids in his long, white beard and his wallet was attached to a chrome chain dangling from his belt loop. "Can our current hobbies originate from past lives?"

"Do you own a motorcycle?" I asked him. He nodded but explained that his bike was currently in the shop. "It's just as well though since I can't ride until the weather warms up."

"My simple answer is yes," I said. "Your current hobbies may have originated from a past life. Here's an example that might be right up your alley." I described a recent past life session where a girl wanted to know about her new boyfriend, Mike. More specifically, she wanted to know about Mike's past lives. I received mental images of his most recent lifetime, which took place in the 1930s. He was a 'gear head', spending long hours in his garage tinkering on cars from the 1920s and 1930s. He wore suspenders and a white t-shirt, and always listened to the radio while working on his cars. I saw images of a stray white cat that wandered into his garage. He befriended the cat and it became his unofficial pet. It rubbed its head against his pant legs, begging for affection as he worked on engines.

As always, the most important part of the past life information was the *feedback* my client then offered. The girl informed me that Mike is still the same today as he was in his past life in the 1930s. She said his favorite hobby is tinkering on cars, specifically classic ones from the 1920s and 30s. She said that Mike *still* wears a white t-shirt with suspenders to hold up his pants. He listens to the radio all day while in his garage. "In fact", she said, "he's so 'old school' that he doesn't own a television because he prefers the radio instead. He's only in his mid-twenties, but he seems much older."

As for the stray white cat I mentioned in Mike's past life, she informed me it's really bizarre because just a few weeks prior to her psychic reading, Mike had befriended a white cat in the neighborhood. It was a stray who continuously wandered into his shop. He started giving it food and water, and the two of them became good pals.

I pointed to the guy and said, "Were you wondering where your fascination for motorcycles came from?" He motioned toward the lady sitting next to him, a woman I presumed was his wife. He said, "Nah,

I was actually asking on her behalf. She's nuts about gardening and has our entire back yard dug up at the moment. I was wondering if maybe she was a gopher in her past lifetime." I had to pull the microphone away from my mouth because I was laughing so loudly. His wife playfully elbowed him in the side. She was laughing as well, so I assumed the joke was well received.

One lady slightly changed the subject and asked if it's true that children select their own parents before coming into the world. This concept is inherently linked with reincarnation and past lives. It implies that a soul is conscious and capable of making decisions before entering the world. I've heard hundreds of cases where children actually remember selecting their own parents prior to being born

Another lady wanted to know if intuition tends to fade as a child grows older. "Sometimes it does and sometimes it doesn't," I told her. "A child can retain a good amount of intuition into adulthood if that ability is fostered or nurtured . . . or at the very least, not *squashed* by the parents." I explained that I've seen really sad instances where a conservative family downplays a child's reports of communicating with spirits, saying it's nothing more than an overactive imagination. *Or worse*, the parents believe psychic abilities to be wrong or evil, and make the child feel guilty for having intuitive hunches.

When outside influences or religious dogma suppresses children's natural intuition, they are less likely to share profound memories and feelings. This could include memories of selecting their parents before they were born, memories of being in Heaven between lifetimes, information about their past lifetimes, or the fact that our children hang out with our deceased relatives in Heaven before being born.

"That's why," I continued, "It's so important for us to be supportive of young children and actually *listen* to what they have to say. If you're looking for wisdom, have a conversation with someone under the age of ten. They are the kindest and most intuitive beings on the planet."

A lady in the front row raised her hand and asked if it's a mutual agreement. "If our kids choose us as their parents for this particular lifetime, do you think we chose them too? Like we have a spiritual contract with our kids or something?"

I nodded my head and agreed that I couldn't think of a more appropriate term. "Yes, it's a contract of sorts. That's a great way to put it."

She threw her hands in the air and snorted as she said, "Well, I don't know what in the heck me and my daughter were thinking when we agreed to this particular journey. She's sixteen and I'm telling you, we're like oil and water, me and her. I swear that girl is responsible for every gray hair on my head." The woman smiled and let out a chuckle as the audience joined in her laughter. Nearby audience members leaned over, whispering condolences to the lady and nodding their heads as though they fully understood her situation.

I took a sip of water before replying, "Oh yeah, you'll have moments like that. Believe me, we all do. Moments where you'll wonder why in the heck you signed up to live a lifetime filled with such turmoil. Filled with people who are hard to get along with. There's one in every family."

I shared with the audience that I wasn't quite at the point of butting heads with my daughter. Not yet, anyways. Her third birthday was on the horizon and I was fortunate that Sky still viewed me as one of her best friends. I'm aware that could change as she eventually morphs into a teenager.

In the days leading up to the past lives lecture, I was having dinner with Sky and Kenzie. Right in the middle of the meal, for no apparent reason, Sky leaned into me and placed her head on my shoulder as she said, "I'll keep you dad." She batted her long eyelashes as she smiled at me. If she had been older, I would have assumed she was buttering me up for something, like giving me a compliment right before asking for a curfew extension. As it was, the nice comment seemed genuine, and it completely melted my heart. Kenzie managed to capture the surreal moment on video as I choked back some happy tears and replied, "I'll keep you too, buddy. Forever and ever."

I later got to thinking and I wondered what she meant by 'keep me.' I assumed our arrangement as father and daughter was a permanent one, for the duration of this lifetime, anyway. I hadn't realized that we were still in the probationary phase. She made it sound like she had been leasing me this whole time and finally decided to commit to the purchase. I relayed this light hearted side-story to the audience, and a few of the members chimed in with funny things their own kids or grandchildren had said in recent months.

After a few minutes of entertaining comments from the audience, a lady in the third row raised her hand to ask, "Has Sky said anything odd or unusual lately?"

I nodded emphatically. "Yeah, actually she said something kind of strange the other day. I was showing her a picture of the Twin Towers because she wanted to know what New York City looked like. She pointed to the buildings and said 'airplanes.'"

The audience gasped audibly as I continued. "And it's so bizarre because I'm absolutely positive she knows the difference between an airplane and a building."

"And there were no airplanes visible in that picture?" asked a red headed gal from the back corner.

"Absolutely not," I responded.

"I bet Sky's so intuitive that she knows what happened on 9-11 just from seeing a picture of those buildings." The lady confidently crossed her arms and leaned back in her seat, as though she was satisfied and had solved the mystery.

Another lady from the other side of the room chimed in. "Maybe Sky was alive back in 2001 . . . you know, like a past life of hers. Maybe she saw the Twin Towers fall and still remembers it."

People whispered opinions to one another and shifted in their seats.

"Well, that's one theory," I said, as I took another sip of water.

"Is that possible?" asked someone else. "Can a person to come into their next lifetime so quickly? It's only been around fifteen years or so since 9-11."

The questions were coming so quickly that audience members were no longer raising their hands. I felt like a judge who'd just lost control of his courtroom.

I gripped my microphone tighter and continued, "If Sky was living another lifetime in 2001 and was born into this life in 2014, that would be a pretty quick turnaround in the grand scheme of things. And keep in mind that even *if* she was alive to witness 9-11, it doesn't mean she *lived* in New York City. I mean, the coverage of the event was worldwide, so perhaps she saw it on TV in her previous life or something." I shrugged my shoulders.

"How long does a soul typically spend in Heaven before coming back for another lifetime?" It was a young lady in the front row who was leaning forward in her seat. She eagerly took notes as if she were a news reporter and my lecture was a press conference.

"It kind of depends on the person," I said. "And the situation. And a whole host of other factors. But typically, a person will spend several decades in the afterlife before coming back again. There are exceptions though, and I've heard of cases where a person will come back for another lifetime as quickly as five or ten years later."

"And kids who come back rather quickly for another life . . . do they more easily remember their past lives?" she asked.

"Bingo!" I said as I pointed to the lady. Had this been a game show, I would have just awarded her the bonus money. "Yes, when a person reincarnates in quick succession, the individual might remember bits and pieces from past lives, *especially* the most recent past lifetime, because it wasn't very long ago. The most recent ones are easier to recall than ancient past lives."

The lady stopped taking notes and leaned back into her chair. She twiddled her pen and scrunched her nose as she asked, "Would trauma from a past lifetime account for night terrors? My son has them all the time. The nightmares are so vivid he wakes up screaming."

I admitted this is a common occurrence for kids who come back rather quickly. Not much time has gone by since their last lifetime, so they're able to recall unpleasant details from the past, much like a memory.

The good news is that night terrors generally fade as children grow older. Once a child gets more settled into his or her current life, echoes from the past seem to drop off a bit as they're replaced with memories from *this* lifetime.

I paused for a second to take another sip of water, and informed the audience I would field one more question about children and past lives before I moved into the subject of soul groups. A gentleman with white hair raised his hand. "So what age do most children have these night terrors? What age do they seem to be most aware of their previous lifetimes?"

"Three or four," I said. "Give or take a few months, it always happens around three or four years old."

Chapter 64

The scream was blood curdling. I threw off the covers and dashed into Sky's bedroom, expecting the worst. Had she fallen out of bed? Was she bitten by a spider? Had she seen a ghost? I found her sitting up in bed, mumbling to herself and crying. She had a case of bed head and her thick, curly hair resembled a lion's mane. She was inconsolable and horribly disoriented. I sat down next to Sky as Kenzie spoke through the speaker of the baby monitor. "Is she okay? What's going on in there?"

"It happened again," I said back to her, knowing she could hear me through the device. "We're okay. I'll lay with her until she falls back asleep."

She was a couple months shy of three years old and had been having occasional night terrors for several months. I wondered what was causing the nightmares, but I thought back to my recent lecture and knew the answer. I snuggled her tightly and within a few minutes, Sky grew sleepy again. I brushed some strands of curly hair out of her eyes and kissed her on the forehead only to realize she was clammy. I knew getting out of bed too soon would cause her to wake up again, so I continued to lay there until she was sound asleep. She nestled into me, resting her head on my chest. I took a deep breath and felt a wave of contentment wash over me.

Her room was a bit stuffy, but the breeze from the portable fan felt nice. The sensation of fresh air circulating around me soothed my soul. The flame of a fire has the same effect on me, which is why I always have a lit candle at my office while giving psychic readings. I suppose all of us are connected to a couple elements of nature, be it earth, air, water, or fire. Kenzie's element has always been water. Sitting on a beach and watching the waves roll in is truly her idea of Heaven.

As for Sky, there was no doubt about it. Earth is her element. I didn't have to look any further than her bedroom dresser for proof. On display was a pile of rocks. Some big, some small, some smooth and others jagged. She'd been collecting them since she was old enough to walk. Sometimes she'd gather them from the trail behind our house, and other times she'd find them in parking lots or down by the pond. There were countless times Kenzie and I heard a god-awful clanking sound coming from our dryer, only to realize Sky left one of her rocks in her pants pocket.

She even had a habit of gifting them to other people. She'd grab a little stone or pebble from the garden and clench it tightly in her hands, insisting it's a special present for the person we were going to visit. Upon arriving at our destination, she'd present the rock to its recipient with pride, as though it were a hunk of gold she panned out of a stream in Alaska.

Looking at the rocks on her bedroom dresser made me smile. I assumed her collection would continue to grow, and I wasn't sure where we'd end up putting them all. Our garage already contained a half dozen boxes full of rocks, fossils, and dinosaur bones I inherited after Grandma Myers died. I wondered if our basement would someday look like Grandma Myers' basement – shelf after shelf of labeled rocks, artifacts, and treasures – all meticulously cataloged like the display cases of a museum.

It suddenly dawned on me that Sky might enjoy seeing *my* rock collection someday – the wooden treasure chest about the size of a shoe box that Grandma gave me on my tenth birthday. It contains family heirlooms in addition to some of the best rocks from Grandma's collection. There's also the red tackle box Grandma gave me that contains snowflake obsidian, petrified wood, fossilized sea shell, and gold pyrite. Sky was turning three in a couple months, and I intended on showing her these collections in hopes she'd finally be old enough to appreciate them.

Sky was now sound asleep with her head resting on my chest. I probably could have slid out of bed without waking her. Yet, I was too comfortable to move. I was enjoying the peaceful ambience in her room. With no cell phone, television, or external distractions to hold my brain captive, I allowed my mind to float around like a helium balloon in the wind.

I wondered what else Sky might enjoy from my assortment of Grandma Myers' treasures. I wondered if she would appreciate the coin collection – a cloth bag filled with assorted currency from all over the globe. There were coins from Panama, Mexico, Canada, Greece, and Spain. Some dated back to the 1700s.

Among the collection were plenty of Buffalo nickels, also known as Indian Head Nickels. They're five-cent pieces which were only created between 1913 and 1938. They were designed by a sculptor named James Earle Fraser and display a buffalo on one side and the profile of a Native American gentleman on the other. Grandma sometimes spoke to me of these buffalo nickels in my youth. She'd bring them out of the closet and we'd sift through them on her kitchen table while she puffed on a cigarette and drank her coffee. She never specifically said the buffalo nickels were her favorite, but I always suspected they were based on how she studied them. She handled them gingerly and marveled at their design. Perhaps she loved buffaloes. Or maybe she loved the coins so much on account of her fondness for Native American culture. Maybe it was both.

Either way, I knew Sky would appreciate the nickels. From the time she was two, she's claimed a buffalo is her favorite animal. I imagined it would blow her mind to see one on a coin. I could appreciate her love of 'tatankas.' In my youth, it was one of my favorite creatures as well. I recall a family vacation to the Teton Mountains in Wyoming. I purchased a little statue of a buffalo that was crafted out of the ash from Mount Saint Helens. The statue was on display in my bedroom throughout childhood. Nowadays, I presume my fondness for buffaloes stems back to the Native American past life with Kenzie. Surely buffaloes played an important role in terms of providing food, warmth, and spiritual significance for our tribe back then.

We'd often take Sky to the Lee G. Simmons Conservation Park and Wildlife Safari. It's a half-hour drive from Omaha. The park consists of a scenic drive that winds through grasslands and forests. It's enclosed and provides habitat for deer, elk, pelicans, cranes, buffaloes, and a few other animals. Every time we drove through the entry gate, Sky sounded like a broken record. "Can we see the buffaloes? Can we see the buffaloes now?"

Eventually, I decided it was time to leave Sky's bedroom and return to my own. I gave her one last kiss on her forehead and eased out of bed, careful not to wake her up. I hoped and prayed that she'd make it through the night without having any more night terrors. Once back in bed, I was sound asleep as soon as my head hit the pillow.

Chapter 65

As always, morning came too quickly. By 6:45, I was awoken by Sky crawling into bed with Kenzie and me. "It's good morning time, Dadda. Can you read me a story?" She grabbed a magazine from my night stand – a copy of *Time Life* that was titled *Greatest Mysteries Revealed: Unlocking History's Most Puzzling Events.*

I was hardly able to open my eyes. My voice was so scratchy it sounded like I had swallowed a cactus. I informed Sky that the magazine was for adults, that it wasn't made for kids. She insisted I was wrong on account of all the colorful pictures inside. *Fair enough.* I obliged, sifting through the pages and trying to find something kid appropriate. There were articles on reincarnation, the Great Pyramids, disappearing colonies, sea monsters, and the controversial prophet, Nostradamus.

It caused me to think of my youth and the time my parents debated on whether or not I should be allowed to watch a show about his prophecies. I thought back to times as a child when Grandma Myers would read me these very same stories of mysterious lands, unknown creatures, and historical enigmas. Grandma got me hooked when I was around eight or ten years old. As for Sky, she was still a couple months shy of three, and I doubted she could comprehend half the words I was reading.

Nevertheless, I pointed to pictures and explained the best I could. "That's King Tut. He lived in a country called Egypt a long time ago. And look, that's the lost city of Atlantis. Doesn't all the water look pretty?" She nodded her head as she snuggled in closer to me. I couldn't help but wonder if moments like these would end up being some of Sky's first memories. I thought back to the den at the Benson house when I'd curl up with a blanket near the metal register vent as Grandma read me stories from *Fate* magazine.

After a few minutes, Kenzie finally woke up and rolled over to face us. She claimed to have dreamt about baby buffaloes. I smirked, wondering if she'd been psychically eavesdropping on my thoughts last night.

"Good morning, Dad. Good morning, Sky. What are you two doing?"

"We looking at King Butt," Sky replied in her little munchkin voice.

"No, sweetheart, it's King Tut," I said through my laughter.

"Hey Dad," said Kenzie with a grimace on her face. "Do you think those articles might be a little too creepy for little kids?"

"Yeah . . . um . . . it's okay. As long as I skip over this part about human sacrifices at Mayan temples."

Kenzie scrunched her nose. "Okay. We'll save some of these stories for later," I said as I tossed the magazine onto my nightstand. Sky reached over me, searching for more reading material. She swiped a copy of my second published book, titled *Inspiration: A to Z*. She looked at the back cover and smiled as she saw my photo. "Dats you, Dadda!"

I squeezed her tighter. "That's right, buddy. And you know what, there are a couple stories about you in this one."

"You read it to me?" she asked with an upward inflection.

I looked over at Kenzie who was yawning. Zico hopped up next to her and buried himself under the covers as Kenzie said, "There's my big handsome wolf." His tail was sticking out of the covers and I could see it wagging from side to side.

I turned my attention back to Sky and said, "You know what sweetheart, I'll read this book to you. But let's wait a few more years, okay?"

She looked slightly dejected. "Okayyyy."

"You know what though?" The enthusiasm in my voice made her perk up a bit and she looked at me with a hopeful expression. "Maybe someday when you're older and can spell more words, we can write a book *together*. How's that sound?"

"Yeah," she squealed. "A book about animals!"

"Animals, huh? What kind of animals would we write about?"

"Um . . . newts and buffaloes. And rainbow tigers!"

"Rainbow tigers? Absolutely!"

Her eyes twinkled with delight, as though she was fully satisfied with her idea.

Kenzie was scratching Zico underneath the covers, and I asked her, "Whatcha think, Momma? Should we write a book about newts and tatankas and rainbow tigers?"

"Yes, but only if you include a chapter about Zico."

Our cat Darwin must have felt jealous because he suddenly jumped onto the bed, seemingly from out of nowhere. It always amazes me how he's so agile and stealthy for a big fella.

"And Dar Dar!" Sky shouted as she giggled uncontrollably.

"Okay, we'll add a chapter about Dar Dar too. We'll put him in the section with the rainbow tigers since they're both felines."

"No, not lions, *tigers!*" Sky whined.

"No, sweetheart, *all* cats are called felines . . . you know what, never mind . . . you'll learn that later on." I glanced over at Kenzie who covered her mouth with her own hand to block a laugh. She placed her other hand over her heart as if to convey the conversation had become all too precious.

By this point in time, Sky was already part of the family business, so co-writing a book with her wasn't much of a stretch. She was part of my marketing team. Sky accompanied Kenzie and me to holistic expos where she'd linger near my booth and wait for potential clients to approach. With her chocolate-stained hands, she'd grab a fist full of my business cards and hand them to the nearest bystander. "Here go. My Dadda has books."

Sky not only helped with my marketing department but also with the technology side of business. She did 'mic checks' for me prior to each event in Omaha. We'd arrive to the venue early in the afternoon to make sure everything was ready for the evening show. She'd grab the microphone and do a sound check by singing "Let It Go" from the Disney movie *Frozen*. She'd belt out the words and sing her heart out as her voice poured through the overhead speakers. I'd adjust the volume levels accordingly and give her a high five afterward.

In February of 2017, I was scheduled to conduct a psychic show in Fort Myers, Florida. It was Kenzie's idea, really. She was craving a little sunshine on the beach to get her through the cold and relentless Nebraska winter. I figured we'd combine business with pleasure. The three of us planned to enjoy the ocean for a few days after my show concluded. We figured we'd even head over to Disney World and let Sky meet all her favorite cartoon characters. Our bags were packed and our tickets were purchased. Unbeknownst to us, the Universe had other ideas. Kenzie received a phone call the evening before our departure. Her Grandpa had died of a heart attack.

We scrambled to cancel our travel plans, and were thankful we'd heard the news *before* we left town. The next day was surreal. We awaited news on funeral arrangements and tried to distract ourselves from the sadness. Thankfully, Mother Nature provided us with an unseasonably warm and beautiful day by February's standards. We only required light jackets to go outside. Kenzie decided she'd cheer herself up by sitting in the driveway and soaking up the sunshine.

Kenzie found the boxes of my grandma's rocks and fossils in the garage. She set them in the driveway and began to sift through the contents. It was an *actual* treasure hunt, as she didn't know what she would find next. Sandstone, dolomite, obsidian, hunks of pumice, and sparkling geodes. She found fragments of teeth and what appeared to be jaw bones. We speculated as to whether it was from an elk, bison, or perhaps even a dinosaur.

A day or two later we called the University of Nebraska at Lincoln and spoke with a paleontologist. We hoped he could help us identify some bones and fossils from Grandma's box of goodies. We strapped Sky in her car seat and drove to the campus. The February weather had returned in full force, and we scurried into the building to get out of the bitter cold. The rocks and fossils were still intact but the cardboard box itself had seen better days. The contents nearly slipped through my grasp. It was like trying to hold a runny pile of gelatin. We scampered into the building and after getting lost in the maze of campus hallways, we eventually found the appropriate department. The paleontologist rummaged through our treasures, identifying what he could, and speculating about some rare pieces that left him stumped.

Not surprisingly, Sky was in her element at the paleontologist's office. She pressed her face against the glass cases to get a better look at the bones on display. She saw a skull of a saber tooth tiger. "That's not a rainbow tiger, Sky," I said in a serious tone. "That's really, *really* old."

We learned from the professor that we had in our possession several jawbone pieces from a Titanothere, more commonly called a Brontothere. It was a large, hoofed mammal that went extinct around twenty-eight million years ago during the Oligocene Epoch. It was essentially a weird-looking second cousin of modern-day rhinos. The professor said the teeth and bones were only as valuable as the tattered box they came in. To us though, they were priceless.

"Dat used to be in the dirt!" Sky interjected as she pointed towards some bone fragments.

"You're right, sweetheart, it was probably in the dirt a long time ago," I assured her.

We thanked the professor for his time and shook his hand. I attempted to pick up the box of fossils, but by this time it was essentially a camping tent that had lost its poles. I cradled the dusty bundle of cardboard and held it close to my chest as Titanothere teeth and hunks of gypsum stabbed me in the sternum. I walked quickly and awkwardly out of the room, trying not to spill Grandma's fossil collection all over the university.

The paleontologist suggested we cross the campus and check out Morrill Hall, more commonly referred to as Elephant Hall. It's home to the world's largest mastodon skeleton, which was a creature similar to a Woolly mammoth. We'd been there plenty of times before. The building is cold and sterile, providing hallway after silent hallway of display cases. Inside are stuffed badgers, trilobite fossils, plesiosaur skeletons, Native American artifacts, and rocks that glow under a black light. This time would be different because we had a particular mission in mind.

The professor informed us that inside the museum was an intact skeleton of a Titanothere should we want to see a fully assembled specimen. I have to admit it's not everyone's idea of an exciting day, but it was a neat feeling to see the creature's entire skeleton inside the official display case while simultaneously holding its twenty-eight-million-year-old bones in my hand. It made me feel like a real-life Indiana Jones.

"Where do you think your grandma found these Titanothere fragments?" Kenzie asked.

"No idea. But I bet her and Boompa wandered miles away from civilization to find these pieces. Maybe they came from the Badlands or some canyon in Utah. At any rate, it was probably a red shirt day."

"Red shirt day?" she asked.

"Yeah, when Grandma and Boompa went hunting for fossils, she usually wore a red shirt. You know, just in case they couldn't find their way back to the car. She figured a red shirt would allow the search and rescue team to spot her more easily from a helicopter."

"I wish I could have met your grandma." Kenzie placed her arm around my waist and leaned her head onto my shoulder. "Can I tell you something, babe?" Her tone was warm and sincere.

"Sure. You can tell me anything."

"I mean this from the bottom of my heart . . . you smell like old dust."

I playfully nudged her away from me and began laughing. "Well, what do you expect? I've been elbow deep in Titanothere teeth all day long."

Sky slid between us, grabbing us each by a hand. We lifted her into the air and propelled her forward like she was on a swing set. She giggled with delight. We perused through other sections of the museum and came upon a hallway lined with Native American artifacts. Looking at the moccasins, drums, and official Sioux regalia made me feel like I'd walked into a déjà vu emporium. I looked at an arrow and instinctively touched my stomach, remembering how one had killed me in a past lifetime. I thought back to the night at the hockey game when Mom rushed me to the hospital with mysterious stomach pains.

I thought of Henry and Sarah Cloud, wondering what they'd been up to since our adventures on the Midwestern plains nearly two centuries ago. *Would they come back for another lifetime after fulfilling their duties as our guardian angels? Would they incarnate together, at the same place and time? If so, would their souls recognize each other here on Earth? Would they fall in love all over again?*

My mind was pondering such notions, for I had grown quite sentimental throughout the day. I was missing Grandma terribly. I suppose holding her old treasures in my hand made me feel closer to her in a tangible way I hadn't felt for a very long time.

As we strolled through Morrill Hall, Kenzie asked questions about Grandma. She wanted to hear more about the adventures her and Boompa took. She wanted to know what Grandma's personality was like, and what she aspired to be in life. I told Kenzie that, once upon a time, Grandma wanted to be an author. Yet, as is often the case, she got caught up in life's current. She was busy raising kids, paying bills, and operating on low energy much of the time. She ended up working for Northwestern Bell telephone company until she retired in 1988. She continued journaling in her diaries throughout her life, and I can only hope that sufficed in terms of satisfying her passion for writing.

For many decades, she and Boompa had season tickets to Nebraska Cornhusker football games. The stadium was merely a block away from Morrill Hall. On crisp fall afternoons, they'd spend the morning walking through the very same museum Kenzie and I were in, passing some time before the afternoon football game. *How many times had Grandma looked at these very same taxidermy badgers and plesiosaur skeletons? How many times had she stood in this Native America section, looking at these very same bows and arrows?*

As we passed by the planetarium, I told Kenzie how my grandma had taken a college course on anthropology. She wasn't working towards a degree, per se. She must have been in her sixties by the time she signed up for the class. She was hopelessly curious, and loved to learn about cultures from the past. Grandma was a true student of life. She was brave enough to explore new concepts, and humble enough to realize there was much more to learn.

"I think your grandma and me would have been good friends," said Kenzie. I silently nodded.

I hadn't received a sign from Grandma in quite some time, and I couldn't help but wonder if she and Boompa would be tickled to know we were inside Morrill Hall. Certainly, they'd be happy to know we were taking such an interest in their dusty old treasures.

The calm ambience was broken when Sky suddenly cried out, "I wanna see the tatankas, Momma!" She ran ahead, dashing down the hallway as quickly as her little legs would carry her. She was going so fast that she tripped over her feet and crashed to the floor. She sprang to her feet and turned the corner, weaving through a group of children who were looking at other exhibits. "I've got her," Kenzie said over her shoulder as she jogged off.

A few moments later, Kenzie rounded the corner. She was holding Sky's hands. Kenzie looked relieved to have found her. Sky looked defeated. Her sense of adventure had prevented her from realizing the dangers of getting lost in such an enormous museum. Nevertheless, we had to admire her enthusiasm.

Kenzie struggled to catch her breath. "Good thing she was wearing that bright red shirt, otherwise I might not have found her."

Chapter 66

A s the city of Lincoln faded in my rear-view mirror, I couldn't help but notice the sunset behind us. It was one for the ages. Goldenrod blended with vermilion, accompanied by brushstrokes of scarlet and crimson, all mixed together on Mother Nature's canvas. It stretched across the western sky from north to south. It was the kind that Grandma would have loved. No camera or lens could do it justice.

Eventually, we were driving down our street and nearing our house. Through her window, Sky spotted the moon up above. She always has a habit of looking up. I suppose she gets that from me. We have a standing agreement that whenever we see the moon in the sky, we howl like wolves. I don't remember how it got started, but we're prone to being silly and it's become a tradition. I suppose we just need to let out our inner werewolf from time to time. Like a wolf pup, she cried out, "Ahhhh Oooooo! Ahhhh Ooooo!"

I cried out with my papa wolf howl. "OWWWWWWW!"

Kenzie just smiled. "My goodness, I'm in a car full of wild animals."

After unloading the boxes of Grandma's fossils back into the garage, I walked into the driveway with Sky. The moon was still visible overhead, so we studied it for a few moments and checked out some stars as well. Sky asked for me to hold her, so I scooped her up into my arms. I saw a particularly bright one in the sky, and pointed to it, saying, "Hey Sky, check out that one. That must be the brightest star in the whole sky!"

"Where?" she said, as her eyes darted back and forth.

"Over there, can't you see it?" I placed my forearm and index finger along her line of sight, and she focused her vision like she was staring through a telescope. "There, do you see it? Look how bright that star is!"

She scrunched her nose and confidently replied, "Dat's not a star, Dadda. Dat's a *planet!*" I cocked my head and squinted my eyes to get a better look, wondering if I could be wrong. I also couldn't help but wonder why Sky would attempt to correct me on a subject she knew so little about.

Kenzie finally walked out of the garage and joined us to stand in the driveway. With arms crossed, she studied the sky. After a few seconds, Kenzie stated, "She's right, babe. That's not a star. That's the planet *Venus!*"

"Nuh uh. Are you *sure?*"

She pulled her cell phone from her pocket. She opened up an astronomy application she had previously downloaded. It allows a person to point the phone towards the sky and the software detects which heavenly bodies are stars, planets, satellites, and constellations.

Kenzie chuckled to herself, "Yup . . . this says it's Venus. Sorry, Dad, but Sky was right." I chuckled to myself as I put my hands on my hips. I've spent my whole life watching shows about astronomy and learning about outer space. Failing to spot the difference between a star and a planet was the equivalent of an NBA player missing a layup. I'd been outdone by my young daughter.

"How in the heck would Sky know that?" I asked Kenzie, completely bewildered.

She exhaled and said, "I guess she's one smart cookie."

Sky perked up and asked, "Can I have a cookie for a bedtime snack, Dadda?"

I caved in, and agreed a cookie sounded wonderful. "Can I have one with you?" I asked. Sky wrapped her arms around me and buried her cold, little nose into my neck for warmth.

Kenzie took one last glance at Venus. "Come on inside my werewolves, it's getting cold out here."

Zico was there to greet us at the door. He wagged his tail and presented us with a rainbow-colored stuffed teddy bear he was holding in his mouth. Sky had won it playing a claw machine game a few weeks prior. We ate our cookies and made our way to the stairs. Sky climbed up to the third step and jumped onto my back, wrapping her arms tightly around my neck. "Giddy up, Tatanka!"

We brushed Sky's teeth and put on her pink footie pajamas dotted with pictures of hearts, stars, and peace signs. We climbed into bed and read her a book. We gave her 'love sandwiches' with extra pickles and cheese.

Kenzie leaned over and turned off the lamp. Sky's ceiling was suddenly illuminated by the glow-in-the-dark stars and planets we'd placed up there a few weeks prior. There was a cluster of stars directly above Sky's bed that resembled the big dipper. The arrangement was a happy accident since I didn't realize I was placing them in such a pattern when I initially stuck them up there. Sky raised her arms and reached towards the ceiling, hoping that if she stretched far enough, she could touch the heavens. It was endearing and whimsical, like a hopeful kid with a glass jar, standing in a dark field of fireflies in late July. I wish we could all stay kids forever, viewing the world as Sky was seeing it – as though everything is magical.

"There's me and you and Momma," Sky said as she pointed over to the corner of her bedroom ceiling. Three stars were nestled together so closely they were nearly touching. Weeks earlier while I placed the stars on her ceiling, Sky insisted that I put three of them next to each other as a representation of our family. She pointed to other parts of the ceiling. "And that one's for Zico, and that one's for Darwin." Kenzie looked at me and winked.

My mind wandered. I looked back to the ceiling and wondered which stars were for Henry and Sarah? What about my dad? Which star was for Grandma?

I reached back and placed my hands behind my head, interlacing my fingers and getting more comfortable. This indoor star gazing session was suddenly making me feel rather nostalgic. I thought back to when I'd proposed to Kenzie inside the Kansas City planetarium after naming a star for her. I recalled seeing swirling galaxies and nebulas through my bedroom ceiling on the night of my spiritual vision. I remembered lying on blankets at Flying Hawks Ranch with Grandma, looking at meteor showers and trying to keep my tired eyes open. It seemed like everything in my life, both past and present, was tied to the sky.

"Hey, look at that one," Kenzie said to me in a playful tone while pointing to a particular spot on the ceiling. "Is that a star or a planet?" I played along and glared at her with a stark frown. She flashed a cheesy smile at me to express she was merely joking.

I leaned in and gave Sky a kiss on her head of curly hair. "At least this little smarty pants knows her stars from her planets," I said. Sky was still reaching upwards, using her finger to trace make-believe constellations. She looked content, curious, and wise beyond her years. She was overflowing with wonder. I closed my eyes tightly and said a silent prayer, asking that she always view the world in this way. I asked she not be jaded by life, that she retains the curious sparkle in her eyes, that she grows into the type of person who finds meaning and answers in the sky . . . up where clouds are shaped like unicorns, and there's a moon to howl at, and golden sunsets that take your breath away, and shooting stars that light up the night like fireworks on the Fourth of July.

I opened my eyes and looked at Sky again. Her gaze was now fixated on a shooting star that was anchored just south of the big dipper. If she thought an artificial shooting star on her ceiling was fascinating, I knew it would blow her mind to see the real deal – hunks of rock streaking across the sky at tens of thousands of miles per hour, leaving behind a trail of fire and ash.

When she's old enough to comprehend astronomy, I'll explain to Sky that shooting stars (meteors) usually come from the asteroid belt located between Mars and Jupiter. They often take a very long time to reach Earth. By the time they flash across our sky and burn up, we're merely seeing the last second or two of a journey that may have lasted millions of years.

We humans are not much different from falling stars. Through the never-ending cycle of reincarnation, we fall into each other's lives as moms and dads, sons and daughters. Yet, when we look at one another, all we're really seeing is the brightest, most recent version of a person. It's the flashpoint, the glowing streak, the final product of a person whose journey may have started eons ago, in places unknown.

My daughter's eyes grew heavy, and as her eyelids shut, I wondered where her journey originated. Like a shooting star, I wondered where she'd come from. *How long had she been on a trajectory toward Kenzie and me? What adventures had she experienced along the way?* One could only imagine. I simply hoped our journey together was far from over, and was overcome with gratitude that she came into my atmosphere this time around. I looked to her ceiling and found my star, which was nestled near two others. I made a wish that we'd take more journeys together in future incarnations.

In hindsight, I wonder what Henry and Sarah were thinking as they watched us say goodnight to our daughter that evening. They must have been grinning, for they knew a simple truth that we humans often forget. We tend to be so focused on the future that we forget about the past. Yet, moving forward can lead us back to things we've left behind. For example, to circumnavigate the globe, one must travel in the same direction. It feels like a straight line. However, when we travel long enough and far enough, we come full circle, arriving back at the very beginning – a familiar place where the journey began.

Chapter 67

It was exactly one week before Sky's third birthday. I'd taken Kenzie and Sky out to dinner at a local Mexican restaurant that evening. Our waiter, David, just so happened to be a client of mine. He was a nice gentleman originally from Venezuela. With the help of a translator, I'd conducted a medium session for him and his family the previous year, relaying messages from David's brother who'd tragically passed away. It was healing and therapeutic for the whole family.

What I remember most is what David's deceased brother told me at the end of their session. He insisted that I not charge the family my usual rates, and instructed me to cut them a significant discount. He wanted the whole family to treat themselves to dinner at a restaurant with the spare money. I relayed the message to the family and heeded the instructions. They were grateful for the discount, and I was thankful for having the chance to meet such a wonderful family.

As we finished our enchiladas, David said he wanted to 'comp' our dinner and insisted it would be on the house. He said it was the least he could do since I previously gave *his* family a discount. I said we were grateful for the offer, but attempted to politely decline. He wouldn't take no for an answer. We chatted for a few moments and he explained how much the medium session meant to his family the previous year. He said it gave them the peace and closure they'd been looking for since his brother's tragedy. He shook our hands. I squeezed tighter than usual and thanked him for the feedback. There are times when my work gets emotionally taxing, so follow-up like that really keeps me going.

On the drive home, Kenzie and I discussed how fortunate we were to know so many kind people. It often seemed like we were bumping into familiar faces at every turn. Nearly every person in our social circle was a direct result of my work. They were people we'd met on ghost investigations, married couples who attended the monthly metaphysical meetings, people who started as my clients and eventually befriended Kenzie and me. We were godparents to their children. We were at their weddings, birthday parties, and back yard barbecues. They all viewed Sky as their honorary niece. We couldn't ask for anything more.

We arrived home from the Mexican restaurant feeling incredibly blessed. Our bellies were full and so were our hearts. Our server, David, had reminded me why I got into this line of work – to offer people hope, closure, and peace of mind; to give them proof of an afterlife, and assurance their loved ones in Heaven are closer than they think.

These are the things that ran through my mind as I sat on the front steps that fine evening. The temperature was perfect. The sky was gorgeous. The air was calm. Sky was playing in the front yard, looking for new rocks and picking some dandelions. Kenzie said she'd join us momentarily, and went inside to put some leftovers in the refrigerator.

Sky stopped what she was doing. She walked up the stairs, joining me on the front porch. She eyeballed my grandma's rocks and fossils that lined the perimeter. Sky was unusually calm and quiet. She shuffled around the porch in circles and it seemed like she was bored. She looked like she was searching for something to explore. Spotting one of the pieces of petrified wood, Sky studied it for a moment or two. She gently placed her foot on top of it, but before she had a chance to push her weight down, I said, "Please be careful of that, Sky. It's very old." Acknowledging my request, she retracted her foot.

"Do you know where that came from, Sky? That belonged to my grandma . . . Grandma Myers." She remained silent and continued to stare at the petrified wood. I suddenly felt a light breeze that blew through her curly strands of brown hair.

"When I was a little kid," I continued, "Grandma had these same rocks on her porch. But now I have them." I lowered my head and leaned in to see her face better. I wondered what Sky was thinking. *Why was she so interested? Why was she so serious?*

Pointing at the petrified wood, she looked at me and remarked, "I gave you that. And I gave you rocks for your birthday."

Chapter 68

Time froze. It seemed like all the background noise of the neighborhood disappeared. My blood ran cold and my legs suddenly felt shaky. Sky stood there on the porch, looking up at me with her big brown eyes. She awaited my response to her comment. I opened my mouth to speak but nothing came out. I bent down to eye level with her and I gently took her hand in mine. With misty eyes and a trembling voice, I softly said to her, "Sweetheart, you didn't . . . um . . . you didn't give me any rocks for my birthday." She blinked a few times. Her expression didn't change. "And this rock right here," I said, pointing to the petrified wood, "It was never yours. It belonged to your Great Grandma Myers."

The sunset illuminated her face. Tiny shimmers glistened from the lucky fleck in her left eye. Sky grinned, looking so pure and innocent. She then lowered her head and stared at her own shoes. She was being coy, like she had a secret to share. Her eyes rose again to meet mine, and she softly said, "*I'm* Great Grandma Myers."

I stood to my feet and stepped back, covering my mouth with my hand. I felt like the wind had just been knocked out of me. I blinked rapidly to block a tear from falling out. My heart was pounding faster and my cheeks felt flushed. I tried not to overreact as I didn't want Sky to think she'd done anything wrong. Thankfully, her focus was back on the rocks and not on me. It was nearly impossible to speak with a lump in my throat, but I mumbled to Sky that I would be right back.

I went inside and saw Kenzie standing in the kitchen. I tried to say something but only managed to stand there motionless. "Where's Sky? Is everything okay?" I took my hat off and ran my fingers through my hair.

Stumbling over my words, I explained what had just transpired. I asked Kenzie if she could go outside with Sky since I needed a moment to gather my thoughts.

"You should call and tell your mom," Kenzie insisted.

"I will. But would you mind taking Sky for a walk while I do that? I don't want her to hear the conversation while I'm talking to my mom."

When my mom answered the phone, she initially thought something was wrong because I was so shaken up. I was struggling to articulate myself, but I assured her everyone was okay.

"Grandma couldn't be back so quickly . . . *could she?*" My mom asked.

"It's not impossible but it's definitely rare. It's also unusual for a person to incarnate back into the same family tree. It's the exception rather than the norm."

My mom and I were perplexed. Our minds ran wild with possibilities. She agreed it was wise for Kenzie and me not to make a big deal out of it. If Sky were to notice we got excited or acted differently when she mentioned Grandma Myers, she may start doing it just to get a rise out of us.

My mom insisted I call and tell Aunt Terry. She's Grandma Myers' only daughter. Terry said she remembered the red tackle box of collectibles, and also recalled the treasure chest of family heirlooms and rocks Grandma gifted me on my tenth birthday. "And you've still got the large rocks and petrified wood near your porch, right? The ones you took from the Benson house?"

"Yeah, Sky was looking at the petrified wood when she made the comment about Grandma."

"You should call and tell your sister," Terry insisted. "See what she thinks."

When I did, Elizabeth was mystified just like the rest of us. We all agreed it wasn't definitive *proof* that Sky was Grandma reincarnated, but it sure was interesting. We all made an unspoken pact not to plant any ideas or suggestions in Sky's head. Meanwhile, we'd wait and see if she offered any more comments or clues on the matter. We continued to treat her the same as we always had. Yet, from that point forward, I couldn't help but look at Sky with a newfound curiosity. Deep in my heart and soul, I wanted to know for sure. *Had I known her before? Could it really be her?*

Chapter 69

That night, Sky's bedtime routine was the same as any other night. She pulled a few items from her pockets that she had squirreled away throughout the evening. Among the collection were three blades of grass, two nickels, and a pebble from the yard. She placed her new treasures next to the rocks on her dresser. We got her pajamas on her, read her books, told her a story about purple buffaloes, and counted the stars on her ceiling. After kissing her goodnight, I walked down to the basement and perused the storage shelves for a few items that were sure to give me a sense of déjà vu.

The red tackle box contained individual compartments lined with cushioned linen, creating a snug little space for each rock to rest. Each compartment was labeled with a little tag identifying the type of rock. I lifted each one out of its compartment and touched them carefully, as though I was a museum curator handling jewelry worn by Cleopatra.

I closed the tackle box and turned my attention to the wooden treasure chest. It wasn't much larger than a shoebox, but housed priceless heirlooms, including the wooden locket that my great-great-great-grandfather carved under a tree between battles in the Civil War. The treasure chest also included buffalo head nickels, some gorgeous rocks, black and white family photos, and a hat that Boompa wore for much of his life – an old-fashioned flat cap, just like the ones I now wear.

Equally priceless was the neatly folded handwritten letter from Grandma Myers, explaining the history and meaning of each artifact. In her beautiful, cursive handwriting, she stated that each heirloom belonged to an important member of our family tree, one from each generation, spanning as far back as she could trace our lineage. I delicately ran my index finger over the handwriting, marveling at the thought she must have put into this collection of goodies.

I stumbled upon a photo album I'd nearly forgotten about. Inside were pictures of the Myers side of the family, including Grandma, Boompa, my dad, Uncle Tim, even some of my great grandparents and distant relatives whose names were vaguely familiar. Some photos were in black and white, showing folks in pinstriped overalls. They didn't smile in pictures back then. Times must have been tough. Grandma had eliminated the guess work by labeling most of the photos by year, location, and who was in the photo.

Flipping each page of the album was like fast-forwarding through the decades. I came across a picture of my dad fishing in the ocean off the side of a boat. He was young and handsome, wearing a white t-shirt and sporting a nifty haircut.

I stumbled upon the 1970s and saw photos of Grandma and Boompa. He was wearing suspenders and she was in a red shirt. Most pictures showed their vehicle in the background, parked on the beach. Or in the foothills of some mountain. Or in a prairie field. They were young, thin, and full of life.

I swam in a pool of nostalgia looking at the old photos. Kenzie was always asking me questions about Grandma, so I knew she'd appreciate some of the pictures. I found her folding a pile of laundry on the living room couch, so I sat down next to her.

"Whatcha got there?"

"It's an old photo album I found in storage," I said. "It's a bunch of pictures from the Myers side of the family. I got it from Grandma Myers a long time ago. Some of them are black and white. And others are more recent, like from the 70s and 80s."

Kenzie leaned in to study the pictures. She smiled as she delicately turned the pages, asking questions about each picture. One showed a man and woman jointly holding a catfish that dangled from a fishing line. The gargantuan fish looked like it must have weighed sixty pounds. Kenzie pointed and asked who those people were.

"It's Grandma's sister, Vilma, and Vilma's husband, Jim. They've always loved fishing. One summer when I was a kid, we visited them in Missouri. Vilma took us out to a special fishing hole and we caught eighty-six bluegills on a single day. Eighty-six!"

"Whoa! Are you serious?" Kenzie reeled.

"It was so crazy that I've never forgotten the exact number of bluegills we caught."

"You can remember *that*, but you couldn't remember to take the trash out yesterday?" she playfully joked.

"My long-term memory is better than my short-term," I reminded her. "Anyways, Grandma, Vilma, and my dad cleaned and cooked the bluegills for dinner that night. Me 'n Dave just had Grandma's potato salad though, because after watching them filet the bluegills, we lost our appetite for fish."

"Is Vilma your grandma's older sister or younger sister?" Kenzie wondered.

"Um . . . younger. Why?"

Kenzie's eyes grew wide. "Oh my God . . ." she whispered.

"What?" I asked, unable to follow Kenzie's train of thought.

"Do you remember what Sky said the other day . . . when you two were in the garage?"

"Huh?" I shook my head and stared at the floor, trying to recall what she was talking about. Just then, it came to me. "Oh. My. God." Goosebumps formed on my arms. I looked back at Kenzie. Her eyebrows were raised and she was speechless.

Chapter 70

A few days prior, I'd been playing with Sky in the front yard. We were blowing bubbles and drawing rainbows on the driveway with sidewalk chalk. Sky wandered into the garage to take a sip of water. Suddenly, she became rather quiet and serious, as if something was wrong. I asked if she was okay. She responded, "Dadda, I miss my younger sister."

We hadn't been talking about brothers, sisters, siblings, or anything related to the topic. It caught me off guard and seemed out of context. I bent down and gently informed her that she didn't have any sisters. "Do you mean you'd *like* a sister?" Sky remained silent and stoic. "You want Mom and I to have another kid so you have a sibling to play with?" My heart ached. I felt guilty that she was an only child.

"No," she finally responded. "I just . . . I just miss my little sister." She scrunched her nose as she wiped a bead of sweat from her eyebrow.

I was confused and didn't know how to respond. "I'm sorry you feel that way, sweetheart." Just as I was searching for something more articulate to say, Sky lost interest in the conversation. She scampered into the driveway, grabbing her bubble wand and spinning in circles until bubbles floated all around her.

At the time, I found Sky's comment odd, but with no further context, I merely told Kenzie what had happened and then quickly forgot about it. Given the recent turn of events, we were now viewing Sky's comment in a different light. *Could she be referring to Vilma?*

Chapter 71

May 19th was on a Friday that year. She was now three years old. Kenzie and I took Sky to dinner at a local restaurant which doubled as an arcade. She wore a pointy birthday party hat with the number three on it. She ate corndogs for dinner that night, staining her outfit with ketchup and mustard. Once our food was gone, Sky took me by the hand and we headed toward the arcade games. We came across a hunting game where the objective is to shoot big game animals on a safari. She furrowed her brow in disgust, insisting she didn't want to play that game because it wasn't nice to animals. "I want to be a betwanawian," she reminded me. Later, we won a stuffed animal in a claw machine game and took it home for Zico to gnaw on.

We arrived home exhausted from having so much fun. Sky climbed to the third step of the staircase and jumped onto my back for her nightly tatanka ride. We went through the bedtime routine, reading her a few books as Zico lay on the floor chewing on his new stuffed animal. Kenzie and I gave Sky some goodnight kisses. She insisted on wearing her birthday hat to bed. The rubber band chin strap had already broken off, so we let her, figuring there was no safety risk.

I made my way downstairs and let Zico outside to do his business. I stood there on the front porch with folded arms, breathing in the fresh air of late spring. Compared to the noise and flashing lights of the arcade, the quiet ambience of the neighborhood was refreshing. I made a mental checklist of things that were needed for Sky's upcoming birthday party that weekend. Between the cake, the decorations, the presents, and the food, it was a lot to keep track of.

I looked around the porch and front garden, pausing to notice the petrified wood and other assorted hunks of rock that once belonged to my grandma. I wondered how many years they rested outside Grandma's house in Benson. *Where did she get them? How old were they?* Part of me wondered if my daughter might know the answer . . . somewhere in her subconscious, in the deposit box of her soul, where memories of Heaven and past lives are kept.

Chapter 72

It was a relatively small party, attended only by family members. My mom was there, along with Aunt Terry and Terry's husband, Al. My brother and sister were present along with their spouses and kids. Sky loves seeing her cousins. With two older cousins and two younger cousins, she's basically the estrogen inside a testosterone sandwich.

She tore into her presents. My mom gave her some adorable new outfits. Someone else gave her a magnifying glass and bug catching container. It came with water dishes, jungle gyms, and bunk beds for the little critters she'd inevitably find. We joked that it must be a grasshopper's equivalent to the high roller's suite at a Vegas hotel. Kenzie and I gave her an art set. She's loved creative activities since she was old enough to hold a crayon. After opening all the other presents, Sky was given a plain and inconspicuous present from my Aunt Terry.

It was the very last present of the day. Terry instructed her to open it very carefully. Sky followed the directions and gently peeled away the wrapping paper. It was a small, white book, no larger than a cell phone. We realized it was an encyclopedia of rocks, crystals, and gemstones. On the front cover was an assortment of colorful rocks, including amethyst, rose quartz, jade, pyrite, and a few geodes. Inside was an alphabetized catalog of each rock, complete with a thorough description of its composition.

Everyone was silent, not quite sure why such a gift would be given to a three-year-old. *How could such a simple present stack up against bug catchers and hula hoops?* Sure, Sky liked collecting rocks. Everyone knew that. Still, I felt anxious, assuming I'd be offering Terry an apology once Sky tossed it to the side and lacked interest. To everyone's surprise, Sky was fascinated with the booklet. She meticulously looked at every inch of it. She turned the pages carefully, studying the material as if there were a test afterwards.

In a sweet and soft voice, Terry explained, "This used to belong to Andy's grandma, Frances." Still staring at the book, Sky's expression was serious and inquisitive. It seemed like she was trying to remember something. "But ever since Grandma passed away," Terry continued, "I've had this book about rocks in my dresser drawer. And I thought to myself, 'You know what, I bet Sky would just *love* to have it.'"

She slowly looked up from the book and locked eyes with Terry. Sky didn't say a word. She merely blinked her long eyelashes as she stared at Terry for ten whole seconds. The room was silent. Perhaps she didn't have the vocabulary to articulate what she was feeling, but her expression was a mix of nostalgia and gratitude. The edges of her ruby red lips curled upward slightly as she gave a little smile. "What do you say, Sky?" I prompted.

"Dank you," she said as she thumbed through more pages.

"Terry, that was *so* thoughtful of you," said my mom.

I placed my hand over my heart and looked at Kenzie. "Oh my God," I silently mouthed. The moment was precious. Terry offered me a wink from across the room. Her gift was clearly a hit. I was curious to know if Sky had held that exact book in her hands a few decades prior. *Could the book still contain Grandma's fingerprints?* From a DNA standpoint, it would be the equivalent of a person touching genetic material of their own body from a past life. It was a mind-blowing notion.

A few minutes passed, and the kids wanted to get up and play some more. Sky softly placed the mini rock encyclopedia on the floor and gave it a gentle pat or two, as if it were a family pet she was instructing to *sit* and *stay*. Fearing it could get lost or thrown away with the wrapping paper, I grabbed the gift and placed it in a safe location.

Kenzie and I agreed that we were running low on energy, so we decided to brew a fresh pot of coffee. Sky and her cousins chased each other around the house as we stood waiting by the coffee maker. She leaned her head on my shoulder as we stood there silently, taking a moment to ourselves. I kept thinking about the rock book and about Grandma. *Would we ever know for sure? Would there be more clues along the way?*

The coffee finished brewing. I poured some for Kenzie into a mug we bought in Portland on our honeymoon. I added in some milk but accidentally poured in too much, turning her coffee from dark brown to beige. It reminded me of how Grandma used to drink it. I apologized and offered to get Kenzie a new cup. Just then, Sky came galloping into the kitchen and demanded a taste. I dipped my finger in, and placed a drop or two on her tongue. "Mmmmmm, dats good."

Soon it was time for cake. We placed three candles on top and sang the happy birthday song. The kitchen was crowded, but thankfully spirits don't take up much space. I knew a few others were singing along with us, even if we couldn't see them. Surely, my dad was there. Henry and Sarah wouldn't have missed the occasion. Boompa had stopped by, perhaps giving her an extra gust of wind as Sky blew out the candles. As for Grandma, I hadn't felt her presence in any tangible way for quite some time. I was beginning to think I knew why.

Chapter 73

Inside my bedroom closet, I was searching for something to wear. I grabbed the dark blue t-shirt which displayed a caffeine molecule. As I pulled the shirt over my head, I heard hangers clinking together next to me. Looking down, I realized someone had snuck in there with me. Sky ran her hand along a row of metal hangers, causing them to play a little melody.

Her expression told me she was bored. "What you doin' Dadda?"

"We're getting ready to go for a drive, sweetheart."

"Where we goin'?" she asked, as she eyeballed the closet for something interesting to play with.

"Not sure. Let's just drive and see where we end up. Should we bring Zico in case we end up playing at a park?"

Sky didn't answer me. She'd found something that looked interesting. In the corner of the closet was a rubber storage bin. On top rested an old photo I'd been looking at days earlier when I was feeling nostalgic. The picture was taken on Easter morning in 1989. It showed Grandma along with my brother, sister, and me. The four of us were on the porch of the Benson house. My brother, sister, and I held new guitars, which were Easter gifts from Grandma and Boompa. It must have been a sunny morning because I was squinting my eyes from the overhead light. The photo showed us all wearing funny silver headbands, making us look like Martian aliens with antennae.

Sky picked up the photo, trying to get a better look. I gently pulled it from her hands.

"Sky, this is very old and delicate. Could I hold it for you?"

Her eyebrows furrowed as she studied the picture intently. She pointed to my brother and asked, "Who's dis?"

"That's your uncle, Dave, when he was younger." She nodded.

"Who's dis one?" she pondered, pointing to the little girl.

"That's your aunt, Elizabeth. Isn't her dress pretty?" Again, Sky nodded. "And this is me when I was a little boy," I said, pointing to the blond-haired child in the striped yellow shirt.

"Who's dat lady?" Sky wanted to know, as her index finger touched Grandma.

"Oh, that's my Grandma Myers. She got those guitars for us. Wasn't that nice of her?"

Sky remained silent for several seconds and continued to stare at the photo. With confidence in her voice, she said, "That's me. I'm Grandma Myers."

My stomach fluttered like I was riding a rollercoaster that had just dropped. My mouth hung open as I searched for something to say. Nothing came out. Sky lost interest and exited the closet. There I sat on the floor, goosebumps all over my body. I stared at the photo in my hand, moving it out from under my chin in case a tear fell down.

Sky had rounded the corner and met Kenzie in the master bathroom where she was applying makeup. "We going to da park, Momma."

"Oh, that sounds like fun," Kenzie replied. I stuck my head out the closet and saw Kenzie applying mascara in the mirror. She glanced over and looked me in the eye. "What's wrong, babe?" I didn't know how to reply. "What's wrong? What happened?" With a trembling hand, I simply held up the photo for her to see.

As I tried to collect my thoughts, Sky scampered into the upstairs hallway. From around the corner, we heard her cheerfully announce, "We goin' for a ride, Zico. I will get da leash." Sky had no idea what kind of impact she'd just had on me. She knew not the significance of her words.

Life itself is a grand theater. It's a stage where we come to perform. Each lifetime is a different production, involving comedy, tragedy, and plenty of drama. *Had Sky become her own sequel – reincarnating back into the same family tree only two generations later?*

If so, she was now playing a different role. Perhaps the theater itself had changed a bit since last time she was here. Yet, she was surrounded by familiar cast members. It was now clear to me why my daughter had always felt familiar in ways I couldn't pinpoint. Kenzie had always wished she'd gotten the chance to know my grandma. In a sense, it appeared she now had that opportunity.

Easter morning photo

Chapter 74

The year that followed was quite simply an onslaught of interesting comments from Sky. I diligently added them to the *Sky Diaries* journal, being sure to include the date on which each incident happened. Including the date was a habit fostered by Grandma. In my youth, when I wrote a poem or drew a picture, she always insisted I flip the paper over and include the date. "That way," she'd tell me, "When you're older, you'll know when you created this little masterpiece."

Sky's journal contains countless moments where she dropped clues or comments related to her prior lifetime. She became fascinated with the Easter morning photo from 1989. For several weeks, she repeatedly pointed to Grandma in the photo and said, "That's me. That's me when I was big!" When we would refer to the lady in the picture as "Grandma Myers," Sky responded with, "That's my *other* name. That's my nickname."

Another example came on a day I was sitting on the back deck with Sky. She asked me what the word *memory* means. I gave her a brief definition, phrasing it in a way that made sense to a three-year-old. "What are some of your memories, Sky?" I assumed she'd mention eating ice-cream the previous day, or something fun like playing video games at the arcade.

"I remember when you worked at a grocery store."

Comments like these were becoming commonplace. The shock factor was starting to wear off. "Yeah, I remember that, too." I propped my legs up on a side table, and interlaced my fingers behind my head to get more comfortable. Inhaling a deep breath, I gazed upon the forest below. The two of us sat there in peaceful silence, enjoying the nice weather. Memories came back of watching *Jeopardy* with Grandma and leaving just before the final round so I'd make it to my shift at the grocery store on time. "Yeah . . . I worked at the grocery store all through high school," I said to Sky.

"What's hike school?" she asked with squinted eyes.

Another example in her journal documents the time I was scrolling through some old photos on my Facebook account while Sky was on my lap. I came across a picture of the Benson house. Without hesitation, she blurted out, "I used to live dare. Dat used to be my house!"

"Oh, that's interesting. Mom and I used to live there too . . . before you were born." She looked at me with skepticism. *How dare I claim a house that clearly belonged to her?*

There was an entry in the journal from February, 2018. Kenzie walked into Sky's playroom and noticed she was playing kitchen. She pretended to cook some plastic food on her plastic stove. "Oh wow, you're such a good chef, Sky. What are you making?" asked Kenzie.

"It's bluegill, Momma," she said in a matter-of-fact tone. She seemed annoyed, as if Kenzie should know that's the best type of fish to cook.

"How does she even know that's a type of fish?" Kenzie asked me. I just smiled, thinking back to the time in Missouri when Grandma, Vilma, and the rest of us caught eighty-six of them.

I documented an evening when we tucked her into bed, offering bedtime stories of rainbow tigers, purple buffaloes, or any other whimsical creature she could imagine.

"Tell me a story about Great Grandpa."

"Boompa?" I asked.

"Uh huh," she eagerly insisted.

I could see the smile in her eyes, even though her blanket was pulled up to her nose. I remembered a bone-chilling true story my grandma relayed to me, about a time in Kansas when she and Boompa came upon a ghost truck and a phantom farm house. I always shared that tale at my Halloween lectures, and it's quite a doozy. Yet, I knew something less ominous would be required for a bedtime story. So, I told Sky about a practical joke her great grandpa once played on me when I was seven years old.

Boompa had a small manila envelope labeled "rattlesnake eggs." He handed it to me with a serious look and warned me to open it with caution. With my jaw clenched, I held it away from my face and slowly opened it. The envelope rattled and vibrated, sounding just like a rattlesnake. I threw the package on the floor and ran away. Boompa chuckled, explaining the sound was caused by a small, metal washer inside the envelope which was fitted to a twisted rubber band. Sky started cracking up. "Wattle snakes are funny, huh Dadda?"

The next morning, we were watching cartoons and eating cereal. Sky turned to me and said, "I want to see a picture of Boompa."

I explained I could probably find a picture of him in my storage bin after I made a pot of coffee. My answer didn't suffice. She grew more impatient by the minute, first asking, and then *demanding* to see a picture of Boompa. "Okay, sweetheart. Please be patient. I'll get it in a minute, okay."

She walked over, and took me by the hand. With assertiveness in her voice, she said, "No, Dadda, *now* please. I want to see a picture of Boompa right *now*."

I gave in, and we went upstairs to find a photo of Boompa. It was a unique request. It wasn't like she was throwing a tantrum while asking for candy in the grocery store checkout lane. I could tell this meant a lot to her.

"Why do you want to see him so much?" I asked.

"Because I miss him." Her expression was somber. Her tone was serious.

"You know, he passed away a long time ago, before you were even born."

"I miss Boompa and I love him," she insisted.

We found a photo album and brought it downstairs to the kitchen table. Sky paid no mind to the cartoon playing on the TV. She was mesmerized by each picture, taking in every detail. She looked at the photographs like she looked at the rock encyclopedia at her birthday party. It was a far-off, soulful expression. *Was she sad? Was she remembering something? Did she find what she was looking for?*

She looked at pictures of Grandma, Boompa, Vilma, and numerous others. She pointed to a photo of my dad and declared with excitement, "There's Grandpa Steve!" Her enthusiasm was infectious. She'd seen plenty pictures of my dad and we spoke of him often. He was her guardian angel, her protector, her spiritual advocate.

My dad and Sky's arrangement is rooted in karma. My dad was a bit of a hell-raiser growing up, and he certainly gave my grandma some gray hairs along the way. Now, he was making amends by keeping her safe in this current lifetime. It's proof that paying back favors and offering apologies can span multiple lifetimes.

In physics, the First Law of Thermodynamics suggests that energy cannot be destroyed. It merely changes forms. This is true for humans as well. We do not die. We merely change our appearance from one life to the next, much like a stage actor who wears a different costume for each production. We humans look different with each lifetime, but our essence remains the same.

This explains how Kenzie and I knew we had a special connection since the first day we met. It explains why we fell in love . . . again. Our bond is merely a continuation from our past life as Native Americans. Similarly, there's a part of Grandma that will always love Boompa. The love now resides within the heart of a little girl, but it's still there. It merely changed forms.

Chapter 75

Six years, four months, and seven days. That's how long it took Grandma to come back for another lifetime. *Did she get enough rest in the afterlife before coming back?* I certainly hoped so. In terms of reincarnation, it was a remarkably quick turnaround. Then again, Sky's enthusiasm was second to none, so I assumed she wasn't soul-weary. Perhaps Grandma's zest for life was so great, she wanted to come back as soon as possible. She couldn't wait for another spin on this ride called Life – much like a child who reaches the bottom of the waterslide, and sprints back to the top for another turn.

On the other hand, maybe she came back so quickly because her soul has time-sensitive missions to accomplish. *Will she have a hand in slowing global warming before it's too late? Will she be part of a crew that travels to Mars? Did she need to be born in 2014 so she'd be old enough to run for president in the 2052 election?* Perhaps these examples are a bit grandiose. Even if Sky is destined for smaller missions in her own neighborhood or city, it's true that timing is everything. For our souls to experience everything we desire, and for us to accomplish our goals, being born at the right place and time is key.

Part of me wonders if Grandma came back to Earth so quickly because she wanted to help inspire this very book. When Sky began remembering her past lifetime as my grandma, I only put the pieces together because I was already familiar with such concepts. Had she been born into a closed-minded family, her comments may have gone unnoticed. Had she been born into a conservative, religious family, such comments may have been considered blasphemous.

It's so important to *listen* when a child speaks. Sure, children are silly, imaginative, and like to tell stories. Yet, there's wisdom buried deep within each child, and they often speak the truth. They might be young in appearance, but their souls are just as ancient as adults'. When their intuition allows past life memories to rise up, it's our job to provide them with a supportive environment to be heard.

Chapter 76

I packed our vehicle carefully, moving bags and belongings with great thought, as if it were a game of Tetris. I adjusted my cap, and for a brief moment I thought of Boompa. How many times, while wearing a hat just like mine, had he carefully loaded the trunk of his and Grandma's station wagon in preparation for a long road trip? He and Grandma left equipped with a Rand McNally map, cigarettes, and ice-cold Pepsi. As for Kenzie, Sky, and me, we had GPS, granola bars, and bottled water. Some things had changed. Yet, in another sense, nothing had changed at all. Explorers will always explore, and there's always some empty highway to cover.

We were leaving for Stover, Missouri to visit Grandma's younger sister, Vilma, and her husband, Jim. I was embarrassed to admit how many years it had been since I'd seen them. Eight years? *Ten*? They'd never even met Kenzie, let alone Sky. Aunt Terry asked me to go to Missouri to give Vilma and Jim some peace of mind. They'd been encountering some paranormal activity in their home, and were feeling very uneasy.

At the time, they were both pushing eighty years old. Vilma and Jim are salt of the earth type of people, not accustomed to dealing with the supernatural. I assured Terry that we'd do a little paranormal investigating in hopes we could pinpoint the cause of the activity. If a paranormal presence was scaring Vilma and Jim, I suspected it was a ghost rather than a spirit. Spirits feel light and breezy, and come in the form of loved ones visiting from Heaven. Ghosts have a heavier vibration. They're people who have died but have chosen to remain Earth-bound for the time being.

Our friend and paranormal enthusiast, Amanda, joined us for the trip. By this point, she was a regular at our monthly metaphysical meetings.

We figured there was strength in numbers, and besides, having three adults along for the trip meant that Sky would have some company in the back seat. Not that she needed it. The kid was a seasoned pro at road trips. By car, boat, or plane, she'd traversed much of the Midwest already. She's not the type of child who requires movies or electronic devices on road trips. As long as she has a good view from her window, she's always game for a haul down any highway or interstate.

Amanda asked about our recent adventures, wondering what other road trips we'd taken in years past. We told her about the Sundance ceremony Kenzie's uncle had invited us to the previous summer. His name is Gary Elk Soldier, otherwise known as Hehaka Akichita. He was the leader of the event. He'd invited us to attend the weeklong spiritual ceremony on the Yankton Sioux reservation. Kenzie, Sky, and I witnessed firsthand something that few outsiders have ever seen before. We were invited to come inside the ceremonial circle and touch the tree at its center. Doing so was the energetic equivalent of plugging our souls into an electrical socket. We could sense the sprits of Kenzie's ancestors, and its branches were so high we could almost feel the heavens.

At the base of the ceremonial tree, Sky was granted permission to touch the white buffalo head. It's a sacred animal in the Sioux culture. Goosebumps formed on my arms and my eyes welled up with tears. *What would Grandma think?* I looked at Sky and knew the answer. She was mesmerized. Grandma's appreciation for Native American culture had come full circle. This wasn't a buffalo *nickel*. This was the real thing.

After the ceremonies, we were invited back to Hehaka Akichita's house where Sky ran around with other children close to her in age. We overheard Sky using words from the Dakota language that she'd learned from her new friends. It's remarkable how quickly children can absorb new languages. Hehaka Akichita asked me if I knew that the Dakota word for Sky was Mahpiya. I couldn't help but grin. I spared him a very long story and simply replied, "Yes, we learned that a few years ago."

Our road trip continued deeper and deeper into rural Missouri, where we neared the town of Stover. I was feeling a wide rang of emotions.

I was excited to see Vilma and Jim for the first time in many years. I was a little tense wondering what paranormal evidence we might discover inside their home. *Was it safe to bring a young child into a house that was genuinely haunted?* That aside, I was also feeling curious. I wondered how Sky might react when she saw Vilma for the first time. *Would she remember her younger sister?*

When we finally saw Vilma and Jim, all my inhibitions melted away immediately. They must be the nicest people east of the Missouri River. Jim has a handshake that can crush granite. He practically has to duck when walking through doorways, but he's a gentle giant with a remarkable sense of humor. As for Vilma, her resemblance to my grandma was uncanny. Her laugh, her voice, and her facial expressions gave me a sense of déjà vu.

After hugs and introductions, I handed them a signed copy of my three books. They acted as a conversation starter, allowing us to ease into paranormal subjects without overwhelming them. Vilma's niece is my aunt, Terry. The two of them had been in regular contact since Vilma's paranormal activity began, and Terry informed them of what I did for a living. They clearly seemed open to my line of work. That being said, I didn't intend on further overwhelming Vilma with talk of Sky and her past life memories, so I didn't mention it.

By age three, Sky warmed up to other children fairly easily. Every child she encountered was her new best friend. Adults, however, were a different matter. She was generally leery of new adults, keeping her distance and clinging to Kenzie and me.

Yet, it was different with Vilma. Their connection was immediate and obvious. Sky sat right next to Vilma on the couch. The two of them talked, played, laughed, and enjoyed each other's company to the fullest. It was surreal. They didn't seem like they were merely getting to know each other. Rather, they seemed like siblings coming together for a long overdue reunion, and simply picked up right where they'd left off.

Sky and Vilma sat side by side, turning the pages of an old photo album. Vilma pointed to a few family members, telling Sky who they were and when the picture was taken. "Where's me?" Sky asked time and time again. "Where's the picture of *me*?" I knew who she was referring to. I merely looked at Kenzie and winked.

They continued turning the pages, and I spotted a photo from the day we caught eighty-six bluegills. We all looked so young . . . so happy and carefree. Vilma picked up another photo album containing pictures that were even older. "Look, Sky, here's a picture of me and my older sister Frances when we were little kids. See our fishing poles? That must have been taken in Nebraska City."

Sky giggled, and proceeded to tell Vilma about her new *Disney* princess fishing pole she'd been using. I sat silently, shaking my head. I couldn't help but smile. Here they were, all these years later, still bonding over fishing, just like they had in their youth.

Jim began showing Kenzie and Amanda various parts of the house where unexplained anomalies had occurred. Vilma and Sky didn't notice. They were lost in their own little world. I sat silently in the corner, listening to their conversations and observing the fun they were having together.

They were separated in age by seventy-six years. Yet, in the vast expanse of the Universe, they'd found each other once again. They would not be denied – not by time, not by distance, not even by death. Two sisters were reunited. They continued to thumb through the photo albums, taking a stroll down memory lane . . . not quite realizing they'd already walked that path together many times before.

Vilma and Sky

Chapter 77

I t's difficult for me to give psychic readings to close friends and family members because I know them too well. Simply put, I'm too close with them to deliver unbiased intuitive information. So, when my mom or sister need to consult with a psychic medium, they visit with Angie. She's an Omaha based psychic medium who my family trusts and loves dearly. Not long after I'd returned from visiting Vilma and Jim in Missouri, my mom and sister went to Angie for a medium session.

My grandpa (my mom's father) had recently passed away. She was hoping Angie could connect with him to provide some messages, validation, and peace of mind. Angie gladly did so, delivering several specific and comforting messages that hit home for my mom. After that, Angie proceeded to connect with other deceased family members, as was typically the protocol when she meets with my mom. One by one, she was accustomed to relaying messages from Boompa, my dad, and Grandma Myers.

She hit the nail on the head each and every time, providing tremendous validation for my mom and sister. That is, until she came to Grandma Myers. While trying to sense her spirit and establish a psychic connection, Angie suddenly appeared a bit flustered. She stammered and stumbled over her words. This went on for a moment or two until Angie was finally left shaking her head and throwing her hands up in confusion. "I'm trying to feel her energy, but . . . *she's not fully there.*"

My mom took a deep breath. "We should probably catch you up to speed on the things Sky's been saying recently." They filled Angie in on the details. It was ironic how Angie's *inability* to connect with a spirit is perhaps the most validating proof she could have possibly offered. She confirmed what we already suspected – that Grandma had come back to us.

Admittedly, there are certain moments when Sky reminds me of my grandma. One time, Sky stuck her hands in her coat pocket and starting laughing. I asked what was so funny. She pulled a rock from her pocket and explained she'd forgotten it was in there. She claimed she found it on the playground at school and wanted to keep it. We walked into the garage, and she placed the rock in a tattered cardboard box that once belonged to my grandma. The box contained a hundred other rocks Grandma had placed in there once upon a time. I reached for my cell phone and snapped a photo of my young daughter adding to a rock collection that she'd started many decades earlier.

There's still an echo of Grandma resounding deep inside Sky's soul. Sky once told me she wants to turn our spare bedroom into a room for her rock collections. It made me think of the basement of the Benson house, which acted as Grandma's unofficial museum. Yes, the similarities between Sky and Grandma were apparent. I'm sure they always will be. Yet, when I look at Sky, I merely see my daughter. To treat her like my grandma would be ridiculous, not to mention unfair to Sky. She is very much her own person. I encourage her to be unique and different.

She's a little like me and a little like her mom, but mostly she's just *herself*. She's a mix of creative and clumsy, a blend of strong and sweet, equal parts inquisitive and intuitive. She loves gifting little treasures to people, and her empathy is abundant. Sky's still adamant that she'll work with animals when she grows up. I tell her she can be anything she wants to be. We'll be proud of her no matter what. I remind her that, right now, all she needs to focus on is having fun and being a kid. She likes that advice, because she's good at both those things.

We're not entirely sure how we were lucky enough to be her parents this time around. On a planet of nearly eight billion souls, my grandma came back to me in the form of Sky. She found us. She *chose* us to be her parents. It's something we reflect on daily with copious amounts of gratitude. The amount of joy this child has brought into our lives cannot be measured or quantified. It's infinite like the stars in the sky, and ever-expanding like the Universe itself.

Chapter 78

Humans are made of stardust. We are literally composed of the stuff of stars. The iron in our blood, the nitrogen in our DNA, and the calcium in our teeth are comprised of atoms that were forged inside of stars. Some stars explode, spraying elements and particles every which way. Over the course of billions and billions of years, these elements coalesced to form our Earth, our moon, our trees, and even us.

It's mind blowing to fathom the implications. Every part of us is comprised of the cosmos, even our eyes. That being the case, it means that when we gaze at the night sky with wonder, it's almost like the Universe is staring back at *itself*, consciousness observing consciousness.

Stars and planets are so far away that it takes hundreds, thousands, and even *billions* of years for their light to reach Earth. This means if we had a powerful enough telescope, we could actually see *back* in time. We could observe what a planet or star *used* to look like eons ago. The reverse is also true. A telescope on a planet 175 light years away would just now see images of Earth as it was in the mid-1800s. I bet they would see two Native American couples riding horseback together on the Midwestern plains – a beautiful woman named Mahpiya and her husband, along with their best friends, Henry and Sarah Cloud.

Those past life images still exist out there, high above the sky where Heaven meets Earth. Memories from our planet fly into space at the speed of light. This is how it's always been, and this is how it will continue to be. The Universe is the preserver of memories, the keeper of dreams.

Pondering one's place in the cosmos is enough to make a person feel small and insignificant. Yet, I remember those nights from my childhood, sprawled out on blankets with Grandma while looking for shooting stars over Flying Hawks Ranch. She thought the twinkle in my tired eyes was more beautiful than the twinkling stars above. This made me feel quite *significant* indeed. In a Universe bigger than anyone can comprehend, I was right where I belonged. Right next to Grandma.

I tell Sky each day how significant *she* is. I remind her that she matters. I tell Sky that her words and actions can change the world, especially when her words and actions are rooted in love. Each day when I drop her off at school, I tell Sky, "Be brave. Be kind. Be creative." It's a family motto we live by. I tell her that magic is real and nothing is impossible. I hope she follows her heart and chases her dreams, much like my grandma once chased sunsets.

One evening around dusk, I was taking a scenic drive with Sky in the back seat. The weather was perfect and we had the windows down to feel the breeze. The sun was hanging low on the western horizon, like an apple begging to be plucked from a tree. The sky was ablaze in oranges and yellows, bathing the landscape in golden hues. A hawk appeared out of nowhere. It glided majestically towards my vehicle, flying directly over my windshield and clearing us by just a few feet.

I looked at Sky through the rear-view mirror, wondering if she'd seen the hawk as well. Her expression was one of utter contentment. She looked serene, bordering on angelic.

"You doing okay back there, Sky?"

"I okay, Dadda."

"Do you see the pretty sunset?"

As she peered out the window, the golden sky reflected in her soulful eyes. The breeze whipped through her curly hair as the last of the sun rays illuminated her face.

"My grandma would have loved a sky like this. Did you know she used to chase the sunset?"

"Did she ever catch it?" Sky asked with curious wonder.

"You know, I'm not sure if she ever did. But I know she had fun trying."

"Have you ever caught it, Dadda? Have you ever caught the sky?"

Glancing over my shoulder, I locked eyes with my daughter in the back seat. I smiled and said, "I didn't have to, sweetheart. The Sky came to *me*."

Epilogue

It's been three years since I finished writing *The Sky Diaries*. Three whole trips around the sun. Sky is now seven years old. As often happens in life, so much has changed in so little time. Yet, a few things remain the same. Sky still insists she'll work with animals for a living someday. She often talks about driving an RV across the country and giving animal demonstrations in classrooms to educate children on the importance of wildlife conservation. I ask her if I can come along too. "Of course you can," she says. "I'll need someone to handle the snakes for me." We joke that RVs will probably drive themselves by then, which is good, because it will free up our hands to take more pictures of sunsets out there on the open road.

Sky just completed first grade in the midst of the pandemic. One highlight of Sky's year was the day her teacher showed the whole class her *Animal Adventures with Sky* YouTube videos. She felt so special seeing her peers enjoy the videos we'd worked so hard on creating together. On the last day of first grade, her teacher presented her the 'Dreamer' award. She said Sky is a free-spirited little soul who loves to tell stories (some of which have to do with aliens, ghosts, and other mysteries). Kenzie simply laughed and explained Sky gets that from her dad.

In the summer of 2018, shortly after completing this book, my marriage with Kenzie came to an end. Few things are more ironic than a psychic who can't foresee his own future. Nevertheless, it took me by surprise. I've had three years to reflect on it, and I've come to realize something that escaped me back then. Our union may have been destiny, but it wasn't necessarily destined to last *forever*. Upon entering this lifetime, Kenzie and I had a soul contract to fulfill, a mission to accomplish.

Together, we were meant to bring forth this precious little girl. In doing so, and allowing others to hear our story, we've brought awareness to a few truths we hold sacred in our hearts. Most importantly, that guardian angels are real, and that reincarnation is one vessel by which a family's love can cross the divide between lifetimes.

At the exact time these objectives were met and my book was complete, Kenzie's soul realized we'd fulfilled our contract. And so, our lives moved in different directions. Kenzie and I hold each other in the highest regard. We co-parent wonderfully together and I'm happy to report that she is, and always will be, one of my very best friends.

As for Sky, she's navigated life's changes with relentless optimism, enthusiasm, and plenty of humor. She is still the creative, clumsy, curly-haired old soul she's always been. Sky now senses the spirits of my clients' pets that have passed away. She asks me to verify the information with my clients. When I do, it checks out as accurate. Yes, she's incredibly psychic. Yet, her intuition is surpassed by her empathy. She's truly a kind and beautiful human being, inside and out. And she still insists we'll catch the sunset one of these days . . . if we can just buy a faster car or get a really tall RV.

On my bedroom wall hangs a very large collage. I created it a few years ago by cutting and pasting together images I'd found online. They're pictures that remind me of *all* my past lifetimes, including images from every corner of the globe and nearly every period in history. Sky is old enough to understand the concept of past lifetimes, and sometimes she asks about the collage on my wall. One morning a few months ago as we were snuggling in bed, she asked, "Why are there Native Americans and tatankas in your collage, Dadda?"

"It's because I shared a past lifetime with your mom. We were Native Americans, and our best friends were named Henry and Sarah."

Sky continued, "What was *my* past lifetime, Dadda? Can you use your psychic abilities and tell me?"

Before I responded, I squeezed her a little tighter and kissed her forehead. "When you're a little older, I have a book you should read."

Kenzie, Sky, and Andy in summer, 2021

Tatanka ride at sunset

Sky Myers

Chasing the sunset

Acknowledgements

When reading a book, we only see the author's name on the front cover. Yet, the reality of writing is that it's a team effort. There are so many talented individuals I'd like to thank for their constant support, their time, and their energies. Without their help, this project would not have been possible.

Thanks to Lisa Brehm, Sam Maine, Erin Plouzek, Jodi Jorgensen, April Cook, Ashley Schmick, Kristina Dalen, and Art Peters for their assistance with proof reading and editing. The importance of their work cannot be overstated, and I'm thankful for the time and energy they invested in helping with this project.

I'd also like to thank Anna of Anna Mostek Photography for designing the book cover. Anna's artistry and creativity are second to none. Additionally, she captured the family photos seen in this book. I'm forever grateful for her patience and the countless hours she invested in this project with me.

I owe a lot to Pat Safford and Jill Thomas for allowing me to reach so many people through the magic of radio early in my career. I'll cherish those memories forever.

Thanks to Eddie Fossler and Pat Pleiss of the Paranormal Dads podcast for their friendship, support, and humor. You guys are the absolute best!

I'd like to acknowledge my aunt, Terry Myers, for her wisdom, guidance, editing suggestions, and assistance with research. You're one of the most generous and remarkable individuals I've ever known, Terry.

I'd like to thank my sister, Elizabeth Myers, for her tireless work to keep my business running smoothly. I'm not sure what I would do without you, Sis. Thanks for keeping my life organized and for being the best sister a guy could ask for.

I want to acknowledge my mom, Sue Myers, for being so supportive all these years. She's offered assistance with my career in every way humanly possible and she's always put her kids first. Many of the blessings in my life are a direct result of her constant love and support.

Lastly, I want to offer a heartfelt thank you to Kenzie Myers. Without her, the story in this book would have never happened. Thanks for playing a lead role in the most amazing story of all our lifetimes, Kenzie. What a wonderful ride it's been!

About the author

A ndy Myers is a psychic medium, inspirational speaker, life coach, and best-selling author. He's made hundreds of appearances on popular radio stations nationwide, and is one of the most respected psychic mediums in the country. Andy is known for his sincerity, humor, and remarkable insights into the spirit world. He travels often to conduct sold-out psychic events and inspirational lectures in cities around the country. He's been delivering psychic readings for over a decade, and is highly regarded for his expertise in the subject of past lives and reincarnation. To date, he has published three other books, including *Flying Paint Rollers from Heaven*, *Inspiration: A to Z*, and *Not Your Average Angel Book*. Andy resides in Omaha, Nebraska.

Contact Information
Website: www.AndyMyersOnline.com
E-mail: AndyMyersManagement@Gmail.com
"Psychic Medium Andy Myers" on Facebook
"psychicandymyers" on YouTube
"andymyers17" on Instagram